Mushroom Cultivation

Mushroom Cultivation

*for Students of Agriculture, Horticulture, Forestry,
Home Science and Mushroom Growers*

DP Tripathi PhD
Associated Professor
Department of Plant Pathology
CS Azad University of
Agriculture and Technology
Kanpur (UP)

Oxford & IBH Publishing Co. Pvt. Ltd.

New Delhi

(*A Unit of* CBS Publishers & Distributors Pvt Ltd)

CBSPD

CBS Publishers & Distributors Pvt Ltd

New Delhi • Bengaluru • Chennai • Kochi • Kolkata • Lucknow • Mumbai

Hyderabad • Jharkhand • Nagpur • Patna • Pune • Uttarakhand

Mushroom Cultivation

ISBN-13: 978-81-204-1644-4
ISBN-10: 81-204-1644-9

OXFORD & IBH
New Delhi
(A Unit of CBS Publishers & Distributors Pvt Ltd)

Published by **Satish Kumar Jain** and produced by **Varun Jain** for
CBS Publishers & Distributors Pvt Ltd
4819/XI Prahlad Street, 24 Ansari Road, Daryaganj, New Delhi 110 002, India
Ph: 011-23289259, 23266861   Website: www.cbspd.com
e-mail: delhi@cbspd.com

Corporate Office: 204 FIE, Industrial Area, Patparganj, Delhi 110 092, India
Ph: 011-4934 4934   Fax: 011-4934 4935   e-mail: publishing@cbspd.com;
publicity@cbspd.com

Branches

- **Bengaluru:** Seema House 2975, 17th Cross, KR Road, Banasankari 2nd Stage, Bengaluru 560 070, Karnataka, India
  Ph: +91-80-26771678/79   Fax: +91-80-26771680   e-mail: bangalore@cbspd.com
- **Chennai:** 7, Subbaraya Street, Shenoy Nagar, Chennai 600 030, Tamil Nadu, India
  Ph: +91-44-26680620, 26681266   Fax: +91-44-42032115   e-mail: chennai@cbspd.com
- **Kochi:** 42/1325, 1326, Power House Road, Opp KSEB, Power House, Ernakulam Kochi 682 018, Kerala, India
  Ph: +91-484-4059061-65,67   Fax: +91-484-4059065   e-mail: kochi@cbspd.com
- **Kolkata:** 147, Hind Ceramics Compound, 1st Floor, Nilgunj Road, Belghoria, Kolkata-700056, West Bengal, India
  Ph: +033-25633055, 033-25633056   e-mail: kolkata@cbspd.com
- **Lucknow:** Basement, Khushnuma Complex, 7 Meerabai Marg (Behind Jawahar Bhawan), Lucknow-226001, UP, India
  Ph. +91-522-4000032 .   e-mail: tiwari.lucknow@cbspd.com
- **Mumbai:** PWD Shed, Gala no 25/26, Ramchandra Bhatt Marg, Next to JJ Hospital Gate no. 2, Opp. Union Bank of India Noorbaug, Mumbai-400009, Maharashtra, India
  Ph: 022-66661880/89   e-mail: mumbai@cbspd.com

Representatives

Hyderabad	0-9885175004	Jharkhand	0-9811541605	Nagpur	0-9421945513
Patna	0-9334159340	Pune	0-9923910676	Uttarakhand	0-9716462459

Printed at Chaman Enterprises, Daryaganj, New Delhi, India

Preface

The importance of edible cultivated mushrooms in international market has assumed greater significance in recent years, not only due to its nutritional excellence, but also because of their good flavour and peculiar taste. There has been a long felt need for a comprehensive text book on mushroom science which may serve the purpose of the students of botany, agriculture, forestry and home science as well as of growers alike. My book on mushroom cultivation in Hindi served this purpose to certain extent in states of Uttar Pradesh, Bihar, M.P. and Rajasthan. It has been my ambition to write such a text book as this one on mushroom science which may be beneficial to students and all those interested in mushroom cultivation through out the country. The book in hand of such a mushroom lover like you, is the outcome of my humble efforts.

In writing this book, I have reviewed a number of books and articles on the subject and formulated my own method of its presentation. I wish to acknowledge my gratefulness to various authors of such scientific publications which formed the basis of this text.

This book is intended chiefly for B.Sc. classes covering courses as prescribed by the ICAR for various Agricultural Universities and Institutions. Foreign books available on mushroom science do not include enough references of research work done in India as they have been written exclusively for their respective countries. Besides, those books are not in accordance with the needs of the students because most of them have not been systematically presented as a text book. However, the book in hand entitled 'Mushroom Cultivation' includes all the topics on the subject giving information on different aspects of mushroom cultivation started from historical development to its cultivation technology and marketing. Chapters like morphology, taxonomy. edible and poisonous species, cultivation of button mushroom, oyster mushroom, straw mushroom and different other specialty mushrooms along with important insect pests and diseases have been dealt with in much detail in this book. Expected questions in objective forms and different practical experiments related with the cultivation of mushrooms have also been included in the text to facilitate the students and growers. All the chapters have been fully illustrated and presented in a comprehensive manner to facilitate the students and growers to use the book as a step by step guide.

I am greatly thankful and highly obliged to Dr. P. K. Singh, Vice Chancellor, C.S. Azad University of Agriculture and Technology, Kanpur (U.P.) for his acceleration in quality research and teaching which inspired me to write this book and to Dr. K.D. Upadhyay, Dean, College of Agriculture of the University for his constructive guidance, he has given time to time. Our special thanks are also due to Dr. Kumud Kumar, Professor and Head, Department of Plant Pathology of this University for his necessary support. Help rendered by Shri Vibhuti Pandey and Mrs. Kalpana Rani who worked hard untiringly in making related illustrations for the book as we desired, deserve words of special mention and appreciation.

I also owe deep debt of gratitude to all the members of NRCM, Solan (H.P.) and members of the Department of Plant Pathology, C.S. Azad University of Agriculture and Technology, Kanpur for their help in various ways. At last but not least, I thank M/s Oxford & IBH Publishing Co. for untiring efforts in bringing out this book in such a form timely. I hope the book in present form will fulfil the needs of the students and mushroom growers alike. Although all possible precautions have been taken to avoid mistakes, still, omissions and mistakes if found will be accepted cordially and thankfully for improvement. Constructive suggestions from readers, if any, will also be highly appreciated and incorporated in future editions of the book. The book is expected to receive wide acclaim throughout the country.

D.P. TRIPATHI

Department of Plant Pathology,
C.S. Azad University of Agriculture and Technology,
KANPUR – 208002 (U.P.)

Contents

development, Essentials for mushroom breeding, Programme and future breeding prospects.

Different methods of storage, Canning of mushrooms, Freeze-drying method, Pickling of mushrooms, Drying of mushrooms, Vacuum cooling method, Marketing, Difficulties in marketing, Suggestions to improve marketing, Future prospects in mushroom marketing and packaging of mushrooms.

Chapter 1

Introduction and History

Introduction, what are mushrooms?, mushrooms and toad stools, fairy rings, puffballs, History of mushroom cultivation, general view of mushroom cultivation in the world, scope and development of mushroom science, concept of mushroom technology, different methods of mushroom growing, essentials of mushroom science, seven phases of mushroom technology and present scenario of mushroom cultivation.

The term 'Mushroom' is employed to designate edible, fleshy and macroscopic basidiocarpous or ascocarpous spore bearing fungi of certain species whereas toad stool signifies poisonous or inedible species of such fungi. Characteristically, mushroom is a fleshy and spore bearing nutritive organ (fruiting body) of certain fungi that belongs to a group of organisms which differ in many respects from flowering plants and animals. Fungi maybe differentiated from higher plants as under :

Table 1.1
Showing difference between fungi and higher plants.

S.N.	Fungi	Higher plants
1.	Fungi lack chlorophyll, roots, stems leaves and flowers.	They have chlorophyll, roots, stems leaves and flowers.
2.	They have not true seeds and are usually propagated by spores.	They have true seeds and are progated by seed and vegetative means but not by spores.
3.	They cannot prepare their food.	They can prepare food for them.
4.	Fungi may be motile or not motile.	Higher plants are always non-motile.

In ancient time, the popular and wide spread interest in mushroom was developed due to their attractive beauty of forms, colours and also because of the supposed mystery about their origin and growth. The value of mushrooms as nutritive food is not so great and is equal to that of cabbage and some other vegetables. Many mushroom species such as *Mycena lux-coeli, Clitocybe illudens, Armillariella mellea* and few species of *Pleurotus* are bioluminescent and they emit light of a green, greenish white or bluish green colour in the dark. Some times, they cause the woods or leaves of plants attacked by them to become luminous. These fungi are known as luminescent fungi and are considered to be attractive for use as gifted by god.

Mushroom affords variety of flavour and taste. It adds greatly to relish other foods when taken with its various preparations. Mushroom eating is much common in most parts of Europe, America, China, Japan and other countries. The edible and poisonous varieties are better known by all classes of people over there. The use of mushrooms in our country was very limited years earlier and was chiefly confined to the people who were well familiar with the flavour, aroma and taste of various preparations of mushrooms. Now days, the interest of people in mushroom is increasing greatly and steadily due to the awareness about the usefulness of mushrooms.

Species of *Auricularia* is considered as the earliest cultivated mushroom in the world. It is known to be cultivated some 1000 years ago in China. *Agaricus bisporus*, another edible mushroom is reported to be first cultivated in France in 1650. *Volvariella volvacea*, known commonly as straw-mushroom, is reported to be cultivated first time some about 300 years ago in China. At present, more than 2000 edible species of mushrooms are known to exist through out the world. About 180 species belonging to 70 genera have been reported from India alone. Some other edible mushrooms still not reported, are eaten by tribal and hill people scattered in different parts of Himalayas and in nearby foot-hills in our country.

WHAT ARE MUSHROOMS ?

In common terminology, most of us use the term mushroom for all the fleshy, macroscopic basidiocarpous and ascocarpous spore bearing fungi but in its strict sense under mushroom science *'the fruiting bodies of edible species of fungi are usually called mushrooms'*. In case of mushrooms, the seed has no sexual origin and the reproducting unit is called as spore. Spores may be differentiated from seeds as under :

Table 1.2
Showing difference between spore of mushroom and true seed in higher plants.

S.N.	Spore	Seed
1.	Spore is a minute usually microscopic propagative unit of fungi.	Seed is usually the macroscopic propagative unit in higher plants.
2.	Spores lacks embryo.	Seed has well develop embryo.
3.	A spore is a sexual or asexual reproductive unit.	Seed is usually a sexual reproductive unit.

These spores are the sexual propagating units which are invisible to the naked eyes. They send out root like threads in all directions within growing medium and produce fruiting bodies — the

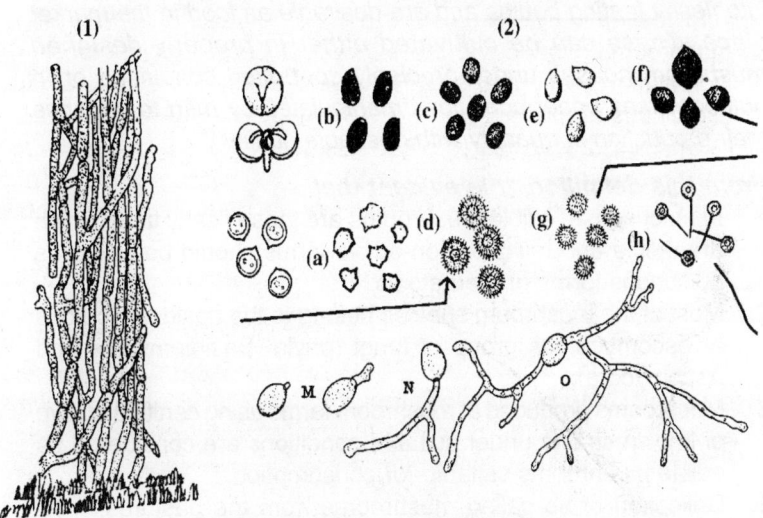

Fig. 1.1 Showing (1) magnified structure of mushroom mycelium (2) Morphology of spores of different species of mushrooms (a) spores of *Entoloma* species, (b) Spore of *Coprinus* species, (c) Spores of *Psalliota* species, (d) Spores of *Clitocybe* species, (e) Spores of *Pleurotus* species, (f) Spores of *Panacolus* species, (g) Spores of *Lactarius* species, and (h) Spores of *Lycoperdon* species, (m), (n) and (o) germination stages.

mushrooms. These usuallly the spores develop inside the cap of the mushroom remain devoid of leaves, stems and flowers as seen in higher plants. Usually, the spores develop inside the cap of the mushroom. The threads (hyphae) in the soil or substratum, which look like roots in appearance, usually develop from these spores in order to search food materials for their growth and development. The food material is transmitted to the mushroom through these thread like structures. Such structures usually fuse together which are known in mass as mycelium. The growers use term spawn for mushroom mycelium. The mushroom first appears as a tiny white ball but later on, it grows forming different parts of the mushrooms including the cap or pileus, the stalk or stripe and the lamella.

Definition of mushroom

Cultivated edible mushrooms may be defined as "Mushrooms are *achlorophylous, macroscopic basidiomycetous or aseomycetous species of certain fungi that bear spores embedded into fleshy fruiting bodies and are desirable as food in the market place. These can be cultivated either in properly designed mushroom houses under precisely controlled conditions or in outdoor areas under conditions manipulated by man to enhance their production in quantity with desirable quality".*

From this definition, it is evident that
1. In strict sense, edible mushrooms are those fleshy fungi which are edible and reliable. Non-edible forms should be called as poisonous forms or toad stools.
2. Most of the mushroom species belong to the basidiomycetous or ascomycetous group of fungi (phyla- Basidiomycota and Ascomycota).
3. Mushrooms produced at mushroom farms using certified spawn of known strains under suitable conditions are considered as edible mushrooms suitable for consumption.
4. Collection of so called mushrooms from the pastures, hills, forests or from any other places are not reliable and should not be consumed at all. Such forms are not advised to be consumed as they many be poisonous.
5. Cultivated mushrooms produced at mushroom farms have their market value in national and international market.

Thus keeping in view the characteristic features of edible

mushrooms, the simple, comprehensive and self explainatory definition of edible mushroom may be given as under :

'Mushrooms are spore bearing fruiting bodies that are desirable as food in the market place and that can be cultivated in quantity either in confined areas or in wider out door areas under precisely controlled conditions mainpulated by man to enhance its production.'

Mushrooms and toad stools

The term mushrooms and toad stools are usually used loosely. The edible species of fungi are usually called as mushrooms whereas poisonous species which are ui.fit to be consumed are called toad stools. In common practice, mycologists generally do not use the term in this way. They use to speak mushrooms, which include all the edible, medicinal and poisonous species. I shall use 'poisonous mushrooms' for not edible species in this text.

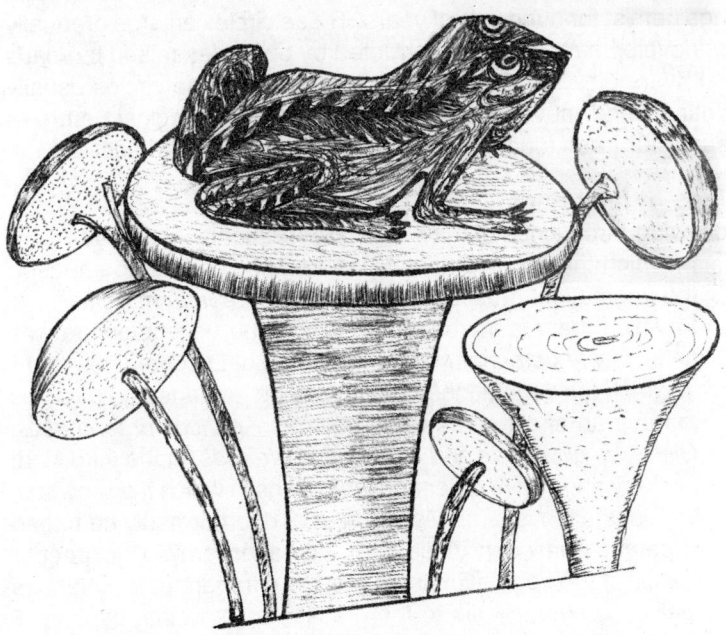

Fig. 1.2 Showing poisonous mushroom known as toad stool because of the characteristic stool like appearance of the cap.

Fairy rings

When we go in the fields and forests in search of mushrooms, we may find a fairy ring. The mycelium of some mushroom species usually grows on the ground forming a circular colony that continues growing year after year and produces a crop of basidiocarps at the periphery of the colony thus forming a ring called a fairy ring. People used to say that fairy-ring arises from the delightful dance of angels. But it is not the real story about fairy-rings. Some times, the spores germinate and threw up mycelium of mushroom. The mycelium spreads onward in all directions from this point in search of food for the next crop of mushroom. It would quickly exhaust the ground rich in food materials and cause much of the grass to die. The bareness of ring is accentuated by the grass growing on either side of it. Inside the ring, the old mycelium usually utilizes the nutrition of that area of the field. As a result of it, the grasses remain temporarily deprived of food material over there. Each year, new circles (fairy rings) with larger diameters are formed. Some fairy rings persist for hundreds of years. These circles enlarge gradually but development may be interrupted by obstacles raised by roads and rivers etc. In such cases, those arches of the circles usually continue and move steadily onwards from the original centre in search for fresh food, independent from the arrested sections.

Kinds of fairy rings

Following three kinds of fairy rings are frequently observed.
1. In which the development of the fruit bodies has no effect on the vegetation/ grasses as observed in *Lepiota morganii*.
2. In which there is increased growth of the vegetation/grasses as in *Lipsta personatum* and members of Lycoperdales and
3. In which the vegetation/grasses may be damaged so badly as to have an effect on its value such as *Agaricus praerimosus*, *Clitocybe gigantean* and *Marasmius oreades*. In the third kind, the fairy rings have outer and inner rings in which the growth of the vegetation is strong with a ring of dead or badly damaged vegetation between these two. Increased growth or greener colour of the vegetation is due to the nitrogenous substances that become available to the grasses as the older hyphae of the fungus mycelium die and disintegrate. The rings are started from a mycelium and the growth of which continue on the outer edges because the band of decaying mycelium and used up soil remain within the ring.

Puffballs and their relatives

Most of the puffballs and their relatives suggest the shape of stomach and a large number of them are usually recognised as stomach fungi. In ancient times, the spore mass of ripe puffballs were used to stop bleeding which was probably due to the good virtue of its powdery nature which exposed a large surface area and caused quick clotting. On account of these reasons, it appears that spore mass of puff balls would be relatively free of filth and bacteria. Besides, puff balls of certain fungi are considered to be the safest edible fruiting bodies. Most of the puff balls are edible and very rare are poisonous. They are at the same time, excellent in taste and flavour. They are also easy to obtain. Genus *Bovista* and *Lycoperdon* are most common puffballs. Puffballs have following distinguishing characteristics.

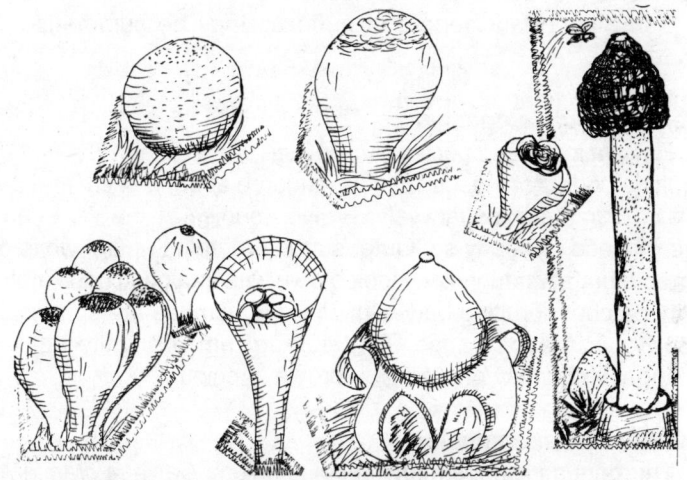

Fig. 1.3 Showing morphological appearance of puff balls and their relatives. (Showing morphological characteristics of mushrooms belonging to Gastromycetales groups).

General characteristics

Some persons consume puffballs in some countries and are familiar with different edible puffballs. Important characteristics of such edible puffballs may be summarized as under:
1. Puff balls are tender in texture, therefore, they may be cooked quickly for consumption. They are easily digestible.

2. They should be cut upon before cooking to see whether they are really puff balls. They should not be too old.
3. If the puff balls are white like cream or cheese and firm inside it showing no yellow or brownish discolouration, they are suitable and fit for consumption.
4. It the interior of puffballs show no special structures and are smooth and homogenous, one may be sure for being puffballs.
5. Puff balls may be cooked in various ways. When used in omelette, they should be stewed first.
6. All kinds, except very small ones, should first be peeled and cut in to slices. After which they may be fried quickly in butter.
7. Smaller kinds of puffballs are thought to be inferior in quality and flavour. Therefore, few specimens of some good mushrooms are needed to mix them with such puff balls to make them attractive and tasty.

Some important genera of puffballs may be summarized as under:

Genus–*Bovista* species

Bovista includes species like *Bovista plumbea* and *Bovista pila*. Fruiting bodies of theses species measure about 2–4 cm and 5–10 cm in diameters respectively. Fruiting bodies of the *Bovista pila* are globose or nearly so. Outer surface remains at first white and smooth but at maturity they look brown with inconspicuous mottled gray patches. Fruiting bodies of *Bovista plumbea* are spherical or nearly so in appearance. The surface remains white but later changes into shiny gray to gray brown in colour.

Genus–*Calvatia* species

The genus includes many species chiefly *Calvatia craniformis*, *Calvatia elat* and *Calvatia maxima*. The genus is characterized by the fruit bodies which are almost spherical, sterile base inconspicuous or absent. Mature spore mass looks greenish in *Calvatia maxima*.

Genus–*Lycoperdon* species

Usually growing on stumps and logs, mostly in clumps, surface of such puffballs are observed to be at first covered with scattered spines. *Lycoperdon pyriforme, Lycoperdon gemmatum* and *Lycoperdon umbrinum* are common species.

HISTORY OF MUSHROOM CULTIVATION

As early as 1630, the cultivation of white button mushroom (*Agaricus* species) was started for the first time in France. The cultivation was done in the open on ridges made out of horse dung manure. In 1707, method of compost preparation was reported and described by Royal Academy of Science, France. Gradually, French method of mushroom cultivation was introduced in England by Miller in 1731. In 1810, a French gardener named as Chambry started growing mushroom in underground quarries at Paris. Callow (1831) grew mushroom in cropping houses and warmed it by fire heat. As a result of it, the yield was increased significantly. Much information about spore germination and growing of mycelium was reported for the first time by Ferguson (1902) from U.S.A. In 1905, Duggar cultured mycelium from tissue of mushroom to be used as propagating material for mushroom crop production. It resulted in setting up of a large number of spawn producing companies in America. In 1915, mushroom growers of U.S.A. practiced complete thermo genesis in shelved compost beds within the growing house before spawning.

In 1917, Flack described the cultivation of *Pleurotus ostreatus* on tree stumps and logs. After sometimes, Lambert in 1929 discovered that productive spawn could also be prepared from single spore culture. After few years, Sinden (1937) observed that about one third of monospore cultures of *Agaricus bisporus* were incapable of producing fruiting bodies. Lambert in 1941, observed the temperature between 50–60°C to be suitable for the preparation of good quantity of compost. During the period between 1950 and 1953, Sinden and Hauser contributed short method of compost preparation. In 1962, Bano and Srivastava reported mass production of mushroom on straw based substrate. They reported increased yield of *Pleurotus* species on paddy straw used as substrate.

Development of different methods of mushroom growing

Very little information on methods of mushroom cultivation in early stages is available. In ancient Chinese literature, the cultivation of *Auricularia* species, *Volvariella volvacea* and *Lentinus edodes* have been recorded. Most probably, Chinese were the first to describe methods of mushroom cultivation. Some important methods in evolution of mushroom growing are summarized as under:

1. Out door ridge beds

This method was first described by Tournament in 1707. The description consisted of beds made in the open, spawned and cased with about one inch thick rotten leaf moulds. The ridge beds were kept 1.2 to 1.5 m. (4–5 feet) wide. Sharp ridges were made which measured (4–5 feet) high and 15 cm in length. Parallel ridges were made side by side with space to walk and perform other cultural works.

2. Ridge beds under cover methods

In England, mushroom growers covered the ridge beds by sheds and also maintained it in glasshouses and green houses. In underdeveloped areas of France, people started utilizing caves for growing mushrooms.

3. Shelf system

This system was the modification of ridge beds. The system consisted of a flat well drained floor bed about 12 m (40 feets) long, 2–4 m (8 feets) wide with back and end walls supported by 0.6 m (2 feets) wide shelves with 15–25 cm (6–10 inches) sides. This system remained in practice for many years in U.S.A. In 1968, improvement in ventilation system was suggested.

4. The rack system

This system was a variation of the shelf system. It included

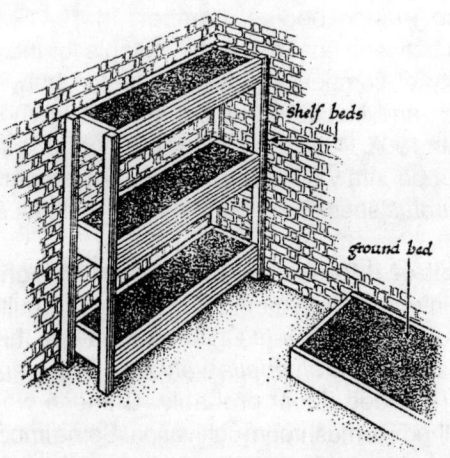

Fig. 1.4 Illustration showing shelf system of mushroom growing.

mechanization similar to tray system and retained single zone shelf method. The racks were made of metal frame-work holding about four tiers of short shelves. This system facilitated easy shifting of substrate for both filling and emptying.

5. *The tray system*
It originated from American shelf system. This system was first introduced by Knaust brothers in 1939. This system helped to carry out 3–5 zones system. It led to the development of mobile shelves with mechanization. Large farm growers started using large trays.

Fig. 1.5 Illustration of tray system of cultivation showing trays placed on metal framework.

6. *Bag system*
The use of bag system in large scale are being done in Italy, France, Ireland and many other Asian countries. It does not require much cost. Plastic bags holding 15–30 kgs compost are filled to a depth of 60–75 cm. (24–30 inches). The development of bulk pasteurisation and spawn running made this system to be more popular. In Ireland, this system is more popular among small growers.

HISTORICAL DEVELOPMENT IN INDIA

After IInd world war, mushroom cultivation was given due importance in more than 800 countries throughout the world. Indians were accustomed to eat mushrooms from very beginning of civilization but art and science of mushroom cultivation came in existence in recent years. A brief review of historical development of mushroom cultivation in India may be summarized as under :

In 1886–N.W. Newton exhibited some specimens of mushroom at annual show organized by the Agriculture/Horticulture society of India. During 1896–97, Dr. B.C. Roy of Calcutta Medical College, Calcutta carried out chemical analysis of mushrooms collected from caves and mines. In 1908, Sir David Pain identified many edible mushrooms and made different illustrations for their identification. During the year 1939–45, experimental cultivation of paddy straw mushroom (*Volvariella* species) was undertaken for the first time by Department of Agriculture, Madras. Thamas and his associates gave the details of paddy straw mushroom (*Volvariella diplasia*) cultivation in Madras. In 1961, a project entitled 'Development of mushroom cultivation in Himachal Pradesh' was started at Solan by the Government of Himanchal Pradesh in collaboration with ICAR. In 1964, the cultivation of *Agaricus bisporus* was started by CSIR at Srinagar in J&K with collaboration of the State Government of Jammu and Kashmir. During the period of 1965–1974, Dr. E.F.K. Mantel and Dr. W.A. Hayes who were FAO mushroom experts, suggested technical guidelines and provided assistance to the Department of Agriculture, Govt. of India for profitable and scientific mushroom cultivation. They guided improved method of compost preparation, management of important parameters in mushroom houses, new compost formulations, casing materials, moisture in casing soil and maintenance of proper environmental factors for profitable mushroom cultivation. In 1977, a mushroom development project was launched under UNDP by the Department of Horticulture, Himanchal Pradesh, where services of Mr. James Tunney were offered to the Department. The project was concluded in 1982, and since then Department of Horticulture (H.P.) is running the project with intensive research and extension work in mushroom cultivation. In 1982, National Research centre for Mushroom (NRCM) was established during VI plan with the assistance of ICAR. The centre conducts research on various problems related with mushroom production, its preservation and profitable utilization. Besides, it imparts training on mushroom cultivation to the scientists, teachers, extension workers and growers. The All India Coordinated Mushroom Improvement Project (AICMIP) was sanctioned by ICAR in 1983 with headquarter located at NRCM, Solan (H.P.). Under the project, six centres were established for research and development of mushroom. These centres were situated at G.B. Pant University of Agricuture & Technology, Pantnagar (U.S.); Punjab Agriculture University, Ludhiyana (Pb.); TNAU, Coimbature (T.N.); V.C. Krishi Vishwa Vidyalaya, Kalyani (W.B.); M.P. Agriculture University, Pune (M.S.) and C.S.A. University of Agriculture and Technology, Kanpur (U.P.).

In recent years, the yield of button mushroom (*Agaricus bisporus*) has increased significantly as a result of continuous research work done by the scientists in our country. The important research centres engaged in research, training and extension works are situated at National Research Centres for Mushroom ICAR, Chambaghat, Solan (H.P.); Division of Mycology and Plant Pathology, IARI, New Delhi; Indian institute of Horticulture Research, Hessar-ghatta, Bangalore (Karnataka); ICAR Research Complex, North Eastern Hills, Shilong (Arunachal Pradesh); Department of Mycology and Plant Pathology, Dr. Y.S. Parmar University of Horticulture and Forestry, Solan (H.P.); Punjab Agriculture University, Ludhiana (Punjab); Tamilnadu Agriculture University, Coimbature (T.N.); G.B. Pant University of Agriculture & Technology Pantnagar (U.S.); Indira Gandhi Krishi Vishwa Vidhyalaya, Raipur (M.P.); Vidhan Chandra Krishi Vishwa Vidhyalaya, Kalyani (W.B:); Mahatma Phule Agric University, Pune (M.S.); Regional Research Laboratory (CSIR), Lalmandi, Srinagar (J & K), C.S.A. University of Agriculture and Technology, Kanpur (U.P.) and N.D. University of Agri. & Tech. Faizabad (U.P.).

Besides above, teaching, research and extension works are being carried out by various Agricultural Universities, Agricultural and Horticultural Departments and KVK centres through out the country.

GENERAL VIEW OF MUSHROOM CULTIVATION IN THE WORLD

Although the mushroom production has steadily been increasing since Second world war, but there has been fluctuation in the yield of mushrooms produced in various countries at different times. About 98% of the total production is obtained from 6 popular genera

Table 1.3
Showing world production of cultivated mushrooms in thousand tons in different years.

Species	1975	1986	1989	1994
Agaricus Bisporus	670.0	1227.0	1424.0	1846.0
Lentinus edodes	130.0	341.0	393.0	826.2
Volvariella volvacea	42.0	178.0	207.0	298.8
Pleurotus species	12.0	169.0	909.0	797.4
Auricularia species	5.7	119.0	400.0	420.1
Others	56.3	175.0	430.0	720.8
Total	916.0	2209.0	3763.0	4409.3

of mushrooms namely, *Agaricus, Lentinus, Volvariella, Flammulina, Auricularia* and *Pleurotus*. Out of these six widely cultivated mushrooms, *Agaricus* species have been found most popular and most widely cultivated mushroom through out the world.

Considerable amount of *Agaricus* species were produced in 14 countries chiefly France, China, Netherlands, United Kingdom and United States of America. These countries, produced almost one-fourth of the world production of *Agaricus*. Remaining one fourth was found to be produced in other countries including Italy, Spain and Germany. An interesting feature of *Agaricus* production was observed in China. It has become chief producer and exporter of this mushroom in recent years. The world wide geographic range in which *Agaricus* species were grown commercially is also note worthy. Available information has revealed that *Agaricus* species were grown abundantly in the continents of North America, Europe, Asia and Australia. Although the optimum temperature for fruiting of *Agaricus bisporus* is above 15–I7°C but certain other methods have been developed for growing it seasonally in subtropical climates also by manipulation in technology. *Agaricus* cultivation is being introduced in such a climate, especially in areas of high and cooler altitude in Thailand and many other countries. *Agaricus* cultivation technology has advanced to such a great extent that this mushroom can now be produced successfully and profitably in different other locations with climate quite different from Europe and America where it is grown profitably and easily from years.

Lentinus edodes ranks second in its production in the world. It accounted more than 16% of the world production. In contrast to

Table 1.4

General view of cultivation of some edible mushrooms with their scientific name and countries of cultivation in the world.

Common name	Latin name	Temperature desired		Place of cultivation
		Vegetative (°C)	Generative (°C)	
Cultivated mushroom (**Button mushroom**)	*Agaricus bisporus*	25 ± 2	16–18	Whole world
Hot mushroom	*Agaricus bitorquis*	29–30	24–25	Netherlands and U.K.
(**Button mushroom**)	*Agaricus avensis*	25	29–30	Belgium and some other countries under research.
Oyster mushroom	*Pleurotus ostreatus*	25	8–15	Japan, France, Italy and India etc.
Pleurotus florida	*P. florida*	25	20–22	—
Branch oyster	*P. cornucopiae*	20	18–22	Asia and Europe.
Abalone mushroom	*P. abalone*	25	25	Taiwan.
Dhindri	*P. sajor-caju*	20–30	20–30	Asia and Europe etc.
Dhingri	*P. eryngii*	25	18	Italy and France etc.
Paddy straw mushroom	*Volvariella volvacea*	30–36	25–35	Asia.
Nameko	*Pholiata nameko*	25	10–15	Asia.
Shiitake (Black forest mushroom)	*Lentinus edodes*	25	16–19	Asia.
Giant stropharia	*Stopharia rugosaannulata*	22	9–11	East Europe and West Germany (in research).
Jelly fungus	*Tremella fuciformis*	25	23	Asia.
Wood-ear	*Auricularia species*	25	18–25	Asia.
Ink cap	*Coprinus comatus*	25	17–29	West Germany.
Bie wits	*Lepista nuda*	25	—	Netherlands.
Winter mushroom	*Flammulina velutipes*	25	10–12	Asia.
Perigord truffle	*Tuber melanosporum*	Perigord-climate (forms mycorrhiza with oak)		France and Italy.

Source : Adapted from Training manual of NRCM, Solan.

Agaricus cultivation which began in France, *Lentinus* cultivation had its beginning in China. Its cultivation was developed to great extent in Japan and until recently it has been exclusive Asian industry. This mushroom became very popular through out the world. In Asia, this mushroom is being cultivated on different substrates which attracted the attention of people in different countries for its cultivation out side Asia.

Presently, different species of mushrooms are being cultivated in about 100 countries with annual production of more than 6.6 million tons. Production of mushroom is mainly concentrated in three geographical regions the world. About 55% production is done in Europe, about 27% in North America and about 14% in East Asia. Consumption of mushroom also differs significantly in different parts of the world. Out of total mushroom production, about 85% is consumed by the G-countries of the world and remaining by the others. Average per capita mushroom consumption also varies in different countries. It is consumed from 2.2 to 7.0 Kgs per capita in different countries like Netherlands, Canada, France, U.K., Sweden, USA, Italy and in Asian countries. In India, per capita consumption is as low as 20 gm only. Preserved mushroom is consumed maximum in Germany and fresh in Netherlands.

In our country, at present three important types of mushrooms are cultivated. These are (1) Button mushroom (*Agaricus bisporus* and *Agaricus bitorquis*), (2) Straw mushroom (*Volvariella volvaceae*) and (3) Oyster mushroom (*Pleurotus* species). Button mushroom chiefly, the *Agaricus bisporus* is the most common mushroom and is extensively cultivated through out the world. It requires very low temperature for its cultivation. Therefore, only cool climatic areas and winter season in the plains of Northern India are suitable for its cultivation. Paddy straw mushroom (*Volvariella volvacea*) is most suitable for cultivation in most parts of our country, but is less suitable owing to its very low yield per unit weight of the substrate. Paddy straw mushroom is still preferred because of its delicious and nutritious property and also for being a kitchen garden crop. Oyster mushroom (*Pleurotus* species) can be grown at moderate temperature ranging from 22°C to 28°C. In some parts of our country including Banglore, this mushroom is grown at commercial scale and it is an item being served as delicious vegetable in hotels situated there on. In North India, different species of mushrooms can be grown in different seasons of the year.

Mushroom production in India and its production schedule

Musroom production schedule in north India may be suggested as under:

Calocybe indica ------------ February to April
Pleurotus sajor-caju ------------ February to mid April
Volvariella volvacea ------------ Mid June to mid September
Pleurotus sajor-caju ------------ September to November
Agaricus bisporus ------------ Mid November to mid March

In India, the annual mushroom production is about 55000 MT. Punjab ranks first in production being at the top followed by Tamil Nadu, H.P., M.P., A.P. and Uttar Pradesh. White button mushrooms contribute about 85% of total production in our country followed by oyster and paddy straw mushrooms.

Volvariella volvacea usually called as straw mushroom is known to be third in total production of mushrooms. This

Table 1.5

Normal range of temperatures and optimum temperatures required for the production of some common cultivated mushrooms.

Mushroom species	Mycelial growth		Fruitings development	
	Temp-range in C°	Optimum temp.in C°	Temp-range in C°	Optimum temp. in C°
Agaricus bisporus	3–32	22–25	9–22	15–17
Agaricus bitorquis	3–35	28–30	18–25	22–24
Auricularia auricula	15–34	28	22–25	15–28
Auricularia polytricha	10–36	20–34	15–28	24–27
Flammulina velutipes	3–34	18–25	6–18	8–12
Hericium erinaceus	12–33	21–25	12–24	15–22
Lentinus edodes	5–35	24	6–25	15 (autumn) 10 (winter) 20 (spring)
Pholiata nameko	5–32	24–26	8–20	7–10
Pleurotus ostreatus	7–37	26–28	25–30	(high tempt. strain)
			16–22	(med.temp strain)
			12–15	(low temp. strain)
Pleurotus sajor-caju	14–32	25–27	10–26	19–21
Tremella fuciformis	5–38	25	20–28	20–24
Volvariella volvacea	15–45	32–35	22–38	28–32

Adapted from Training manual of NRCM, Solan (H.P.)

mushroom needs high temperature with optimum range between 32C°–35C° for mycelial growth and 28C° to 32C° for fruiting.

Although in 1983–84, the production of *Volvariella volvacea* was as low as 4–5% of total mushroom production but now it is very popular in both the tropical and subtropical areas of the world. Countries like China, Taiwan, Thailand, Indonesia, Hong Kong, Philippines, India, Srilanka and others are producing this mushroom with much interest because of the discovery that *Volvariella* could be grown on cotton and other industrial wastes. Cultivation of *Volvariella* was increased in many countries especially in Hong Kong in recent years.

SCOPE AND DEVELOPMENT OF MUSHROOM SCIENCE

The production of mushroom in the world has been increasing steadily day by day. At present, the mushroom is under consumed in our country on a worldwide basis. Being rich source of good quality protein, mushroom is a part of vegetarian food in our country. The market for such a nutritious high proteinaceous food like mushroom with excellent flavour and texture is expected not to be saturated in near future for many years. Mushroom cultivation, maintenance of flavour and texture of mushroom and use of waste products as substrate for profitable production and mushroom preservation in different ways are different criteria which must be kept in mind by the growers. Therefore, for successful and profitable cultivation of mushroom, logical and systematic approaches involving observation of experiments and scientific evolution are desirable for up gradation of quality and yield for various phases of mushroom cultivation. Such observations frequently suggest the growers for changing cultivation methods. Quantitative measurements and objective evolutions are thus essential aspects for such experiments and observations. In this way, development of mushroom industry also requires gradual change with the time.

NEED FOR CONTINUOUS RESEARCH

It has been observed that continuous research is essential for profitable cultivation of mushroom because of the following reasons :

1. To increase the number of species that can be grown commercially at different locations under different environmental conditions.
2. To decrease cropping periods for a number of mushroom species.
3. To identify the use of a wider variety of substrates from different waste products and by products.
4. To improve methods of production and protection from diseases and insects etc.
5. To develop better techniques for mushroom cultivation and preservation.
6. To increase the consumption of mushrooms.

All above objectives can be obtained by continuous and systematic research. On the basis of applications of different technologies in its cultivation and preservation, mushroom cultivation can be appropriately told as mushroom science.

CONCEPT OF MUSHROOM TECHNOLOGY

Concept of mushroom technology is based upon the principles of production of highly nutritious food of excellent taste, with the proper utilization of the waste materials as substrates without making extensive demands upon land or having requirement for expensive equipments. A large numbers of people are undertaking mushroom growing on a commercial basis day by day because of these reasons. The concept of mushroom growing is very simple as stated above. It is a complicated business as it needs training and adaptation of new modern techniques for profitability. Therefore, the art and science of mushroom growing should be known to all those who are interested and serious about establishing a mushroom farm or cultivating it as cottage industry. Concept of mushroom technology may thus be summarized as under:

1. Mushroom is highly nutritive food of excellent taste usually relished by most and all classes of people in India and in foreign countries.
2. Mushroom production is cheap, as it does not require much land like other vegetables.
3. Mushroom is produced on substrates composed of waste materials obtained as by-products from agriculture and other industries. Thus the waste materials are better utilized.

4. Its cultivation does not require much land and expensive equipments.
5. Short-term training of mushroom cultivation may fulfil the desirable need of people who are interested and serious about mushroom cultivation.
6. Mushroom may be utilized in therapeutic diets of patient suffering from different kinds of diseases like diabetes mellitus, over weight, cardiovascular diseases and kidney diseases.
7. Mushroom cultivation may be adopted as small-scale industry and may earn foreign exchange by commercial cultivation.
8. Mushroom can be preserved for long term use. Mushroom in the form of powder and in other forms are used year round by mushroom lovers.

ESSENTIALS OF MUSHROOM SCIENCE

Mushroom science a discipline that is concerned with the principles and practice of mushroom cultivation. As in any other branch of science, mushroom science includes systematic investigations consisting of scientific studies and practical aspects of mushroom cultivation. Principles and practice of mushroom cultivation is, therefore, based upon the study of microbiology, microbial fermentation, mycology, environmental engineering and other related subjects.

Microbiology in mushroom science

Knowledge of microbiology is essential because mushroom itself is a filamentous fungus. Fungi are studied by microbiological techniques. In composting process, the knowledge of microbiology plays a significant role. Similarly principles and techniques of microbiology are also applied in preparation of spawn. The pure culture is used to inoculate the grain medium or other suitable spawn substrate under aseptic conditions. Thus knowledge of microbiology, mycology and environmental engineering is essential for profitable mushroom production.

Biochemistry in mushroom science

Mushrooms are heterotrophic organisms and they derive their nutritional requirements from the substrate. The most suitable and selective substrate is prepared for profitable button mushroom production by the application of the principles of fermentation. The principles of fermentation are involved in phases of composting which is a part of biochemistry.

Environmental engineering

Spawn running phase and the reproductive (fructification) phase are essential to be proper for profitable and economic mushroom cultivation. Both the phases are dependent upon suitable temperature and relative humidity. Thus, for the development of both the vegetative and reproductive organs of the mushroom, application of environmental engineering is of utmost importance. Optimum temperature, humidity and light are maintained in mushroom houses for better vegetative growth and formation of quality fructifications.

DIFFERENT PHASES OF MUSHROOM CULTIVATION

Besides, good knowledge of mycology, microbiology, biochemistry (fermentation) and environmental engineering, following different phases which occur in sequence must be well known to commercial mushroom growers. These phases are as under:
1. Selection of appropriate mushroom species.
2. Selection of desired fruiting culture.
3. Preparation of spawn from desired mushroom strain.
4. Preparation of quality compost.
5. Spawning and spawn running.
6. Mushroom development.
7. Picking, marketing, consumption and preservation.

PRESENT SCENARIO OF MUSHROOM CULTIVATION

From the world production figures, it is evident that *Agaricus bisporus* contributes about one third of the total production followed by Shiitake and *Pleurotus* species. Some years earlier, the trend and the demand of oyster and wood ear mushrooms have shown appreciable increase. In most cases, the total production of different species of mushrooms, has increased more than 5 times during the last 20 years. Now a days, mushroom is being cultivated in more than 100 countries with an estimated annual production of around 6.6 million tons. The Europe shares about 55%, North America about 27% and Eastern Asia produces about 14% of world production. Remaining percentage of mushroom is produced in other parts of the world.

Today the Indian scenario is much more encouraging because of an over all increase in production by five times during the last decade. During the current season, the estimated production is likely to be higher than the present. The quantity of mushroom produced in our country is obviously too small, if the vast market potential of this great country is fully exploited. The present trend of marketing in India is more prone towards export rather than towards domestic consumption. Gradually, we have to make some change in the trend and have to create a balance between production and consumption by increasing domestic market. To achieve this, however, the Indian consumers should be made more aware of the qualities, usefulness and economic importance of mushroom. All the people must also be known about the medicinal importance of mushrooms and its use in diabetes and Cardiac diseases. So that mushroom may occupy due place in the vegetarian food in our country.

RESEARCH WORK UNDER INVESTIGATION

Research works on following aspects are being done at NRCM (ICAR), Solan (H.P.).

Survey and collection and identification of fleshy fungi

At National research center for mushroom (NRCM), cultivation of three new species of *Pleurotus* collected from nature were observed to be successful. Of these, two important species were *Pleurotus eous* and *Pleurotus ulmarius*. *Pleurotus eous* was observed to display intense colouration on pileus and fruiting bodies. This species was found to develop over a wider temperature range.

Genetic improvement

Forty three germplasm lines of *Agaricus bisporus* comprizing of commercial strains, wild collection from India and exotic strains from *Agaricus* Recovery Programme (USA) were evaluated for yield, quality and pest resistance. Brown strains from Agaricus Recovery Programme (USA) produced tough fruiting bodies with increased yield at lower temperature range between 14–16°C when compared with commercially popular white strains. Efforts are being made to develop hybrid strains in *Agaricus bitorquis*. Several hybrids of *Agaricus bitorquis* have been evaluated for yield, quality and resistance against false truffle. However, some hybrids have exhibited resistance against false truffle under natural conditions.

Improved method of composting

Eco-friendly covered bunkers were built at National research center for mushroom. These were used for aerobic phase I fermentation of agro-wastes for compost preparation, followed by traditional phase II in the pasteurization tunnel. The compost thus prepared was observed to yield more mushroom.

Improved cultivation technology

Supplementation of cereal straw substrate with soybean and cotton seed cake increased mushroom yields over unsupplemented substrate.

Standardization of cultivation of specially mushrooms

Cultivation of *Lentinus edodes* on synthetic saw dust logs and of *Calocybe indica*–milky mushroom on wheat straw substrate were standardized with improved productivity. Similarly, cultivation of *Auricularia polytricha* and *Auricularia mesentrica* were also standardized with good yields.

Medicinal mushrooms

Medicinal mushroom-*Ganoderma lucidum* was successfully cultivated for the first time in our country on saw dust and wheat straw substrate. Attempts to cultivate other medicinal mushroom–*Grifola frondosa* is in progress.

Integrated pest management

Disease survey of mushroom growing areas in H.P., Punjab and Haryana were done and two important diseases–wet bubble–(*Mycogone perniciosa*) and dry bubble-(*Verticillium fungicola*) were observed to cause heavy loss to button mushroom. Spraying of Bavistin was found suitable to manage the diseases.

Maximum population of phorids was found in October whereas sciarids were found abundant in the month of May on seasonally grown crops at Solan (H.P.)

Casing and crop management in *Agaricus bisporus*
Use of coir pit, spent mushroom and composted FYM have shown promising results as casing materials in place of peat in button mushroom cultivation. Post composting supplementation with soybean meal and cotton seed meal at casting continued to show yield increase in button mushroom cultivation by over 15% as reported.

Chapter 2

Economics Importance

What is nutrition? Mushroom as food in our diet, nutrition and food, what are nutrients? Mushroom as low caloric food, nutritional consideration, mushroom in therapeutic diets, mushroom in cardiovascular diseases, a simple menu for an adolescent boy and girl, menu for old aged person and for diabetic patients.

Since earliest times, mushrooms have been treated as a special kind of food. Greeks believed from the very beginning that mushroom provides strength for warriors in battle. The Chinese treasured mushrooms as a health food the elixir of life. Some praised mushrooms as a delicacy and the Romans regarded it as food of the gods. In olden days, mushroom was served on festive occasions by Romans. Early man did not consume edible mushrooms for its nutritional composition but because of the taste and flavour of it. After analysis, it is known to all of us that mushrooms are a good source of delicious food with high nutritional attributes. Some species have medicinal values and other uses as well.

ECONOMIC IMPORTANCE
Useful effect of mushrooms
Nutrition and food

Nutrition is a combination of elements by which all parts of our body receive and utilise the materials necessary for the performance of their functions, growth, renewal and renovation of all the components. Food is the substances taken into the body that will help to meet the body's need for energy, maintenance of health, growth and reproduction. Optimum nutrition means that a person is receiving and utilizing essential nutrients in proper proportions as required by the body for all round development and performance of functions. Nutritional status is the condition of the body as it relates to consumption and utilization of food. Nutritional status of a person may be either good or poor. Good nutritional status refers the intakes of a well-balanced diet, which supplies all the essential nutrients to meet the body's requirements. Poor nutritional status refers to inadequate or even excessive intake but poor utilization of the nutrients to meet the body's requirements. Over eating can also result in poor nutritional status of a person. Malnutrition refers to the physical effect of the inadequate dietary intake in quantity and quality on the human body. Under nutrition refers to low food intake. Shiny hair, smooth skin, clear eyes, alert expression and well-developed structures of the body usually reflect good nutritional status. Good nutritional status also reflects the stamina and resistance against the diseases. Poor nutritional status is manifested by poor physique, little stamina, dull lifeless hair, dull eyes, slumped posture, failure and depression. Such people may be grossly overweight or underweight.

What are nutrients?

Nutrients are chemical components of food that supply nourishment to the body and they are required by the body in the right amounts. They must be eaten regularly. Nutrients include— proteins, carbohydrates, fats, minerals, vitamins and water, each performing specific functions in our body.

Mushroom as food rich in protein

Mushrooms have been recognised by Food and Agriculture Organization as food contributing high protein in nutrition. In such a vegetarian country like India, people are largely depend on cereals and vegetables that are not so rich in proteins and many other nutritive elements. The importance of mushrooms in our diet is too much because of the presence of high protein in it. Mushrooms usually contain 20–30% protein (about 3% on fresh weight basis) which is higher than most of the vegetables. Quality of mushroom protein is superior to that of vegetable protein. The word protein comes from a Greek word meaning primary or holding first place, which is an appropriate name for an essential life forming and life sustaining substance of all organisms. Protein makes up the major structure of all living cells and forms most of the dry weight of the body cells. Protein may be defined as organized substances that on digestion yield its constituents—unit building blocks, the amino acids. In other words, amino acids unite to form the complex molecule of a protein. Essential amino acids cannot be synthesized by the body and their requirements have to be met through dietary intake. Mushrooms are rich in these essential amino acids. Chemical composition of twenty essential aminoacids are as under :

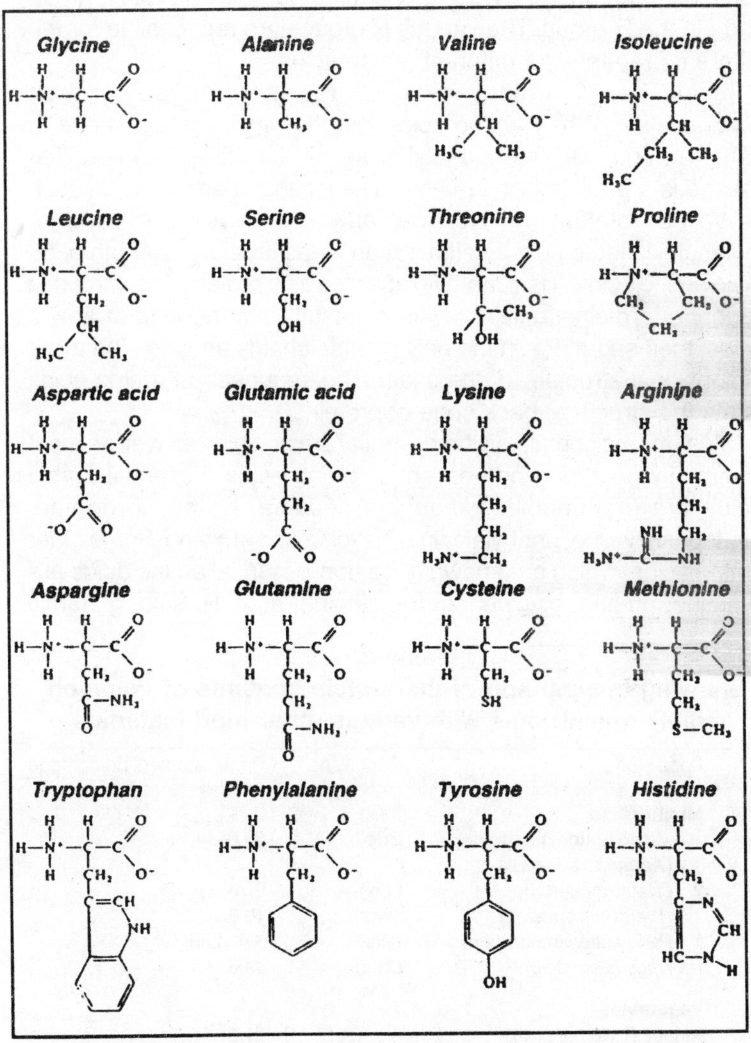

Fig. 2.1. Showing molecular structure of 20 important amino acids found in protein

Amino-acids in protein

Proteins are composed of amino acids. There are twenty different amino acids used as building block molecules for proteins. These amino acids are chemically different from each other but all of them contains (i) an amino (NH 2) group, (ii) a carboxyl (-COOH) group and (iii) the R group. The various R groups are responsible for the different properties of different amino acids.

In all the 20 amino acids linkage is achieved through condensation. When amino acids join the amino group of one, it forms a bond with the carboxyl group of the other. The resulting linkage is a peptide bond (-C-N-). The joining of amino acids such as Valine-, glutamine-, tyrosine- and alanine result in a larger molecule called a poly peptide. When it has reached a length of 50 or so amino acids, it is generally regarded as a protein. The immense variety of proteins in living systems result from the kind of amino acids, their sequence in the poly peptide chains and also the three dimensional structure of the chain. The sequence of amino acids forms the structural back bone of proteins.

Mushrooms contain all the essential amino acids as well as most commonly occurring non-essential amino acids. Essential amino acids are methionine, isoleucine, leucine, lysine, threonine, tryptophan, valine, phenylalanine, histidine and arginine. Some other amino acids, which are known to be non-essential amino acids are cysteine, proline, glycine, serine, alanine, aspartic acid, glutamic

Table 2.1
Showing comparison of the protein contents of common edible mushrooms with various other food materials

S.N.	Food stuffs	Conditions	Protein content percentage
1	**Mushrooms**	Fesh	3.7++
	1. White button mushroom (*Agaricus bisporus*)	Dried	35.0+++
	2. Oyster mushroom (*Pleurotus* species)	Fesh	2.78
		Dried	19.8
	3. Paddy straw mushroom (*Volvariella* species)	Fesh	3.9–4.99
		Dried	28.5
	Vegetables		
	Kidney Beans (Dried)		21.3
	Broad Beans (Dried)		24.0
	Lentils (Dried)		24.7
	Frozen Green Peas		5.4

Dry Peas	24.2
Cabbage	1.5
Carrots	1.1
Cauliflower	2.7
Potato Raw	2.3
Water Cress	2.2
Tomato	1.1
Egg Plant	1.1
Beets	1.6
Fruits and Nuts	
Apricot (Dried)	5.0
Coconut (Dried)	7.2
Roasted Peanuts	26.2
Fresh Apple	0.3
Banana	1.1
Dried Dates	2.2
Yeast, Bread, Cereals	
Compressed yeast	12.1
Dried yeast	38.8
Breads	8.7–9.1
Wheat flour	11.7
Corn flour	7.8
Whole rice	7.5
Maize	3.5
Dairy products	
Raw egg whole	12.8
Cheddar cheese	25.0
Cow's milk	3.2
Meat-Beef. sirloin rib	19.5–21.5
Liver	19.7
Rabbits	20.4
Chicken	19.0–20.6
Pork, loin, cutlet	14.6–18.6
Fish-Mecherel	19.0
Haddock	18. 3
Cod	17.6
Perch, trout	18.4–19.2
Lobster, Crab	16.9–17-.4

Source – Proceedings of specialized workshop on tropical Mushroom cultivation (1992), held at I.I.H.R. Banglore, India

acid and tyrosine. They are also found in most of the mushrooms. These non essential amino acids are usually synthesized by the body. Of the total amino acids, 25–40% is comprised of essential amino acids. Approximately 25–35% of the total amino acids occur as free amino acids and the remainder being combined with the protein. The composition of the growth substrate may also have a significant effect on the composition of amino acids in mushroom without changing the apparent crude protein.

Mushroom as low caloric food

Mushrooms like other vegetables contain about 90% moisture and are basically a low calorie food. Total carbohydrate content is 4–5% which consists of chitin, hemicelluloses and glycogen. Starch is absent and very little amount of free sugar (0.3%) is known to be found in mushrooms. Cholesterol and the sterol known to be dreaded for heart patients, remain absent in mushrooms. In its place, ergosterol is present which is converted by the human body into vitamin D, being very essential for bones and teeth. Fibre content in mushroom is high which is helpful in excretion of wastes from the body and prevention of constipation. Vitamin B complex and vitamin C are found in significant quantities which includes chiefly the thiamine, riboflavin, niacin, biotin and folic acid. Folic acid and vitamin B_{12} normally absent in most of the vegetables, are known to be present in mushrooms. Besides above vitamins, they are fairly good sources of vitamin C also.

Carbohydrates in mushroom

Carbohydrate $(C_6H_{12}O_6)_n$ is a chemical compound made up of carbon, hydrogen and oxygen. The basic unit of carbohydrate is a monosaccharide. It contains a series of carbon atoms linked together in a chain attached with oxygen and hydrogen atoms. Since carbohydrates in the form of glucose cannot be stored in nature on a large scale, therefore, carbohydrates form chain like complex polymeric molecules with removal of water. Carbohydrate

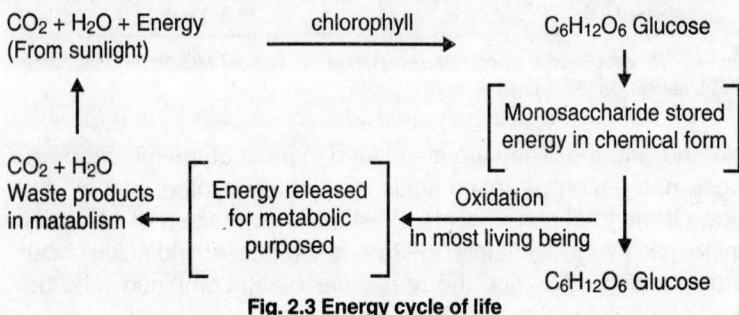

Fig. 2.3 Energy cycle of life

Table 2.2

Showing chemical composition consisting of carbohydrate, crude protein and fat of different edible mushrooms

Species	Sample	Initial moisture percent	Cruide protein	Fat	carbohydrates Total N. free		Fibre	Ash
Agaricus bisporus	Fresh	90.4	28.0	3.1	59.4	51.1	8.3	9.4
Volvariella volvacea	—	88.0	29.5	5.7	60.8	49.6	10.4	9.8
V. diplasia	—	90.4	28.5	2.6	57.4	40.0	17.4	11.5
Pleurotus ostreatus	—	90.8	30.4	2.2	57.6	48.9	8.7	9.8
Pleurotus species (Indian var.)	—	91.0	21.6	7.2	60.5	48.6	11.9	10.7

Source: *Proceedings of specialized workshop on tropical Mushroom cultivation* (1992), held at I.I.H.R. Banglore, India.

is usually found as starch in plants and glycogen in animals. These starch and glycogen when required are broken down to their simple form in glucose in the presence of water. Glycogen is the stored starch in animals and is found in liver and muscles from where it is mobilized as soon as glucose levels in blood dip below the normal. Fresh mushrooms contain relatively large amount of carbohydrate and fibre. *Agaricus bisporus* contains pantoses, hexoses, disaccharides, amino acids and alcohols as well as undefined uronides and methyl sugars. Mannitol occurs in high concentration.

Among the polymeric carbohydrates, glycogen and chitin as polymer of N-acetylglycosamine are found as the structural components of fungus cell wall. In young specimens a-trehalose (mushroom sugar) occurs in significant quantity which is hydrolysed to glucose as mushroom matures.

Fats in mushroom

Fats are a more concentrated form of storage of energy than carbohydrates. They are found in the adipose (fatty) tissue of animals. An ingested fat undergoes emulsification, digestion and absorption. In the presence of an adequate supply of carbohydrate, fat is stored in the adipose (fatty) tissue. An excess of daily intake of carbohydrate also results in its conversion into fat and storage of such fat in the fatty tissues. Hence, over weight persons should not only avoid an excess intake of fat but also an excessive daily intake of carbohydrate. Fat is a complex molecule constituting a mixture of fatty acids and an alcohol generally glycerol. Like carbohydrates, it contains carbon, hydrogen and oxygen. It differs from carbohydrate as it contains more carbon and hydrogen and less oxygen. Different species of mushrooms contain little amount of fat and; therefore, may be taken by persons without the risk of being overweight. Fresh mushrooms usually contain insignificant amount of fat and no cholesterol at all.

Vitamin in mushrooms

Mushrooms are known to be rich in potash, iron as well as in certain vitamins. In fact, mushrooms contain more of the vitamins B_{12} and niacin than any other vegetable. Mushrooms are also low in sodium and are, therefore, useful to adding flavoured dishes served to heart patients who have been advised not to take common sodium salt. Mushrooms are ideal for inclusion in vegetarian diets as they increase variety and flavour. Mushrooms can be frozen for considerable period while retaining much of their nutrient contents. During cooking, there is inevitably a loss of vitamin B-complex in the juice but in a soup, the vitamins will remain in the dish. There are more than 100 different varieties of edible mushrooms, which serve as valuable source of nutrients and can be made available whole of the year.

Vitamins are the vital substances. They are needed in small quantity for growth and good health. These are vital body regulators. Most of the vitamins are synthesized by the body while others must be supplied through diet. Requirement of very few of the vitamins may be met by the synthesis in the body. Mushrooms are rich in vitamin B-Complex which is very essential for our well being. Vitamin B Complex contained in mushrooms are Thiamine (B_1), Riboflavin, Niacin (Nicotinic acid or pellagra preventing factor), Pantothenic acid (formerly vitamin B_3), Pyridoxine (B_6), Biotin (co-enzyme R), Folacin and Cyanacobalamine (formerly B_{12}). Besides B-complex, mushrooms contain ascorbic acid which is also known as vitamin C.

Minerals in mushrooms

Mushrooms are rich in minerals. A mineral is an inorganic element occurring in the form of its salts such as calcium, phosphorus, potassium, sodium, iodine, iron, copper, molybdenum, sulphur,

Table 2.3
Deficiency symptoms, important sources and therapeutic importance of different vitamins present in edible mushrooms

Name of vitamin	Deficiency Symptoms	Important sources
Thiamine (Vitamin B$_1$)	Anorexia, fatigue, constipation, depression, irritability, tenderness of leg calf with some loss in muscular co-ordinations and abnormal carbohydrate metabolism	Mushroom, meat (especially pork), whole grain and enriched cereals, organs (especially liver), nuts and peanuts, butter, legumes (especially soybean), milk, eggs, yeast and wheat gems.
Riboflavin (Vitamin B12)	Burning and itching eyes, blurred and dim vision, eyes sensitive to light, inflammation of the lips and tongue, lesions in angles of mouth, digestive disturbances, greasy and scaly skin.	Mushroom, dairy foods, organs especially liver, meat, legumes, eggs, whole gains cereals, green leafy vegetables, yeasts and liver concentrates.
Niacin (tryptophan precursor)	Fatigue, dermatitis, sore mouth especially tongues, gastrointestinal disturbances (diarrhoea and vomiting), nervous disturbances, mental depression, weakness and anorexia.	Meat especially liver, fish, poultry, whole grains, cereals, legumes, nuts, peanuts, liver concentrates and mushrooms.
Ascorbic acids (Vitamin -C)	Fatigue, dermatitis, sore mouth especially tongue and skin, many other skin diseases and bleeding gums etc.	Fresh fruits especially citrus, milk and fresh mushrooms

chlorine, magnesium and manganese etc. Minerals help to build tissues, regulate body fluids and various other body functions. Like the vitamins, they are also required in small quantities and are of vital importance for the well being of the body. They should be supplied daily as they are excreted through the kidney, the bowel and the skin. They may be present in the body as organic and as inorganic compounds. Organic compounds are phosphoproteins, phospholipids, haemoglobin, thyroxin and inorganic compounds include sodium chloride, calcium phosphate and certain free ions.

These important minerals are known to be present in different edible mushrooms. Minerals present in mushrooms may be classified under three important groups:

1. **Major minerals or macro minerals**
   Macro minerals are calcium, phosphorus, sodium and chlorine. These are required in large amounts at least 100 mg/day.

2. **Minor minerals**
   These are required in small quantities less than a few mgs. Iron, sulphur and magnesium are important minor minerals needed in our body.

3. **Trace elements (micro minerals)**
   Trace elements are required in very little quantities. Iodine, molybdenum and zinc are some of the important trace elements needed in our body.

Functions of minerals
   Different minerals usually found in different edible mushrooms vary widely. Important functions of these minerals may be summarized as under:
1. They are structural components of bones, teeth, soft tissue, muscles, bloods and neve cells.

Table 2.4
**Showing mineral requirements and deficiency
symptoms of different important minerals**

Tissues of body parts	Elements especially needed	Deficiency symptoms
Bones and teeth	Calcium and phosphorus	Stunted growth, weekend or soft bone, malformed or decaying teeth and rickets
Hair, nails, skin and soft tissues	Potassium, phosphorus, sulphur and chlorine	unhealthy looking
Nervous tissue	Phosphorus	Nervous weakness
Blood	Iron, calcium, sodium, phosphorus and copper	Lack of iron or copper results in less than normal amount of haemoglobin in blood called nutritional anaemia.
Glandular secretion		
Gastric	Chlorine	—
Intestinal	Sodium	—
Thyroid	Iodine	Goitre
Pancreas (insulin)	Zinc	—

2. They help in regulating the activity of nerves with regard to stimuli and contraction of muscles.
3. They help to maintain acid-base balance of fluid in the body.
4. They control the water balance by means of osmotic pressure and by regulating the permeability of cell membranes.
5. They help in the process of digestion.
6. They are structural parts of the molecules of hormones and enzymes.
7. They act as enzyme activators and regulate cellular oxidation.

Mineral requirements

Our body needs different minerals for performance of different functions. Different parts of our body exhibit deficiency symptoms of various descriptions. Some of the important elements and their characteristic deficiency symptoms have been shown in the table given ahead.

Table 2.5
Showing contents of vitamins and minerals found in some common edible mushrooms
(*in milligrams per 100 g of dry weight*).

Contents of vitamin

Species	Sample	Thiamine	Riboflavin	Niacin	Ascarbic acid
Agaricus bisporus	Fresh	8.9	3.7	42.5	26.5
	Canned	1.0	0.2	17.9	0.0
Volvariella volvacea	Fresh	1.2	3.3	91.9	20.2
V. diplasia	Fresh	—	—	—	—
Pleurotus ostreatus	Fresh	4.8	4.7	108.7	0.0

Contents of minerals

Species	Sample	Ca	P	Fe	Na	K
Agaricus bisporus	Fresh	71	912	8.8	106	2850
	Canned	119	738	9.5	—	4762
Volvariella volvacea	Fresh	71	677	17.1	374	3455
V. diplasia	Fresh	58	1042	17.7	—	3333
Pleurotus ostreatus	Fresh	33	1348	15.2	837	3793

Source - Based on reports of Food and Agriculture Organization. (1972)

In general, mushrooms contain significant amount of phosphorous, sodium and potassium with lesser amount of calcium and iron. Fresh specimen of *Agaricus bisporus* was found to contain some undesirable minerals like traces of lead, cadmium and selenium. These undesirable elements, however, have no any adverse effect on the health because these are destroyed during cooking of the mushroom.

Nutritional consideration

A comparison of nutritional indexes shows that high value mushrooms rank above all the vegetables and legumes except soybeans. Mushrooms are a stable food in the diet of various cultures of people in different countries. Edible mushrooms are usually considered to be highly nutritive and are liked by most of the people for their flavour and condiment value. Comparision of

Table 2.6
Comparison of nutritive values of various foods as compared to mushrooms

Name of food	Nutritional indexes
Chicken	59
Beef	43
Pork	35
Soybeans	31
Mushrooms	5–28
Spinach	26
Milk	25
Kidney beans	21
Peanuts	20
Cabbage	17
Cucumbers	14
Corns	11
Turnips	10
Potatos	9
Carrots	6
Tomatos	8

Note: Ranking based an nutritional indexes as calculated against the FAO reference protein pattern.

nutritive value of different food materials are given below:

MEDICINAL VALUE OF MUSHROOMS

Mushrooms are known to have medicinal value. Some of the species have been used in different diseases. Years ago, people were more interested in the medicinal properties of the mushrooms than in their basic value as a source of food. Medicinal value of mushrooms may be summarised as under:

1. Haematological value

Lectins are plant proteins isolated from different species of mushrooms. These are used in various ways. Lectins isolated from *Agaricus compestris* is a tetramer with an estimated molecular weight of 64,000. A lectin purified from *Flammulina velutipes* was estimated to have a molecular weight of 20,000. Volvatoxin A is the lectin produced from *Volvariella volvacea*. It has been shown to reduce haemolytic activity towards group 'O' red blood cells. Pleurotolysin is the lectin isolated from *Pluerotus ostreatus* and is a haemolytic agent for mammalian red blood cells *in vitro*.

2. Antiviral value

There are reports that antiviral substances were present in mushrooms. Extracts from the fruiting body of *Lentinus edodes* and the spores contained therein have been observed to own antiviral activity against influenza virus infection in mice. A phenol fraction of mushroom extract was capable of conferring the antiviral activity. It has further been observed that virus like particles were present in several mushrooms chiefly in *Lentinus edodes*.

3. Anti-tumour effect

The virus like particles isolated from *Lentinus edodes* are known to be able to suppress a peculiar type of carcinoma in mice. Anti tumour activity is not confined to *Lentinus edodes* only since it is also present in other mushrooms. Anti carcinogenic action of water stable and alcohol insoluble fraction obtained from the culture medium of *Lentinus edodes* mycelia was composed of a xylose containing polysaccharide and protein.

4. Antibacterial effect

Antibacterial effects have been observed in phenolic and quinoid derivatives isolated from *Agaricus bisporus*. Other edible fungi also contain such derivatives but do not dominate the list of sources of antibacterial compounds such as polyethylene, phenolic compounds, purines or pyrimidines, quinones and terpenoids. *Pleurotus, Polyporus* and *Tricholoma* species are common mushrooms which have also been characterized for the presence of substances of antibacterial activity.

5. Anti fungal effect

There are certain edible fungi who have antifungal activities. These edible fungi include *Lentinus edodes*, *Coprinus comatus* and *Qudemansiella mucida*.

6. Cardiovascular and renal effect

The cardiovascular diseases are generally manifested due to overload of work on the heart against its rated capacity. Alteration in the walls of arteries usually results in obstruction of the normal blood flow due to cholesterol, high caloric diets and excessive electrolytes. Ingestion of *Lentinus edodes* has been reported to reduce the serum cholesterol level in human. An anti-platelet substance was also isolated from the aqueous extract of *Auricularia polytricha*. This substance could inhibit platelet aggregation. This substance has recently been identified as adenosine. It has been observed that atherosclerosis is very low in incidence among people who consumed *Auricularia polytricha* regularly. Reduction in high blood pressure towards normal, extended life span of chronic renal failure patients and reduction in plasma glucose tolerance in diabetic patients have also been observed in patients who consumed *Pleurotus sajor-caju*, and *Coprinus comatus* regularly.

Volvatoxin A is a cardio toxic protein isolated from *Volvariella volvacea*. Its carcinogenic toxic effect has been observed in mice. In human, it has very little ill effect of insignificant importance and can be eliminated after heating for 5 second at 100°C. Despite these two negative observations, consumption of mushrooms may confer the benefits of being antifungal, antibacterial, antiprotozoal and antiatherosclerosis. Although much information has been accumulated about the physiological and therapeutical effects of most of the edible mushrooms but very little is known about the mechanism of these effects.

Mushroom in therapeutic diets

Infancy, childhood, adolescence, adulthood and old age are the various stages in life cycle of a man. A balance and simple diet at every stage can be beneficial to the health and well being of a person. A pregnant and lactating mother has greater responsibility towards the health of her child since her nutritional status during these periods affects the baby's physical and mental development. Balanced diets for every stage of life have been specified according to the need of energy. Mushrooms may be taken by the persons of all age groups and may be consumed both by male and female.

Adolescence (12 to 18 years)

Adolescence period is characterized by the heavy demands of energy (calories) and protein. The appetite of the child during this period usually increases and tends to consume more carbohydrate foods and fewer protein foods. The need for calcium and iron to support bone and muscle growth continues especially in case of girls due to iron losses during menstrual cycle which may predispose her to simple iron deficiency anaemia. Therefore, it is necessary to take more care of girls than boys because girls may be vulnerable to malnourishment. If the physical activity of the girl does not match her food intake, it may result in excessive fat deposits and fatness of the body. Similarly, if she is figure conscious, she may follow some crash diets which will predispose her to malnutrition. In real sense, a simple list of natural and easily digestible items of food is considered most suitable for proper development in adolescence period.

Table 2.7
A simple menu for an adolescent boy and girl
Menu Plan

Break fast	Bread toast	2–3 slices with butter
	Boiled egg	1
	Fruit juice / milk / mushroom soup	1 glass
Lunch	Potato paratha or chapati	2
	Mushroom and potato mixed vegetable	1 cup
	Salad	As much as desired
	Rajma / Urad Dal	1 cup
	Rice	1 cup
Snacks	Banana	2
	Milk or fruit juice	1 cup
	Rava laddu	1
Dinner	Chapati	2
	Mushroom mixed vegetable	1 cup
	Rice	1 cup
	Dal palak	1 cup
	Curds	½ cup
Bed time	Milk with Proteinex	1 glass

Note: For adolescent girl milk may be reduced if so desired to avoid fatness.

Mushrooms for the aged person

Young adulthood is characterized by the years of building one's career and establishing one's own home. In these years (18 to 40 years), the adult struggles for himself and his family. Middle adulthood covers the age of 40 to 60 years and older adulthood covers the age between 60 to 80 years and above. In late adulthood over weight and obesity, diabetes mellitus, mal-absorption, constipation, anaemia, hypertension, bones and joint diseases, atherosclerosis and coronary heart diseases are common in occurrence. Mushrooms are very useful in management of these diseases and can be substituted against meat.

Table 2.8
Diet plan for an old man (60–80 years) based on energy requirement of a normal old person

Menu Plan

Tea	—	1 cup
Break fast	Bread	1
	Mushroom soup or milk	1 cup
	Banana	1
Lunch	Chapatti	1
	Rice	½ cup
	Dal	½ cup
	Potato palak mixed with mushroom	1 cup
	Curd	½ cup
	Oranges or sweet lime	1
Tea	—	1 cup
Dinner	Chapatti	1
	Rice	1 cup
	Curd	½ cup
	Salad (carrot, cabbage, khira)	As much as desired
	Mushroom	1 cup
Bed time	Warm milk	1 cup

Note: Old persons with any specific disease may be advised the menu with some modification.

Mushroom in diabetes mellitus

Diabetes mellitus, commonly known as sugar disease is a metabolic disorder. It indirectly arrests carbohydrate metabolism. The disease is characterized by high blood sugar level and high level of sugar in urine. It is accompanied by secondary alterations of fat and protein metabolism resulting in an array of physical disorders. Although the fundamental principles of dietary control in patients suffering from diabetes mellitus, is based upon the fact that necessary calories according to the requirement of ones body's daily requirement should be given. The total calories advised will vary among different patients. The obese patient who is required to reduce his weight must take lower caloric diet whereas under weight patient requires a comparatively high caloric diet. It has been found that reduction of body weight alone results in better functioning of the beta cells and increased sensitivity to insulin action in diabetic patients. Mushrooms have been found to be suitable in all the cases of diabetes mellitus and may be liberally taken up as soup and vegetable. It is also used by meat-eaters as substitute due to its similar taste if cooked with meat spices.

ANCIENT PREPARATIONS FOR THE TABLE

Ancient and sophisticated mushroom preparations listed here, have been tried out and proved acceptable by many mushroom lovers in different countries. The skilful house-wife and dietetian may find many ways of improving these recipes according to their need and taste. They may also devise new and original methods of great interest and taste.

1. Mushroom fried in butter on toast

One of the most palatable dishes may be made of any or all the edible mushrooms by the use of plenty of fresh and good butter.

Method of preparation: Place a frying pan containing butter on the fire and allow the butter to turn brown. Now add the whole sliced or cut up mushrooms and cover with a lid. Stew slowly for about ten minutes or longer if the quantity is large. By the time the mushrooms are sufficiently cooked, the lid should be removed. When superfluous water is evaporated, the butter should be added in sufficient quantity to avoid the preparation from burning and not to make the dish too greasy.

How to serve: Meanwhile, make toast ready, place the preparation on the toast and serve on the table.

Note: In the preparation, no salt and pepper has been added. However, it can be add if so desired.

2. Fried mushrooms and eggs
Fry the mushrooms in the manner already described above. Just before they are ready to be served, break one or more eggs in to the clear center of the pan, season and cover with lid until white of egg is set.

3. Fried mushrooms and scrambled eggs
Fry the mushrooms as above. Meanwhile prepare as usual, eggs for scrambling. Now add the fried mushrooms to the eggs and scramble them in a buttered pan in the usual manner.

4. Simple mushroom omelete
Fry the mushroom as above. Prepare butter for omelette in the usual manner. Now fill the fried mushroom when served.

5. Mushroom sweet breads
Mushrooms fried in the above manner , when served with daintily prepared sweet breads, constitute a most palatable and appetizing and nutritious food.

6. Stewed mushrooms
Cut the mushrooms in small pieces and place them in the frying pan with a small amount of butter. Stew well, under lid for ten minutes or more. Meanwhile beat a little flour in water or cold broth, add finely chopped parsley, salt to taste and pour over mushrooms in pan. Instead of using butter alone, peanut butter maybe added, which gives a pleasant flavour. Instead of water and flour, use milk for a change or milk and egg beaten together. The addition of parsley enhances the flavour.

7. Breaded mushrooms
Mushrooms may be used as whole. In foreign countries, puffball are cut or sliced in pieces. It is now buttered, seasoned with salt and pepper and rolled in eggs and bread crumbs. Afterwards fry them briskly in butter.

8. Mushroom soups
Mince the mushroom finely. Add to hot broth and boil for twenty minutes. Brown some flour in butter, beat slowly into the soup, add salt and pepper and chopped parsley according to taste. Strain or serve unstrained.

SOPHISTICATED MUSHROOM PREPARATIONS

Different delicious preparations are known to be liked by mushroom lovers in India and abroad. They are usually used as vegetables made with the potato, tomato, onions, eggs and different other materials. Besides this, some most common mushroom preparations including both common in India and abroad (exotic preparations) are being given below:

(Adapted from training manual of NRCM, Solan, H.P.)

1. Lentil Mushroom Soup
Ingredients

Lentil		50.0g
Onions (sliced and chopped)		10.0g
Mushrooms		150.0g
Celery stalk (Chopped)		5.0g
Carrots (sliced)		15.0g
Tomatoes (Pureed)		30.0g
Salt		2.0g
Pepper		2.0g
Stock or water		1.0 cup
Vinegar	(teaspoonful)	1.0
Oil	(teaspoonful)	1.0

Method of preparation

Boil the stock and add lentil slowly. Reduce to a simmer and cook for half an hour. Meanwhile, saute the onions and mushrooms in oil. Set aside and combine all ingredients except vinegar and seasoning. Cook half an hour. Add vinegar, salt and pepper before serving.

2. Mushroom Souffle
Ingredients

Mushrooms		150.0g
Floor		5.0g
Butter		5.0g
Onions		30.0g
Milk		60.0g
Cheese		50.0g
Pepper		2.0g
Egg	(in numbers)	2.0

Method of preparation

In a large sauce pan, melt butter and add onion. Cook until onion is soft but not brown. Remove pan from heat and blend in flour. Stir sliced mushroom in milk. Place pan on heat and stir until mixture boils and retains thickness. Cool a little and break the egg putting yolks, cheese, salt and pepper in it. Heat egg whites until stiff and mix mushroom mixture to it. Now heat the egg whites quickly and lightly. Pour mixture into grease free soufflé dish and bake at 18°C for 30 minutes. Serve hot.

3. Mushroom Pizza

Ingredients

Refined flour		60.0g
Fresh yeast		5.0g
Salt	(teaspoonful)	½
Mushrooms		50.0g
Tomatoes		75.0g
Onions		20.0g
Cheese		20.0g
Butter	(teaspoonful)	1.0
Garlic	(flake)	1.0
Chilli powder	(pinch)	1.0

Method of preparation

Sieve the flour and mix salt and yeast in it. Warm it to make the dough. Cover the dough with a wet cloth until it becomes double in size. Knead the dough and roll it out making 1.0 centimeter in thickness. Grease the pizza tray and place the rolled out dough in the tray. Chop the onion, tomatoes and mushrooms. Saute the onion, garlic, tomatoes, mushrooms, chilli powder and salt. Cook for 5–10 minutes and spread the mixture over the rolled dough and sprinkle with grated cheese. Bake in a very hot oven for 20 minutes.

4. Mushroom Pulao

Ingredients

Mushrooms	150.0g
Rice	75.0g
Onions (sliced)	40.0g
Ghee	30.0g
Paneer	40.0g
Salt	1.0g

Peas		50.0g
Green chillies		1.0g
Water	(cups)	3.0

Method of preparation

Fry onions in ghee till it changes to golden brown in colour. Stir in the drained rice, mushrooms, paneer and salt. Now add shelled peas, chillies, hot water (double the amount of rice) and cover. Simmer it till cooked. Serve hot.

5. Tomato Mushroom Bhujia

Ingredients

Tomatoes	100.0g
Mushrooms	150.0g
Onions	75.0g
Green chillies	2.0g
Garlic	5.0g
Ginger	2.0g
Turmeric	2.0g
Chilli powder	2.0g
Salt	2.0g
Garam masala	2.0g
Oil	20.0g

Method of preparation

Take a flat bottom vessel and pour oil in it. When oil is hot, add chopped onion and dry till it changes to light brown in colour. Now add all the other ingredients including chopped mushrooms. Cook till it becomes gravy in thickness.

6. Palak Mushroom

Ingredients

Spinach	150.0g
Mushrooms	150.0g
Onions	50.0g
Garlic	1.0g
Potatoes	80.0g
Red chillies	1.0g
Turmeric	1.0g

Ginger		1.0g
Cloves		1.0g
Ghee		10.0g

Method of preparation

Wash and chop spinach, onions and coriander leaves. Boil and mash potatoes. Grind cloves, red chillies, garlic and ginger make it a paste. Heat ghee and add the spiced paste and make it dry. Now add mushrooms to it and heat slowly for some time. Cook spinach and grind well along with mashed potatoes in an electric blender. Now add the spinach potato mixture to the coriander and chopped mushrooms. Add salt and turmeric. Cook for 2 minutes and serve it with lime.

7. Mushroom Pattice
Ingredients

Potatoes		60.0g
Mushrooms		100.0g
Peas		25.0g
Onions		20.0g
Oil		10.0g
Salt		2.0g
Chilli powder		1.0g
Garam masala		1.0g
Lime	(in number)	¼

Method of preparation

Boil potatoes and peas. Mash potatoes into cups and stuff with mushrooms and pea mixture. Bind the edges together and flatten them. Fry it slowly till it becomes crisp and brown in colour.

8. Mushroom Omelette
Ingredients

Eggs	(in number)	2.0
Mushrooms		100.0 g
Pepper		2.0g
Salt		1.0g
Fat		10.0g
Cheese		20.0g

Method of preparation
Break the eggs into a bowl and season with pepper and salt. Mix properly the yolks and whites of the eggs with mushroom cut into thin pieces. Wipe thoroughly the omelette pan, add fat/ghee to it and heat as usual. Move the mixture continuously and half fold the solidifying preparation at right angles to the handle. Now lift it out and serve hot.

9. Mushroom Samosa
Ingredients

Flour		40.0g
Fat		10.0g
Salt		2.0g
Mushroom		100.0g
Potato		20.0g
Peas		20.0g
Onions		20.0g
Green chillies	(in number)	2.0
Coriander powder	(teaspoonful)	2.0
Amchur	(teaspoonful)	1.0
Chilli powder	(teaspoonful)	1.0
Salt	(teaspoonful)	2.0

Method of preparation
Sieve flour, melt fat and mix the flour and salt to it. Add water and knead to stiff dough and leave aside for ½ hour. Boil potatoes and peas. Saute the chopped onions, green chillies, the seasoning, mashed mushrooms, peas and dried potatoes. Make small balls of dough and roll out into very thin rounds. Cut the rounds into half, form into a cone and put in the stuffing. Seal the two edges together. Deep fry till crisp and changes medium brown in colour. Now it is ready to use.

10. Mushroom Pakora
Ingredients

Mushrooms	150.0g
Onions	55.0g
Cabbage	30.0g
Coriander leaves	6.0g
Chillies	4.0g
Gram flour	100.0g

Garam masala	3.0g
Salt	3.0g
Oil	60.0ml

Method of preparation

Chop onions, cabbage, coriander leaves, chillies and mushrooms finely. Add gram flour to bind the vegetable mushroom mixture. Add salt, chilli powder, garam masala and mix well. Shape into round balls. Fry and serve.

11. Mushroom pickles
(1 kg content)

Ingredients

Mushroom (small size)	1.0kg
Zira	6.0g
Coriander	10.0g
Kalauji	6.0g
Salt and chillies	30.0g
Ginger	15.0g
Garlic	15.0g
Onion	30.0g
Methi	8.0g
Ajwayan	5.0g
Cinnamon (Dalchini)	1.5g
Jaifal (in number)	1/4
Mastard oil	500.0ml
Vinegar	6.0ml
Citric acid	trace

Method of preparation

Clean mushroom and remove all dirts adhered to it. Fry it in mustard oil till it turns brown and then cool it. Now cut onions into small pieces and add garlic, zira, kalouji, salt and other spices like ajwayan, cinnamon, jaifal etc., after grinding it properly. Make it like a paste. Mix the ground paste with the mushroom, vinegar and citric acid. After mixing the contents well, submerge the entire contents into mustard oil. Keep it in sun for two days. Pickle is ready. Consume it when desired. Pickle should remain submerged in mustard oil up to date otherwise it would get spoilt by moulds.

EXOTIC RECIPES OF MUSHROOMS

12. Mushroom and apple chutney

Ingredients

Onion	(in number) minced	1
Apples (cooking apples, peeled, cored and chopped)		500.0g
Mushrooms chopped		500.0g
Red pepper chopped		125.0g
Green tomatos chopped		375.0g
Garlic cloves	(in number)	2.0
White vinegar		1200.0 ml
Sugar		375.0g

Method of preparation

Put the onions into a saucepan just covered with water. Soak it until it becomes tender. Most of the water usually evaporates during this period. Add the apples, mushrooms, pepper, tomatoes and half of the vinegar. Crush the garlic and put it into pan. Simmer the mixture until it thickens and then add the remaining vinegar gradually. When it becomes thick in consistency, add sugar and continue to cook until the liquid evaporates. Stir the mixture. Pour the chutney into clean, dry jars and cover it with air tight vinegar proof seal. Label and store it in cool place. Now it is ready for use.

13. Mushroom Ketchup

Ingredients

Wiped mushrooms	2.0kg
Salt	125.0g
Pepper corns	10.0ml
All spices	10.0 ml
Mace	5.0ml
Ground ginger	5.0ml
Ground cloves	2.5 ml
Cinnamon	2.5ml
Vinegar	800.0ml

Method of preparation

Cut the mushrooms into small pieces, sprinkle with salt and leave in a bowl for about 120 hours. Rinse the mushrooms and mash them with a wooden spoon or popular. Add vinegar and spices and simmer in a closed pan for half an hour and later strain through a sieve. Pour it in to hot bottles when it is hot and seal at once. Slacken screw caps and put into a pan of hot water and keep this simmering for half an hour. Remove from pan, tighten screw caps. It yields about 1200 ml ketchup.

14. Red Tomato and Mushroom Chutney
Ingredients

Ripe tomatoes	2.5kg
Thin sliced onions (in number)	3.0
Green peppers (in number)	3.0
Sliced mushrooms	1.0kg
Malt vinegar	1.5 liters
Salt	60.0g
Grated rind and juice of lemons (in number)	2.0
Ground mixed spices	7.5ml

Method of preparation

Cut the tomatoes into pieces and remove most of the seeds. Put flesh and juice into large pan. Add all the other ingredients and boil gently for at least one hour until the chutney becomes thick in consistency. Put it into sterilized jars, cover with airtight vinegar proof seal. It yields about 1.5 kg of chutney.

15. Pickled Mushrooms
Ingredients

Mushrooms	2.0kg
Salt	7.5g
Vinegar	800.0ml
Pepper corns	10.0ml

Method of preparation

Wash the mushrooms thoroughly and dry it on blotting paper. Now put it into a large sauce pan and sprinkle salt over mushroom. Cover the pan with a well fitting lid and simmer gently until the mushrooms become tender but not soft. Boil the vinegar with the pepper corns in another pan. Fill sterilized jars with the mushrooms. Strain off excess juices, leaving about 1 table spoon of liquor in each jar. Now fill the jar with boiled vinegar and cover it with air tight vinegar proof seal. Pickled mushroom is ready to use. Label it properly.

16. Lemon and mushroom soup
Ingredients
Butter	50.0g
Plain flour	40.0g
Chicken stock	600.0ml
Milk	400.0ml
Minced mushrooms	225.0g
Chopped parsley	30.0ml
Lemon juice (add desirable amount for taste)	
Double cream	142.0ml

Method of preparation
Heat the butter in a pan, stir in the flour and cook for a few minutes. Stir in the stock and bring to a boil. Add milk, mushroom and parsley. Season it with salt, pepper and lemon juice for taste. Cook for 5 minutes. Stir in the cream, chill it when serving cold. Reheat gently if required hot.

17. Mushroom and Carrots
(For 6 persons only)
Ingredients
Butter	50.0g
Oil	30 .0 ml
Parsley (Chopped)	15 .0ml
Small carrots	450.0g
Mushrooms sliced	450.0g

Method of preparation
Heat butter and oil in a shallow pan. Add parsley and chives, season with salt and freshly ground black pepper. Now put a carrots into the pan, add the mushrooms and turn over moderate heat for a minute. Reduce the heat and cover the pan and simmer gently for about 15 minutes. The product is ready to use.

18. Mushroom in Foil
Ingredients
Open or cup mushroom	450g
Salt and pepper	as desired

Method of preparation
Take a large sheet of cooking foil and place it flat on the

table. Now clean the mushroom and put these in the centre of the foil. Sprinkle salt and pepper to it. Seal the foil and put the parcel into oven. Serve it as vegetable.

19. Grilled Mushrooms

Ingredients

Open mushrooms	450.0g
Butter	50.0g
Salt and pepper	as desired

Method of preparation

Remove the grid from the grill pan and heat the grill. Trim the mushroom stalks level with the edges of the caps (use in another dish) and melt the butter in the grill pan. Dip the mushroom caps in the butter and put them into the grill pan. Grill for two minutes. Turn the mushrooms and sprinkle with salt and pepper. Return the pan to the grill for 2 to 3 minutes further. Serve on hot buttered toast as part of a mixed grill

20. Royal Mushrooms

Ingredients

Butter	50.0g
Button mushrooms	450.0g
Onion minced	30.0ml
Black pepper	as desired
Pinch tarragon	as desired
Sherry	30.0ml
Tomato pulp	450.0ml
Cream cheese	100.0g
Chopped parsley	Add as desired

Method of preparation

First heat the butter in saucepan and add mushrooms and onions. Sprinkle salt and freshly ground black pepper and cook it for two minutes. Scatter the tarragon over the vegetables and pour in the sherry. Pour in the tomato pulp and cook until tomato has reduced to half. Stir in the cream cheese over the heat. Serve it hot by sprinkling with parsley.

MUSHROOM USED AS SALAD

22. Mushmom and Bean Salad

Ingredients

Broad bean	175.0
Trim button mushroom	225.0g
Spring onions (in number)	4.0
Plain yoghurt	142.0 ml
Salt and pepper	as desired

Method of preparation

Cook the broad beans in salted water until it becomes tender. Drain and allow to cool. Wipe and slice the mushrooms thinly maintaining the stalk as it is. Chop the onions and mix all the ingredients with yoghurt. Season it for taste.

23. Curried Cream Salad

(For 4 to 6 persons)

Ingredients

Curry powder	1.0tsf
Soured cream	2.5 oz cartons
Mango chutney sauce	1.0 tsf
Lemon juice	as much desired
Button mushroom sliced	225.0g
Salt and pepper	as much desired
Ham, diced	175.0g (6 oz)

Method of preparation

Turn the soured cream into a bowl and blend in the curry powder and chutney sauce. Add salt and pepper and lemon juice to taste. Stir in the mushrooms. Now arrange in a dish garnished with the remaining jam and sprinkled with a little curry powder.

These are the important vegetarian preparations. Besides these, a number of non-vegetarian preparations like pork, bacon and mushroom loaf and many other non-vegetarian preparations are also prepared and consumed in India and other mushroom growing countries.

Harmful effect of mushrooms

Besides being very tasty and nutritionally rich for consumption, certain species of mushrooms are poisonous to human beings and many species are known to cause diseases in plants affecting the quality and yield of the plants affected. Some important diseases caused by mushroom species are given in following Table.

Table 2.9
Showing a partial list of diseases caused by different species of certain fleshy fungi may be summarized as under

S.N.	Name of mushrooms	Diseases caused by mushroom species
1.	Pellicularia filamentosa	Black scurf like disease of potato.
2.	P. salmonicolor	Rot of orange trees.
3.	Sterum species	Heart rot of oak.
4.	S. purpureum	Silver leg disease of palm and other fruit trees.
5.	Polyporus sulphurous	Wood rot of oats.
6.	P. versicolor	Wood rot timber trees.
7.	P. hispidus	Wood rot of conifers.
8.	P. betulinus	Wood rot of birch wood.
9.	Fomes applanatus	Rot of peach wood.
10.	Lenzites separia	Wood rot of trees.

Chapter 3

Morphology and Taxonomy

Mushroom morphology, variations in edible mushrooms, different parts of a typical mushroom, taxonomy of edible fungi, classification according to natural habits, classification according to colour of spores, keys for identification of mushrooms, classification according to morphology, recent classification, sexuality in cultivated mushrooms.

Mushroom in the eyes of the mushroom growers includes all edible fleshly fungi that are cultivated in mushroom houses or in specified places where the environmental conditions have been manipulated by them to the growing conditions for the mushroom under cultivation. However, the word mushroom has no significance in distinguishing the edible forms from poisonous one. The term toadstool, on the other hand includes all those fleshly fungi, which are popularly looked upon as poisonous to eat. Edible and so called toadstools belong to a group of plant kingdom known as fungi. They lack chlorophyll and therefore, are unable to synthesize their own food and depend on organic substances for their nutrition. They grow saprophytically on various dead substrates and parasitically or symbiotically on or with other organisms.

Morphology of mushrooms

Mushrooms consist of two portions—one the fruiting bodies or the mushrooms itself and the other one is thread like structures growing extensively in substrate comparable to the roots of higher plants. These thread like structures are known as mycelium which supplies nutrients from substrate to fruiting bodies. There are lot of variations in fruiting bodies. Many mushrooms have caps and stalks whereas, there are some other varieties with different shapes and sizes and are usually devoid of stalks. Some varieties do produce underground fruiting bodies also. About 25 species out of many are under cultivation in India and in different mushroom growing countries. Three to four species are well known and share major part of mushroom production in the world. As much as about 2 million tonnes fresh mushrooms are produced per annum.

DIFFERENT PARTS OF TYPICAL MUSHROOMS

Two important parts of the mushroom are the thread like structures called mycelium and the fruit bodies or sporocarps formed above it under suitable growth conditions. The typical mushroom may represent following different parts. These parts are the cap or pileus, the gills or lamellae, the veil, the annulus, the stipe or stalk and the volva.

1. The cap or pileus

This part is thick, fleshy, membranous or corky with some variation in its shape, size and colour. The surface of the pileus may be scaly, hairy, rough or smooth.

2. The gills or lamellae

These are usually situated below the cap of the mushroom starting from the apex of the stalk to the margins of the pileus or cap. Gills also called as lamellae, bear the spores in most cases.

3. The veil

The veil covers the gills and extend from the margin of the cap to the stalk. When fruiting body matures, the veil expands along with the cap and breaks away resulting in some of its part commonly attached to the margin of cap.

4. The annulus

A ring is formed around the stipe, known as annulus. Annulus may be present or absent in different varieties.

5. The stipe or stalk

Stipe or stalk may be present or absent in different species of mushrooms. In most of the genera, it remains centrally attached to the cap. In some others, it may be located laterally. Stipes may be solid or hollow in structure. They may be cylindrical or spindle shaped in morphology with or without bulbous structure at the base.

6. *The volva*

In many varieties, fruiting bodies remain covered by a veil. With the development of fruiting body, this veil breaks and some of its parts may remain present at the base forming a cup like structure known as volva. It usually surrounds the base of the stalk. The presence or absence of volva is an important factor in classification of mushrooms.

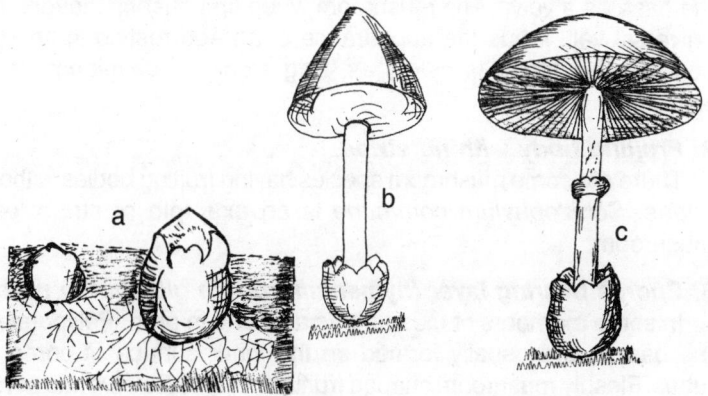

Fig. 3.1 Showing different stages of a typical mushroom. (a) shows the button stage and mycelia of a growing mushroom. (b) and (c) show the full grown mushroom.

VARIATIONS IN MUSHROOM MORPHOLOGY

Different varieties of mushrooms may differ in their morphology from typical morphological characteristics described above. Some of the variations may be summarized as under:

1. *Mushroom with cap, gills, stripe and volva*

The most familiar types of mushrooms, usually have the cap, gills, stripe and volva. The cultivated paddy straw mushroom-*Volvariella volvacea* can serve as an example of this type of mushroom. The fruiting body when young remains surrounded by a layer of tissue called the universal veil. There is pileus or cap and below the plieus are gills on the lower surface. The pileus and gills are supported by the stipe (stalk). The stalk arises from a cuplike structure known as volva as seen in *Volvariella volvacea*. In the genus *Agaricus*, there is no volva since there is no universal veil. A partial veil extends from the margin of the pileus to the stripe in some of the species. As the pileus enlarges and stripe elongates, this veil ruptures leaving tissue from the veil as a ring (annulus) on the stripe. Prior to enlargement of pileus and elongation of stipe, the existing growth stage of the mushroom is called as the 'button stage'. In *Volvariella volvacea*, the elongation of stipe causes the rupturing of universal veil, and some parts of it may be observed at the base as a volva. The mushroom when first pushes thought the universal veil, it has the appearance of an egg resting in an egg cap. So this stage is called as 'Egg stage' of development of *Volvariella volvacea*.

2. *Fruiting body with no stripe*

There are some mushroom species having fruiting bodies without stipes. *Schizophylum commune* is an example of stripe less mushroom.

3. *Spores bearing layer (hymenium) not in gills but in pores*

In some members of mushrooms as found in order Polyporales, the basidia are usually formed on the inner surface of pores or tubes. Fleshly mushroom shaped fruiting body of *Boletus* has pores and not gills. Some species of *Boletus* are poisonous but *Boletus edulis* is a highly prized edible mushroom.

4. *Funnel shaped fruiting body with hymenium layer in folds on underside of body*

The genus *Cantharellus* has a funnel shaped fruiting body with folds, somewhat like gills on the under side of the fruiting body.

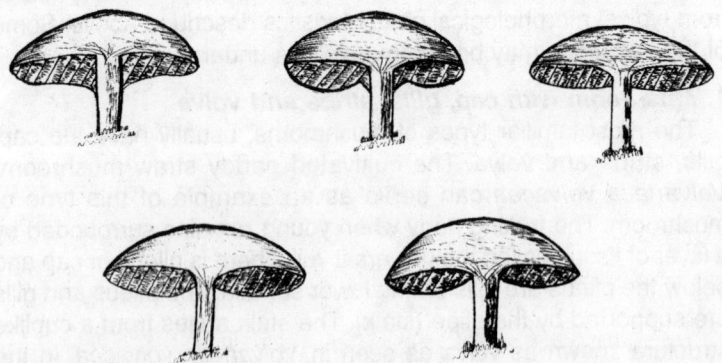

Fig. 3.2 Showing different shapes of caps and attachment of gills to the stipe.

These folds constitute the hymenium layer. *Cantharellus cibarius* is an edible wild species.

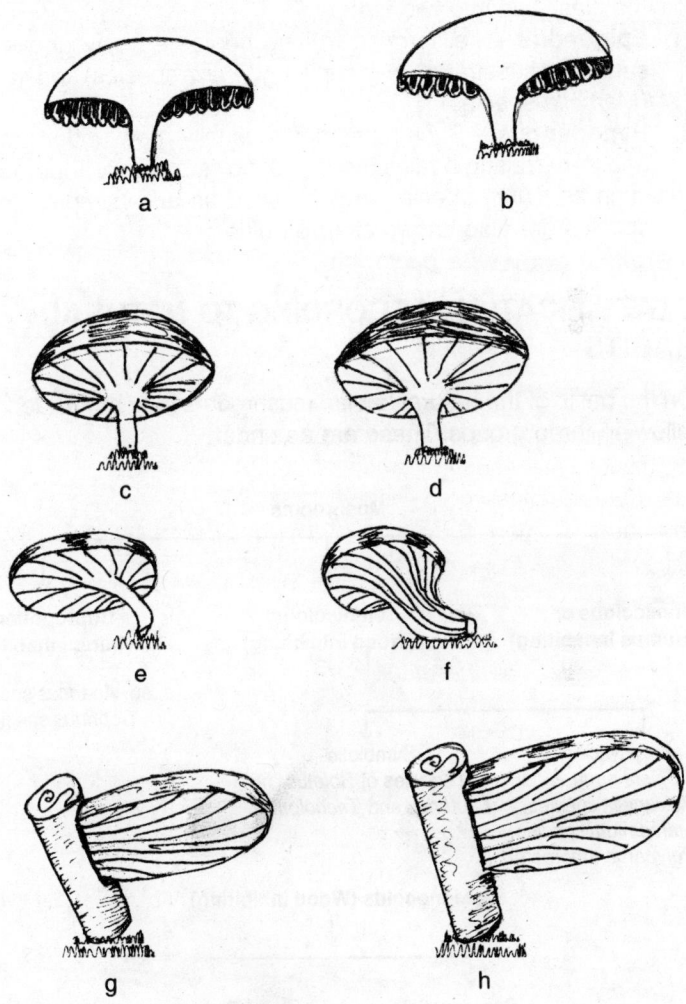

Fig. 3.3 Showing morphological characteristics of white spored mushrooms, (a) and (b) *Lentinus* species, (c) and (d) white spored mushrrom with stem centrally located, (e) and (f) stem laterally located and (g) and (h) stem lacking.

CLASSIFICATION ACCORDING TO THE OCCURRENCE

On the basis of the occurrence of fruiting bodies, mushrooms may be classified into two groups:

1. **Epigenous** – i.e. forming fruiting bodies entirely above the surface of substratum, e.g. cup fungi (*Pizza* species) and morels (*Marcella* species).

2. **Hypogenous** – Such mushrooms usually grow under ground and form fruiting bodies therein. Species of family Tuberaceae such as *Tuber* species may be cited as an example. These species are also known as true truffles.

CLASSIFICATION ACCORDING TO NATURAL HABITS

On the basis of the natural habits, mushrooms may be divided into following three groups. These are as under:

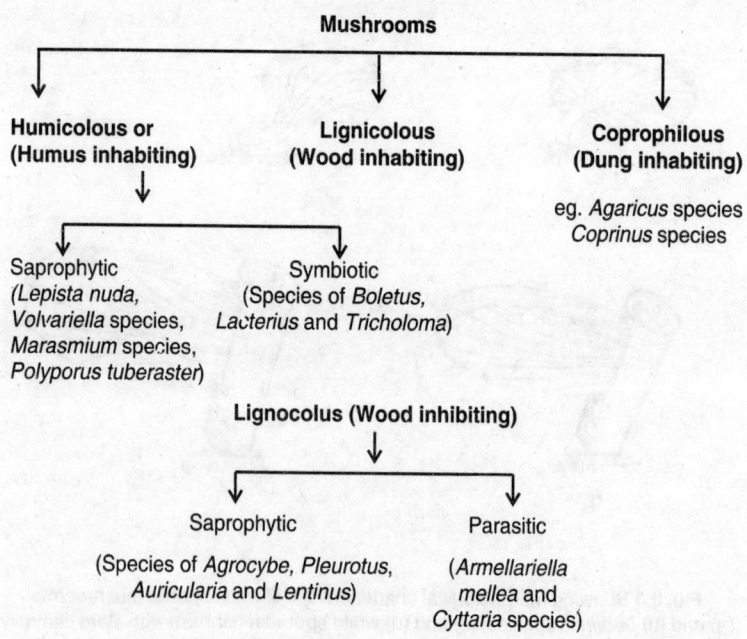

CLASSIFICATION ACCORDING TO THE COLOUR OF SPORES

On the basis of colour of the spores produced, mushrooms can be classified in to five categories as under:

1. White spored mushrooms

It includes species of *Amanita, Armillaria, Cantharellus, Clitocybe, Lacterius, Lentinus, Lepiota, Pleurotus, Russula* and *Tricholoma.*

2. Yellow brown spored mushrooms

It includes *Flammulina, Inocybe* and *Paxillus* species.

3. Pink spored mushrooms

Species of *Entoloma* and *Volvariella* are included in the category.

4. Purple brown spored mushrooms

It includes *Agaricus, Hypholoma* and *Stropharia.*

5. Black spored mushroom

Coprinus, Panaeolus and *Psathyrella* species are included in the category.

KEYS FOR IDENTIFICATION

White Spored Mushrooms
Lentinus
Family – Lentinaceae

Edge of the gills prominently and irregularly serrated. Fruit bodies are tough and leathery.

Fig. 3.4 Showing morphological characteristics of different *Lentinus* species.

Armillaria
Family – Tricholomataceae
Gills adnexed or short decurrent; stipe not separating readily from the cap; ring often disappearing quickly

Tricholoma
Family – Tricholomataceae
Gills sinuate; stipe with neither ring nor volva.

Cantharellus
Family – Cantharellaceae
Gills not noticeably triangular or waxy, gills decurrent, gills in the form of thick, fold like ridges, often forked.

Clitocybe
Family – Tricholomataceae
Gills thin and plate like, decurrent, not noticeably triangular or waxy.

Marasmis (=Chamaeceras)
Family – Tricholomataceae
Cap and stipe tough, withering but not decaying when dried and reviving when moistened.

Russula (= Russuelina)
Family – Russulaceae
Cap and stipe tough, withering but not decaying when dried, not reviving when moistened; flesh of cap very brittle and almost granular.

Lactarius (=Lactariopsis = Lactariella)
Family – Russulaceae
Flesh of cap exuding white or coloured juice when broken. Cap usually depressed in the centre.

Amanita
Family – Amanitaceae
Stipe with both volva and ring.

Amanitopsis
Family – Amanitaceae
Stipe with volva only having no ring.

Lapiota
Family – Agaricaceae

Gills free, ring prominent, stipe separating readily from the cap. No volva, stipe with ring only.

Pleurotus
Stipe eccentric or lateral; gills not splitted; cap thin tough and leathery

Shizophyllum
Gills longitudinally splitted

Panus
Stipe eccentric or lateral; gills not splitted, cap thin, tough and leathery texture.

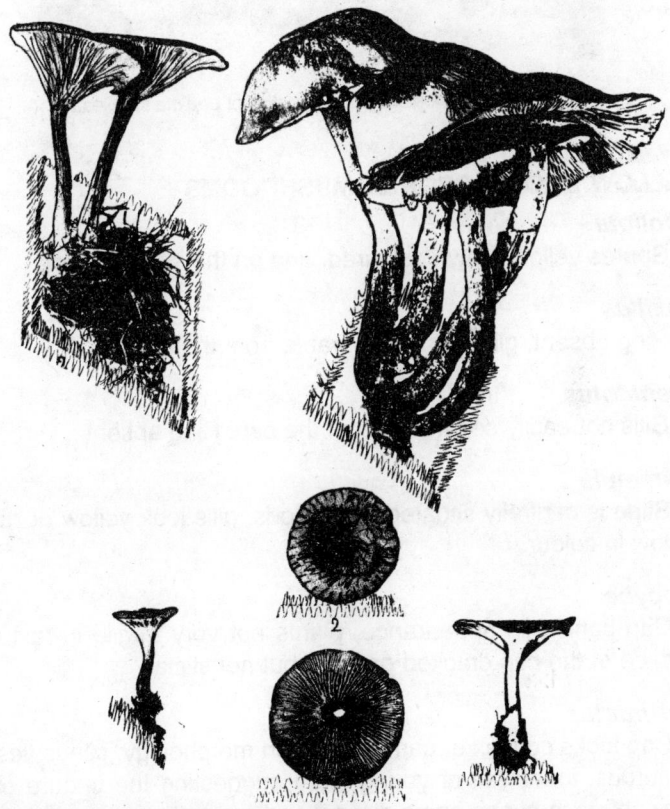

Fig. 3.5 Showing two different species of mushroom-*Clitocybe*.

Fig. 3.6 Morphological characteristics of *Lepiota* species.

YELLOW BROWN SPORED MUSHROOMS

Pholiota
Spores yellow brown coloured, ring on the stipe present.

Paxillus
Ring absent, gills easily separable from the cap.

Crepidotus
Gills not easily separable from the cap. Ring absent. ,

Flammula
Stipe is centrally situated. On woods, gills look yellow or rusty yellow in colour.

Inocybe
Cap conical in appearance, plants not very fragile in texture, surface of the cap cracked or scaly but not sticky.

Cortinarius
Cap looks convex or campanulate in morphology; pileus fleshy or fibrous; inner veil of young plant suggesting the texture of a cobweb; each hypha being distinct and separate.

PINK COLOURED MUSHROOMS

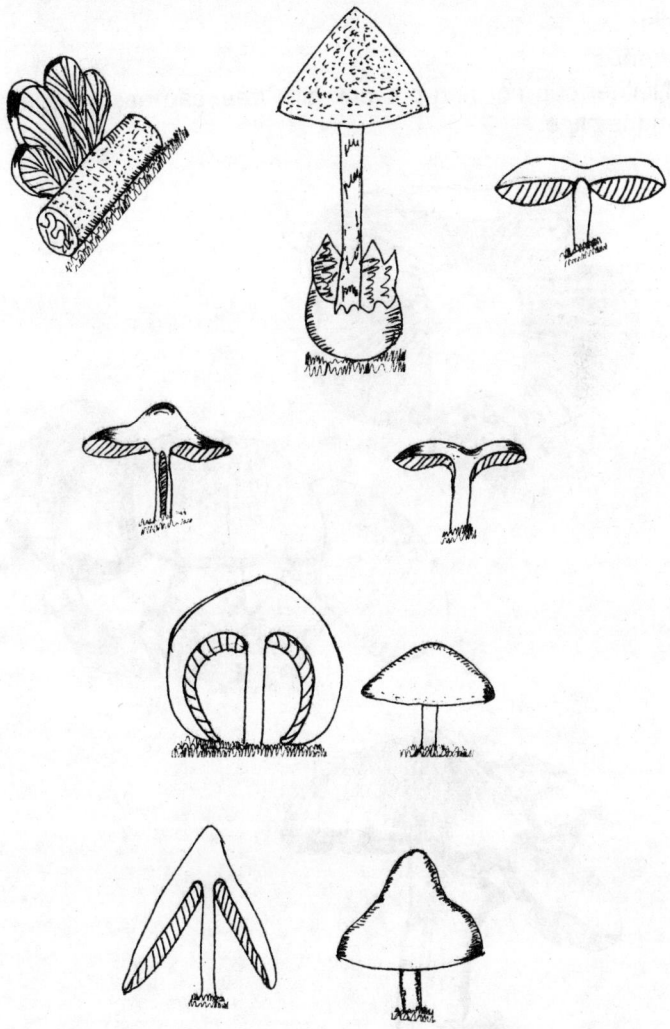

Fig. 3.7 Morphological characteristics of pink spored mushrooms showing characteristic structures of different species.

Claudopus

Stipe lateral or absent on wood.

Volvaria

Stipe central; cup present at the base of the stipe; no ring on the stipe.

Pleuteus

Neither cup nor ring present; gills free; cap easily separable from the stipe.

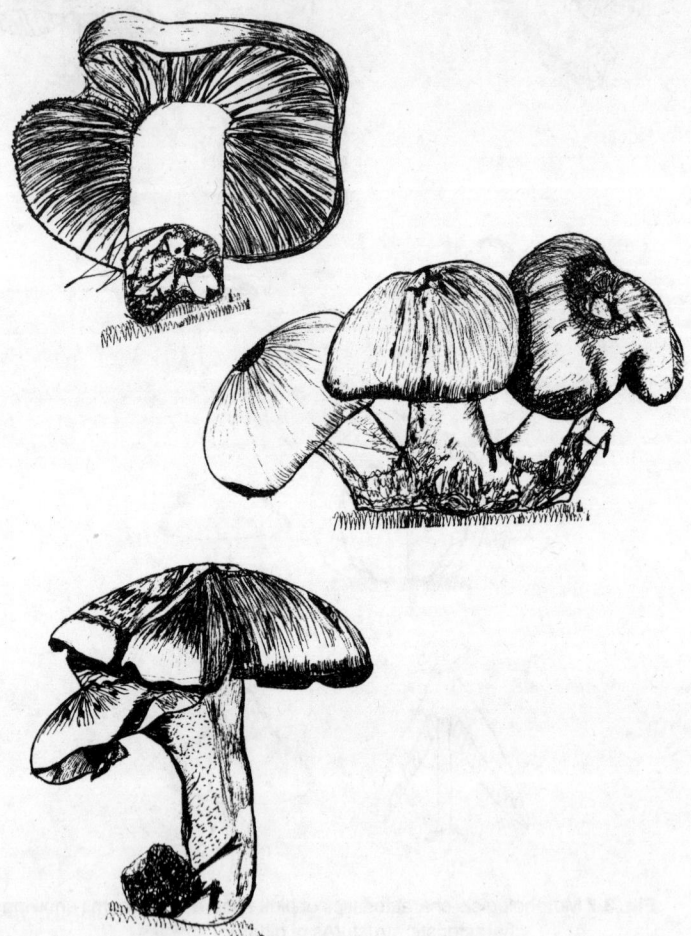

Fig. 3.8 Showing morphological appearance of mushroom – *Entoloma* species.

Fig. 3.9 Morphology of mushroom – *Entoloma* species.

Entoloma
Pileus fleshy or fibrous; gills mostly sinuate.

Clitopilus
Pileus fleshy or fibrous; gills decurrent or adnate.

Laptonia
Gills nor decurrent; pileus convex, margins at first incurved.

Nolanea
Gills not decurrent; pileus bell shaped or conical, margin at first straight.

PURPLE BROWN SPORED MUSHROOM

Fig. 3.10 Morphological structures of different species of purple—brown spores species, (a) *Agaricus* showing free giills, (b) *Stropharia* with gills attached to the stipe and (c) showing an other species with veil.

Agaricus
Ring present on stipe, gills free.

Stropharia
Ring present on the stipe, gills attached to the stipe/stem.

Hypholoma
Ring absent on the stipe, veil present, and the remnants of it hanging from the margin of the cap.

Psathyra
Ring absent on the stipe, veil absent or evanescent, stipe slender, margin of the cap first straight.

Psilocybe
Ring absent on the stipe, veil absent or evanescent, stipe slender, margin of the cap first incurved.

BLACK SPORED MUSHROOMS
Coprinus
Cap and gills liquefying, beginning at the margin and progressing toward the centre of the cap.

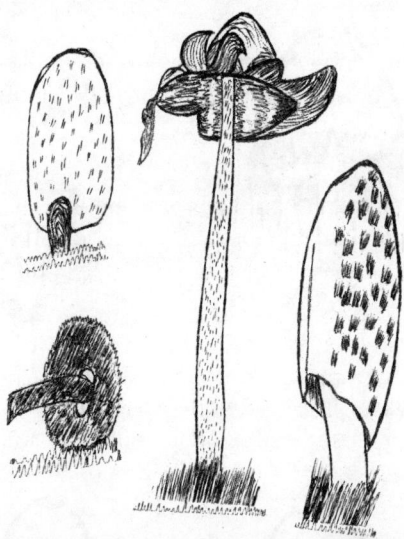

Fig. 3.11 Morphological characteristics of *Coprinus* species.

Gomphidies
Caps and gills not liquefying, gills decurrent, waxy, cap sticky.

Psathyrella
Gills not decurrent, cap striated or furrowed.

Panaeolus
Gills not decurrent, cap not furrowed.

CLASSIFICATION ACCORDING TO THE MORPHOLOGY

Fungi described in this treatise may be divided into two main groups:
1. First main group – Basidiomycetous mushrooms
This group may be divided into two sub groups:
  • **Fruiting layers exposed to the air** – This sub group has further been divided in to 5 categories
    1. *Gill fungi* – Characterized by presence of gills. Gilled fungi have further been divided in to five categories according to the colour of the spores, namely, (1) White coloured spores, (2) Pink coloured spores, (3) Brown coloured spores (4) Purple coloured spores and (5) Black coloured spores.

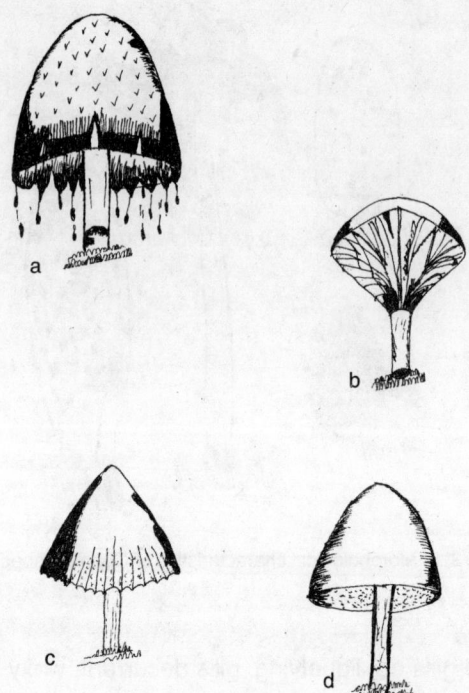

Fig. 3.12 Showing morphological characteristics and species of black spored mushrooms, (a) *Coprinus* species, (b) *Gomphidius* species, (c) *Psathyrella* species, and (d) *Panaeolus* species.

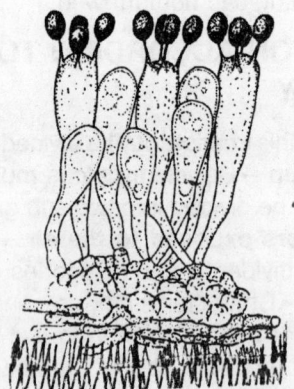

Fig. 3.13 Morphological characteristics of basidia producing basidiospores as observed in Basidiomycetous mushrooms.

2. **Pore fungi** – Characterized by the absence of gills and presence of tubes or pores.
3. *Teeth fungi* – Fungi without gills or pores but with prickles or teeth.
4. *Club or coral fungi* – Fungi without gills, pores or teeth, but are club or coral like in shape.
5. *Jelly fungi* – Fungi without gills, pores or teeth, forming soft, jelly like masses when moist.

- **Fruiting layers not exposed to the air** – This sub group may be divided into two main categories

  1. *Stem like receptacle arising from a definite egg - stage, with volva at the base of the stipe.* This category includes three important genera.
     - *Dictyphora* - Characterized by the fruiting body at apex prominently differing in dimensions from stipe, more cap like with more or less netted veil.
     - *Ithyphallus* - Similar to the above, but no trace of a veil.
     - *Cynophallus* - Fruit body at apex with same dimension but differing in colour having no trace of veil.

  2. **Stem like receptacle absent or rudimentary, volva absent.** It includes five genera.
     - *Geaster* - Fruit body opening at maturity with round holes at apex. Plants star shaped.
     - *Lycoperdon* - Fruit body opening at maturity with round holes at apex. Plants not star shaped, globular, flask shaped, Base sterile.
     - *Bovista* - Fruit body opening at maturity with round holes at apex. Plants globular with distinct apical mouth. Base not sterile.
     - *Calvatia* - Fruit body not opening at maturity with round holes at apex. Slightly sterile base.
     - *Cyathus* - Fruiting body never wholly intact or closed. Mature forms resembling minute bird nest.

2. **Second main group** – Ascomycetous mushrooms
   This group may be divided into three sub groups.
   - **Plants with prominently pitted or gnarled cap** – This sub group have been divided into two genera:
     1. *Morchella* – Cap irregularly pitted.
     2. *Gyromitra* – Cap irregular gnarled mass.

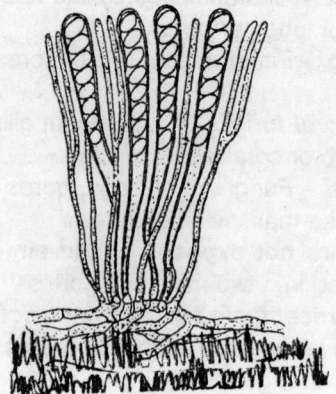

Fig. 3.14 Showing morphology of ascocarp and asci, characteristically formed in Ascomycetous mushrooms.

- **Plants with cap formed by saddled-shaped** – It includes one important genus:
  1. *Helvella* – It has above characteristics.
- **Plants saucer, cup, or goblet-shaped** – It includes following four genera:
  1. *Plicaria*
  2. *Pustularia*
  3. *Sarcoscypha*
  4. *Geopyxis*.

CLASSIFICATION BASED ON STRUCTURE AND TEXTURE OF FRUIT BODIES

GILLED FUNGAL MUSHROOMS
(Family – Agaricaceae)

The species belonging to this group are characterized by the presence of gills or lamella which bear spores. It includes species of *Agaricus* and *Amanita*.

Fig. 3.15 Showing morphological characteristics of a gilled mushroom.

PORE FUNGAL MUSHROOMS
(Family – Polyporaceae)
Distinguishing characteristics
The family includes those fleshy fungi in which the fruit bodies are tough, leathery or woody and the pore layer can not be separated easily from the context or flesh.

Fig. 3.16 Showing morphology of *Polyporus umbellatus*.

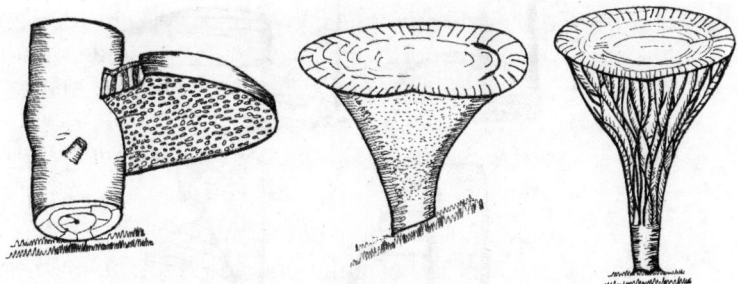

Fig. 3.17 Morphological characteristics of mushrooms belonging to family – Polyporaceae.

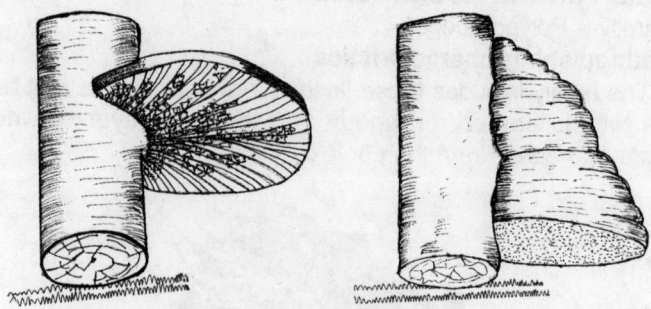

Fig. 3.18 Shwoing shape and attachment in different species of pore fungi.

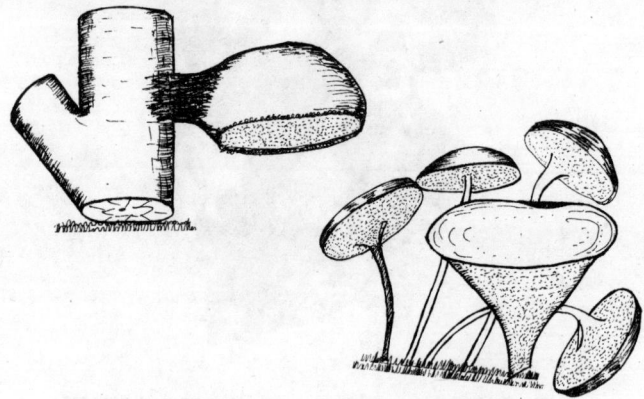

Fig. 3.19 Showing shape and attachment of pore fungi.

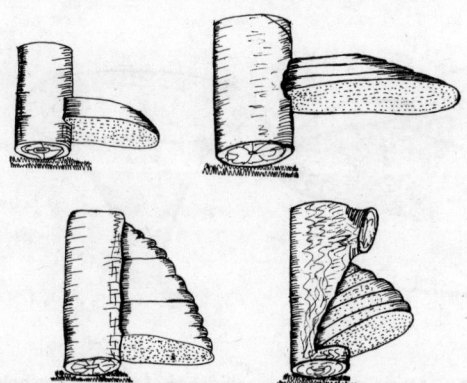

Fig. 3.20 Showing shape and attachment in pore fungi.

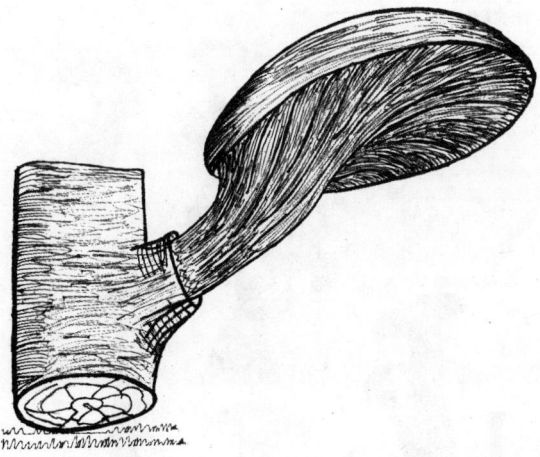

Fig. 3.21 Showing morphological characteristics of different species of gilled mushroom.

Keys to common genera of polyporaceae
Fomes
Fruit bodies are perennial, usually very hard and woody.

Fistulina
Fruit bodies annual, soft and fleshy, 8–16 cm wide, thick , semi circular or kidney shaped with a lateral stem; flesh soft, white red streaks; pores 3 to 7 mm. long, each pore separate and distinct from its neighbor. Usually found on hard wood stumps.

Trametes
Pores meating the context in an irregular, uneven line.

Favolus candensis

Pores diamond shaped, fruit body kidney shaped, pores are reddish brown to tan or white with a lateral stem.

Polyporus

Pores round, angular or irregular. Different species of Polyporus are economically important. These include *Polyporus arcularius, Polyporus lucidus, Polyporus umbellatus, Polyporus perennis* and *Polyporus melanopus.*

TOOTH FUNGAL MUSHROOMS
(Family – Hydnaceae)

Fig. 3.22 Showing different stages of *Hydnum* species.

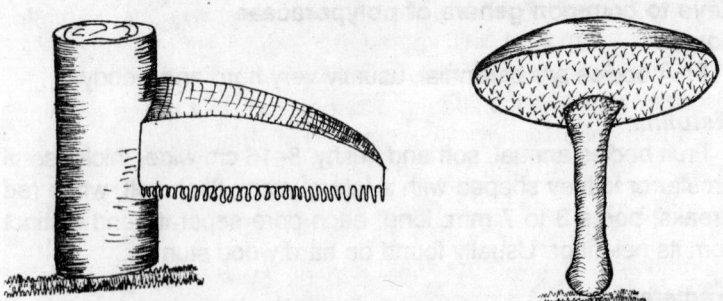

Fig. 3.23 Showing characteristics features of tooth fungi belonging to family – Hydnaceae

Keys for identification of species of *Hydnum*
Hydnum septentrionale

Fruit bodies white, usually in a clump of several, one above the other, each shelf 10–30 cm wide on living hard maple.

Hydnum corallloides

Fruit bodies tan to brown, on hard wood decaying logs.

Hydnum caputursi

Fruit body a dense clump, tapering tooth upto 2 cm long, branches consealed.

Other species are *Hydnum aurisclapium*, *Hydnum velutium*, *Hydnum albonigrum*, *Hydnum amicum*, *Hydnum rapandum* and *Hydnum cyathifirme*.

BOLETACEOUS FUNGAL MUSHROOMS
(Family – Boletaceae)

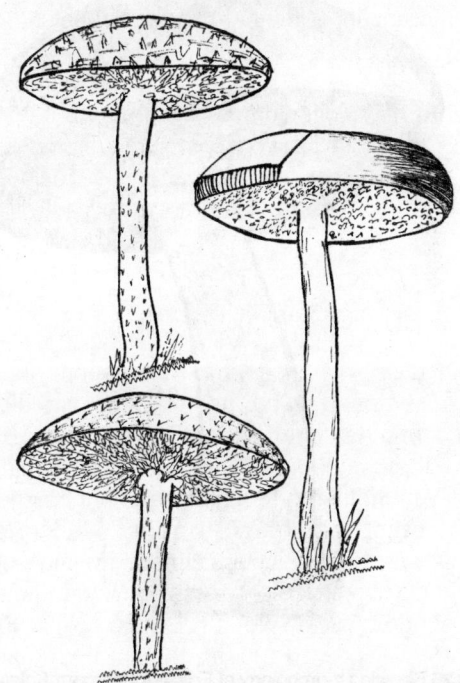

Fig. 3.24 Showing morphological characteristics of mushrooms belonging to family – Boletaceae.

Fig. 3.25 Showing morphological characteristics of different stages of *Boletus edulis*.

Fig. 3.26 Showing morphology of Edible mushroom *Boletus versipellis*.

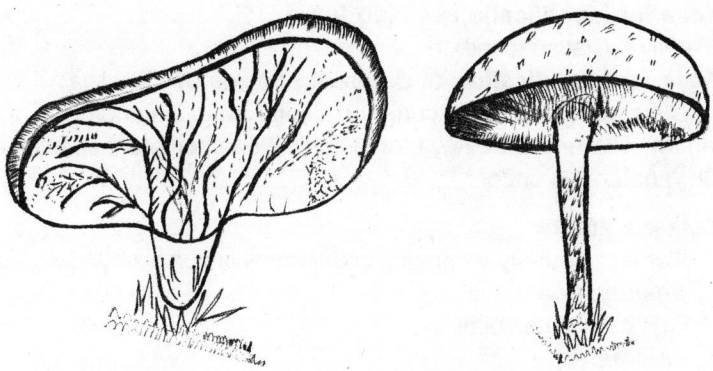

Fig. 3.27 Showing morphological features of members belonging to family Boletaceae.

Keys for identification of *Boletus* and *Boletinus* species

Boletaceous fungi belong to the family – Boletaceae whose many species can be distinguished among them only by microscopic characteristics. With the aid of the microscope also, the species are difficult to differentiate with each other.

Boletinus

Pores shallow, pore layer not easily pealed from flesh of the cap.

Boletus

Pores deep, pore layer easily peeled from flesh of the cap.

CLUB SHAPED MUSHROOMS

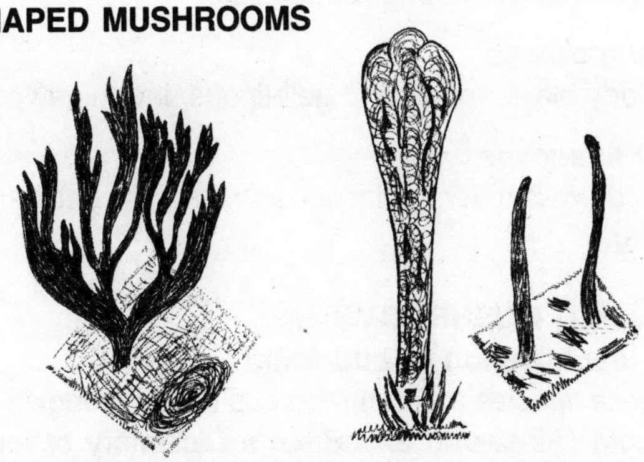

Fig. 3.28 Showing morphological appearance of club mushrooms belonging to family – Clavariacae.

Keys for identification of club fungi
(Family – Clavariaceae)
Keys for identification of different species of *Clavaria*
Clavaria is the most common fleshy fungi belonging to the family—Clavariaceae. Keys for identification of different species of Clavaria are as under :

Clavaria stricta
Plants repeatedly branched, usually growing on decayed woods.
C. amethystina
Fruit body pale voilet.
C. cinerea
Fruit body ash geay in colour.
C. flava
Flesh of pileus and its branches turning red brushed.
C. aurea
Flesh not turning red when bruised.
C. pistillaris
Fruit bodies tan in colour, often thick at the top and tapering downward.

JELLY FUNGAL MUSHROOMS
Keys for identification of Jelly fungi
This group of fungi was named because some of the species have a consistency suggesting jelly when moist. Most of them grow on woods and only one of then is known to be edible. However, it should not be consumed to remain safe.

Exidia grandulosa
Fruit body black, tough and geletinous, irregularly convuluted.

Tremella lutescens
Fruit body yellow, very gelatinous and translucent, hemispherical or irregular.

CUP SHAPED MUSHROOMS
Keys to identification of cup fungi
Morchella species are common cup fungi belonging to phylum-Ascomycota (Ainsworth and Bisby's Dictionary of fungi, 1995). Some other species are *Verpa, Patella, Helvella* and *Xylaria*.

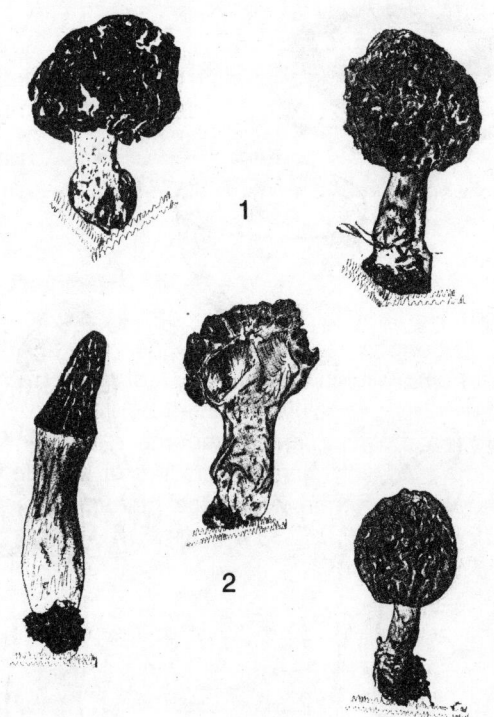

Fig. 3.29 Two different species (1) and (2) of mushroom – *Morchella* species.

Fig. 3.30 Showing morphology of Ascomycetous mushrooms.

Fig. 3.31 Showing morphological characteristics of Ascomycetous cup fungi and their relatives.

Morchella esculenta
Cap sub-globose or cylindrical, with a rounded top.

Morchella conica
Cap conical with pointed top.

PUFFBALLS AND ITS RELATIVES
Keys for identification of puffballs and its relatives
Species of *Lycoperdon, Calvatia, Geaster* and *Bovista* are called as puffballs. Puffballs are fruit bodies without a stalk extending through the enterior.

Lycoperdon
Fruit body tapering toward the base, base composed of spongy mycelium that does not form spores.

Calvatia
Wall of the upper part of the fruiting bodies breaking up and disappearing at maturity, exposing the spore mass.

Geaster
Outer wall of the genus looks splitting into star like rays and folding back at maturity.

Bovista
Fruit body of the genus is spherical and without a sterile base.

CLASSIFICATION BASED ON FRUIT BODIES AND SPORES

Ainsworth *et al.* (1973) classified mushrooms into two subdivisions— Ascomycotina and Basidiomycotina. These two groups contain most of the edible fungi. Mushrooms belonging to these subdivisions may be described as under:

Subdivision – Ascomycotina
Ascomycetous edible fleshy fungi include mainly species of *Morchella*, also called as morels, species of *Tuber* also known as truffles and species of *Terfezia*. These fungi produce sexual spores called the ascospores inside a club shaped or cylindrical structure called the ascus.

Class – Discomycetes
Species described above belong to the class Discomycetes in which asci are formed in a fertile layer or hymenium usually in a cup shaped fruit body called apothecium. Important species are as under:

Morcella
Moreella is one of the oldest known genus of order Pezizales. Six species of this genus have been reported from India. They are *Morchella semlibera*, *M. angusticeps*, *M. deliciosa*, *M. crassipes*, *M. conica* and *M. esculenta*. The member of this genus grows abundantly in the hilly regions of J & K, Himanchal Pradesh, Utter Pradesh and Maharashtra.

Terfezia

The members of this genus have fruiting bodies which are subglubose or pear shaped in morphology, measuring about 2–10 cms in diameter. Surface of the fruiting body is smooth, whitish or cream coloured with characteristic faint smell of cherry laurel. Asci are large and ascospores are globose and coarsely warted.

Tuber species (truffles)

Tuber *melanospermum* is the important species liked by the most people. Other species are *T. aestivum*, *T. mangatum* and *T. refum* etc. The growth and fructification of truffles may be observed in well-drained calcareous soils. These species are artificially propagated in France where the soil is inoculated with truffle mycelium in oak plantations.

Subdivision-Basidiomycotina

Subdivision-Basidiomycotina contains the largest number of genera of edible fungi. Basidiospores are mainly borne in basidia on sterigmata.

Class – Gasteromycetes

There are six economically imporant orders of this class. These are order Podaxales, Phallales, Sclerodermatales, Pymenoganterales. Melanogastrales and Lycoperdales.

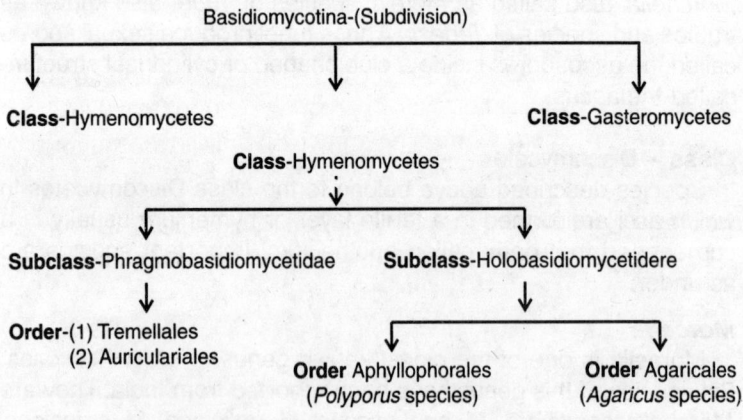

Basidiomycotina-(Subdivision)

Class-Hymenomycetes   **Class**-Gasteromycetes

Class-Hymenomycetes

Subclass-Phragmobasidiomycetidae   **Subclass**-Holobasidiomycetidere

Order-(1) Tremellales
(2) Auriculariales

Order Aphyllophorales
(*Polyporus* species)

Order Agaricales
(*Agaricus* species)

Class – Hymenomycetes

This is the important class of sub division Basidiomycotina. It includes two important sub classes namely, Phragmo-basidiomycetidae and Holobasidiomycetidae. These two sub classes may be characterized as under:

Sub class – Phrgmobasidiomycetidae
The mushrooms belonging to this subclass may be characterized by the gelatinous and waxy basidiocarps, producing spores abundantly. Edible members belong to orders Tremellales and Auriculariales. Cultivated species are *Auricularia polytricha, A. auricula, Tremella fuciformis* and *T. mesenterica*.

Sub class – Holobasidiomycetidae
This subclass consists of two orders namely Aphyllophorales (Polyporus fungi) and Agaricales. Polyporus fungi are extremely polymorphic in their morphology. The fruiting bodies are annual or perennial, fleshly, corky or woody with lamellate hymenophores (*Lenzites* species). In Agaricales, basidiocarps are fleshly, subfleshly, leathery, membranous or fragile. Basidia may contain 2, 4, or 8 basidiospores. These spores are one celled at maturity. Basidiocarps consist of long or short stipe, fleshly pileus with radiating plates (lamellae) on the under side. *Agaricus, Lentinus, Pleurotus* and *Triciholoma* are important genera belonging to this order.

Order – Agaricales
The order Agaricales contains about 17 families, namely, Polyporaceae, Hygrophoraceae, Tricholomataceae, Amanitaceae, Pluteaceae, Agaricaceae, Coprinaceae, Bolbitiaceae, Strophariaceae, Cortinariaceae, Crepidotaceae, Entolomataceae, Paxillaceae, Gomphidiaceae, Boletaceae, Bondarzewiaceae and Russulaceae. Some of its families are economically important as they contain cultivated genera like *Pleurotus, Tricholoma, Fammulina, Agaricus* and *Volvariella* etc.

RECENT CLASSIFICATION

The 8th edition of Ainsworth & Bisby's *'Dictionary of fungi'* has been published during the year 1995 from International Mycolological Research Institute. According to this classification, ger era have been placed within families all under 11 fungal phyla

Table 3.1
Showing taxonomic position of some of the cultivated / propagated fleshy fungi as suggested by Ainsworth (1973).

Class	Subclass	Order	Genus
Subdivision			
Basidiomycotina			
Hymenomycetes	Holobasidio-mycetidae	Agaricales	Agaricus
			Coprinus
			Lentinus
			Pleurotus
			Tricholoma
			Flammulina
			Calocybe
			Stropharia
			Pholiota
			Kuehnero-myces
			Hypholoma
	Aphyllo-phorales		Volvariella
			Hericium
	Phragmobasi-diomycidae	Auricularials	Auricularia
		Tremellales	Tremella
Subdivision			
Ascomycotina	Class–Discomycetes	Tuberales	Tuber
	Subclass–Hymenoasco-mycetidae		species

in the dictionary. A key to the phyla is followed by the keys to the families described under each phylum. Each phylum has further been divided into classes and subclasses for convenience. All the eleven phyla in alphabetical order are 1. Acrasiomycota, 2. Ascomycota, 3. Basidiomycota, 4. Chytridiomycota, 5. Dictyostellomycota, 6. Hyphochytrimycota, 7. Labyrinthulomycota, 8. Myxomycota, 9. Oomycota, 10. Plasmodiophoromycota and 11. Zygomycota. All the mushroom species usually fall under phyla Ascomycota and Basidiomycota. Phylum Ascomycota has been divided into 281 families whereas Phylum Basidiomycota includes approximately 77 families.

Phylum Ascomycota
The phylum is characterized by the mycelium which remains

absent and vegetative cells usually proliferate by budding or fission; Ascomata remain absent, asci are formed singly or in chains from morphologically undifferentiated cells.

Phylum Basidiomycota

The phylum is characterized by the karyogamy somatogamous, often forming a visible basidiome; saprophytes, symbionts (ectomycorrhizal) or parasites; Basidiospores (meiospores) *ballistosporic* or *statismosporic*; clamp connection present or absent.

Mushrooms and their species belonging to different families are being summarized with their distinguishing characteristics as described in the 8th edition of Ainsworth & Bisby's *'Dictionary of fungi'*.

Family Agaricaceae

The members of the family are ballistosporic, basidiome agaricoid and lamellate. It includes species of *Agaricus* and *Lapiota*.

Family Amanitaceae

Ballistosporic, basidiome agaricoid with lamellae often with velar layers, spores globose to elongate or ellipsoid. Members are terrestrial. It includes *Aminita* species,

Family Pleuteaceae

Characterized by the spore print white to cream or dull pink, hymenophoral trama bilateral with convergent lateral strata. It includes *Volvariella* species.

Family Entolomataceae

Ballistosporic, basidiome agaricoid, lamellate. It includes *Entoloma* species.

Family Tricholomataceae

Ballistosporeic, basidiome agaricoid, lamellate, spores ornamentation various statismosporic. It includes species of *Clitocybe*, *Tricholoma* and *Flammulina*.

Family Boletaceae

Basidiome robust, stipe stout with a scabrous or reticulate

surface, hymenophore sinuato-adnexed, always tabulate, basidio-spores either ovoid or fusoid-cylindric and smooth or subglobose with a reticulo-redged ornamentation. It includes species of *Boletus.*

Family Cantharellaceae
Basidiospores hyaline, thin walled and basidia 2 to 8 sterigmate. It includes species of *Cantharellus.*

Family Auricularaceae
Basidiome resupinate, orbicular or auriform, gelatinous to waxy, basidiospores cylindrical, often curved, ballistosporic, repetition and budding with curved microconidia. It includes *Auricularia* species.

Family Hidanaceae
Hymenophore spinose. It includes species of *Hydnum.*

Family Lycoperdaceae
Peridium not splitting radially, dehiscence either by an apical pore or by apical fragmentation. Capillitium septate or not, typically branched, not forming a columella. It include species of *Lycoperdon* and *Bovista.*

Family Lentnaceae
Hymenophore lamellate, basidiome centrally to laterally stipitate, sometimes sessile, hyphal system monomitic or dimitic with skeletal or scleto-ligative hyphae, basidiospores cylindrical. It includes species of *Pleurotus* and *Lentinus.*

Family Polyporaceae
Basidiome stipitate, stipe frequently with a black crust, skeleto-ligative hyphae present. It includes species of *Polyporus.*

Family Russulaceae
Basidiospores ballistosporic, asymmetric, bearing asuprahilar plage and tapering hilar appendix, basidiome agaricoid to gasteroid, always stipitate. It includes species of *Russula* and *Lactarius.*

Family Schizophyllaceae
Basidiome pleurotoid, hymenophore with aggregated cupsules

compressed radially to produce a split lamellate condition. It includes species of *Schizophyllum.*

SEXUALITY IN CULTIVATED MUSHROOMS

Sexuality in different edible mushrooms have been studied in much detail. Different modes of sexuality as observed in some important mushrooms may be summarized below:

1. *Volvariella volvacea*

Primary homothallism is found in this cultivated subtropical mushroom—*Volvariella volvacea* (Fr.) sing. This mushroom is commonly known as the paddy straw mushroom. In addition to presumed sexual cycle, *Volvariella volvacea* has an asexual cycle via multinucleate chlamydospores. The vegetative spores are borne as spherical cells on specialized swollen cells of the multi-karyotic mycelium. Clamp connections are not present in the mycelia of this species.

2. *Agaricus bisporus* Lange

The most widely cultivated mushroom *Agaricus bisporus* is a secondary homothallic species. The formation of two binucleate spores on each basidium is the normal pattern of development of this species. Occasionally, a basidium may bear more than two spores. In normal case, only two spores are formed.

3. *Agaricus bitorquis* (Quel.) Sacc

Sexuality in this cultivated wild species (*Agaricus bitorquis* (Guel.) Sacc) usually differs in an important respect from that of *Agaricus bisporus. Agaricus bitorquis* is heterothallic rather than homothallic. *Agaricus bitorquis* like most members of the genus produce four-spores rather than two spores. Heterothallism and presence of uni-factorial incompatibility system has revealed it through a recent genetic analysis.

4. *Pleurotus ostreatus* (Fr.) Kummer

Pleurotus ostreatus commonly called as oyster mushroom, is the only one of the several cultivated species of its genus with known sexuality. Bifactorial heterothallism has been detected in this species by analysis of clamp formation.

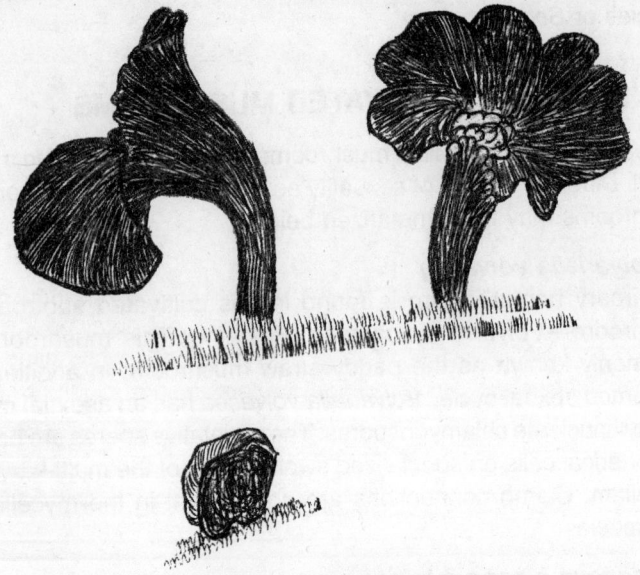

Fig. 3.32 Showing morphological characteristics of edible mushroom – *Cantharellus* species.

Fig. 3.33 Showing morphological characterstics of *Pholiota* species.

5. *Pholiota nameko* (T. Ito) S. Itoet Imai

This cultivated Japanes mushroom is apparently heterothallic with unifactorial control. The basidium bears four spores and each spore is characteristically uninucleate. Most germinated spores develop into homokaryotic selfsterile mycelia with monokarytic cells. Both homokarytic and dikaryotic mycelia may have asexual cycles, either thought oidia and or thought basidiospores.

6. *Auricularia auricula* (Hook.) Underw

Auricularia species are members of the order Auriculariales and family Auriculariaceae. *Auricularia polytricha* was reported to be the first mushroom, having been cultivated in China around 600 AD. This species was designated as heterothallic with unifactorial control. An asexual cycle through the formation of clustered oidia occurs in the monosporous, presumably homokaryotic mycelium of this species. *Auricularia polytricha* (Mont) Sacc., has been reported to be heterothallic with bifactorial control. Asexual cycle through uninucleate oidia in the homokaryon of this species, has also been reported.

7. *Lentinus edodes* (Berk.) Sing

This mushroom is popularly known as shiitake mushroom. Bifactorial heterothallism has been clearly observed in *Lentinus edodes*. Careful cytological studies have revealed the fertile mycelium as clamped and dikaryotic. Evidence for meiosis in the basidium and the subsequent development of four uninucleate spores on the basidium have also been observed. Asexual cycles have not been observed in *Lentinus edodes*.

Sexuality in different edible species of mushrooms have been studied by different scientists. Different characteristics of different edible species related with sexuality may be summarized as under:

Table 3.1.
Summary showing characteristics of life cycle and sexuality in some important cultivated edible mushrooms.

Cultivated fungus (mushroom)	No. of spores per basidium	No. post-meiotic N/spore	Homokaryon No. N/cell	Homokaryon Fertile	Fertile heterokaryon No. N/cell	Fertile heterokaryon Clamps	Asexual cycle Homoka-ryon	Asexual cycle Hetero-karyon	sexuality Incompat Factor (s)
Volvariella volvacea	4	1	Many variable	Self	-	-	Yes	-	None
Agaricus bispores	2	2	-	-	Many variable	No	-	No	A
Agaricus bitorquis	4	1	Many variable	Cross	2	No	No	No	A
Pholiota nameko	4	1	1?	Cross	2	Yes	Yes	Yes	A
Auricularia auricula	4	1	1?	Cross-?	2	Yes	Yes	No	A?
Auricularia polytricha	4	1	1	Cross-?	2	Yes	Yes	No-?	A, B
Lentinus edodes	4	1	1	Cross	2	Yes	No,?	No,?	A, B
Flammulina velutipes	4	1	1	Cross	2	Yes	Yes	Yes	A, B
Pleurotus ostreatus	4	1	1	Cross	2	Yes	Yes	No	A, B
Coprinus fimetariuc	4	1	1	Cross	2	Yes	Yes	Yes	A, B

From the above table it is evidient that different kinds are sexuality ocuur in different species of mushrooms.

Chapter 4

Edible and Poisonous Mushrooms

Mushrooms for beginners, common rules to select mushrooms for consumption, description of some edible mushrooms, a partial list of some edible mushrooms, some critical edible mushrooms, poisonous mushrooms, characteristics of poisonous mushrooms, mushroom poisoning, different types of mushroom poisoning, nature of poisonous mushrooms, guidelines to avoid poisonous species and key to poisonous species of mushrooms.

The common field mushrooms grow in low grass on meadows or on rich, moist upland pastures being common after rains. The upper surfaces of such common field mushrooms, are seen to be white with brownish fibrils or scales. Under the side are beautiful salmon-pink structures when young, changing gradually to almost black or brown when old. Years earlier, people were very much interested to collect common field mushrooms. Popular edible mushrooms were known to them which and where to collect such mushrooms for their consumption. Now a days, the majority of people usually limit themselves entirely to only one or very few kinds of mushrooms well known to be edible. All knowledge regarding the edible and poisonous properties of mushrooms are based on experience of the people who were very fond of mushrooms. They tested them either intentional or unintentional in order to identify these edible or poisonous forms of mushrooms.

MUSHROOMS FOR BEGINNERS

The only safe rule is to confine oneself to known edible forms until other forms are proved to be harmless. If one is a beginner, he should ask a person experienced about that mushroom. Owing to the vast number of similar forms among the mushrooms, it is very difficult for a person to distinguish the edible forms from that of poisonous forms. There are a few mushrooms that contain poisons so deadly as that of the rattle—snake or copper head mushrooms. These were responsible for practically all the deaths due to mushroom eating. These poisons are narcotics rather than irritant and their effects are usually very slow to appear. Within 4 to 5 hours after eating, such poisonous forms exhibit their effects on our body. It may be very probably a case of indigestion or minor poisoning which should readily yield to a prompt emetic. If however, 8 to 12 hours have lapsed since eating the mushrooms, disagreeable symptoms should be taken very seriously. Since it is certain that one of the deadly poisons is at work, a physician should at once be called and the heart action should be stimulated by a hypodermic injection of atropine sulphate, known to be the antidote of mushroom poisoning. The injection of atropine sulphate, should be repeated again if so desired. If the deadly *Amanita* has been cosumed, it may paralyse the nervous system controlling the action of heart. In case, of the deadly *Amanita*, the atropine sulphate probably cannot save the patient and death will surely follow if the amount taken is sufficient.

The deadly *Amanita* is a very conspicuous and beautiful object occurring throughout the summer and autumn in open fields along the edge of the dense woods. Neither its odour nor its taste is disagreeable. It must be recognised by a careful study of its form and parts which are fortunately very characteristics. The most important part of deadly *Amanita* is the sheath at the base of the stem known as the "death cup". The ring of stem is similar to that of common mushroom but the gills are white both when young and old. In common edible mushrooms, the gills remain first pink changing black with the advancement of age. Therefore, nothing may be said about the colour of the upper surface of the cap. It varies so much being pure white, yellowish, brownish or blackish. When there is gathering of different kinds of mushrooms, it is important to get the entire stem and not leave a portion of it in the ground since the death cup may thus be overlooked. Mushrooms should not be gathered in the "button" stage from the field or pastures unless mature specimens are growing in the same place. Otherwise, a button shaped poisonous mushroom may be collected by mistake.

The fly *Amanita* species is beautiful and extremely dangerous. The cap is usually bright scarlet, yellowish or orange and sometimes fading to nearly white in colour and usually covered with conspicuous warts. The death cup also remains on the surface of the cap that should always be looked carefully. No mushroom of this group should be collected or eaten, although some forms of them may be excellent. Common mushroom, morel, button mushroom, paddy straw mushroom, beet steak and sulphur coloured polypore, common ink cap, glistening ink cap and all puff balls are known to be consumable provided they are white, tender and homogenous in texture within them. All coral fungi may not be poisonous if they are fresh, crisp, tender and neither have bad door or bad taste. The oyster mushrooms and their near relatives with white gills and short stems are also consumable. Most of these mushrooms usually grow on dead wood and above the ground in forests and orchards.

Rules for selecting mushrooms for consumption

There is no single and general rule or test by which it can be determined whether a given mushroom is edible or poisonous. If one intends to eat wild mushrooms especially in places where edible mushrooms produced by any mushroom farm are not available, the only safe procedure is to learn to recognise some of the common, easily identified and almost unmistakable kinds with absolute certainty. Mushrooms collected from different places, should never be used for consumption. Following principles must be followed as useful tips for selection of mushrooms to be consumed.

1. Mushroom eaten by others, should only be taken for consumption with safety.
2. Mushrooms produced at mushroom farms should be purchased for consumption. Such mushrooms are quite safe and free from all kinds of adverse effects.
3. Mushroom collected from fields, forests and pastures and from any other places, should not be consumed, as they may be fatal.

HOW TO RECOGNIZE MUSHROOMS

Different kinds of mushrooms may be identified on the basis of the illustrations given in this text. Suppose you find a gilled fungus and you wish to identify it, compare the diagram with the mushroom you wish to identify. Also, compare the spore colour with the colour described in the text. Colour of the spore can be printed by 'spore print technique'. Method of collection of spores for identification and for obtaining pure culture through spore culture method may be described as under:

SPORE PRINT TECHNIQUE

(Spore print method – The spore print is a simple method used for selection, identification and collection of pure spore culture. This method is most frequently used for identification of gilled fungi. When the cap of mushroom is held stationary on a paper in a cooled chamber for a long period, the impression of pattern of gills is printed and the spores are accumulated onto the paper. The invisible spores appear coloured. Single spore collected in this way may be used for pure spore culture).

Material required

Desired mushroom species, knife, a half black and half white paper, a glass bowl and light microscope.

Procedure for spore print

1. A fresh mushroom of desired species is taken and with the help of a sharp knife a gill is cut properly.
2. Now place the gill side down of the cap on a half black and half white paper in such a way that half of the gill should be towards black side and half towards white side.

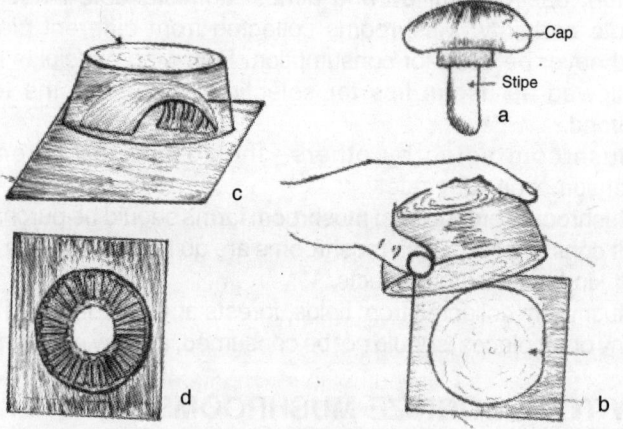

Fig. 4.1 Showing *Spore impression (print) method* that demonstrates (a) gilled mushroom selected for the study (b) bowl is ready to be placed (c) half black and half white paper on which cap of the mushroom is held stationary and (d) spore print of *Agaricus*.

3. Place a drop of water on the cap of mushroom and cover it by a glass bowl.
4. Leave this set up for about 8 hours or overnight undisturbed.
5. Next day gently remove the glass bowl and cup from the paper.

Results
On the paper, prints of the gills and spore deposits should be observed carefully.

Observation
Gills pattern and spore colours may be compared with the colour of the spores given in the text for identification.

EDIBLE MUSHROOMS KNOWN YEARS EARLIER

Some more than 50 years earlier, Dr. Charles H. Peck, former state Botanist of New York studied fungi. The following list comprises some of the edible species recognized by him. Mushrooms listed below are slightly different from the current nomenclature in some cases:

Table 4.1
A partial list of edible mushrooms identified some 50 years earlier

Agaricus abruplus Pk., *Agaricus micromegethus* Pk. *Agaricus placomyces* Pk., *Agaricus rodmani* Pk., *Agaricus diminutivus* Pk., *Agaricus haemorrhoidarius* Schulz, *Boletus edulis* Bull, *Boletus pallidus*, *Boletus eximius* Pk., *Boletus frostii* Russell, *Boletus granulatus* L., *Boletus laricinus*, *Boletus grisellus* Pk., *Boletus subaures* Pk., *Boletus albidipes* Pk., *Boletus versipellis* Fr, *Boletus bicolour* Pk., *Amanita caesarea* Scop, *Bovista plumbea* Pers. *Canthrellus lutessens* Fr, *Cantharellus cinnabarinus*, *Canthrellus minor* Pk., *Hygrophorus cantharellus*, *Hygrophorus chlorophanus*, *Clitocybe monadelpha* Morg, *Clitocybe rnultiformis* Pk., *Hygrophorus flavodiscus*, *Clitocybe ochropurpurea* Berk, *Clitocybe abortivus* B. & C., *Clitocybe prunulus* Scop, *Lactarius lignyotus*, *Coprinus comatus* Fr, *Cortinarius collinitus* Fr, *Cortinarius evernius* Fr, *Lepiota cepaestipes* Sow, *Entoloma grayanum* Pk., *Lycoperdon atropurpureum*, *Morchella angusticeps* Pk., *Hydnum caput-ursi* Fr, *Morchella conica* Pers, *Morchella diliciosa* Fr and *Morchella semilibera* DC etc.

SOME COMMONLY CULTIVATED EDIBLE MUSHROOMS

Agaricus bisporus
It is predominantly a crop of temperate region but it has successfully been introduced in subtropical countries like Mexico and Taiwan. With the technical advancement, the cultivation of

this species has spread all over the world. In our country, the production of *Agaricus bisporus* is increasing day by day with the simultaneous increase in number of people consuming it.

Agaricus bitorquis

In relatively short period, this species of button mushroom has attained its own status in the mushroom industry. It has many desirable attributes such as resistance to virus and tolerance to relatively high temperature. Fruit-bodies of this mushroom is white, solid and brownish in colour as compared to *A. bisporus*. Other species of white button mushrooms like *Agaricus arvensis* and *A. subrufescens* also seem promising to be exploited for cultivation on industrial scale.

Volvariella volvacea

It is an edible and fast growing mushroom of tropics and subtropics with relatively simple technology involvement. It has prospects for cultivation as cottage industry in both rural and suburban areas of tropical and sub tropical regions of the world. Common species which are cultivated, are *Volvariella volvacea, V. diplapsia* and *V. esculenta*. Recently, some other species have also been brought under cultivation with possibilities of domestication. In nature, *Volvariella* species are found growing on rotten paddy heaps or on other carbohydrate rich substrates during rainy season in tropics and subtropics. It requires high temperature (30–36°C) and relatively high humidity (70–90°C). This mushroom is mainly cultivated in Asian countries.

Pleurotus ostreatus

Among different cultivated edible mushrooms, species of *Pleurotus*, also known as oyster mushrooms are easiest and cheapest to grow throughout the world. This mushroom has distinct flavour with excellent drying and keeping quality. It is likely to assume a unique status as poor man's food and substitute for vegetables. Oyster mushrooms include many species, such as *Pleurotus ostreatus, P. sajor caju, P. florida, P. eryngie, P. cornucopiae, P. flabellatus*, and *P. pulmonaris*.

Lentinus edodes

It has taken an important place in the agricultural industry of Japan, Korea and China. This mushroom is commonly known as shiitake in Japan. It has got good international reputation as food and is exported from Japan to many countries in dried from.

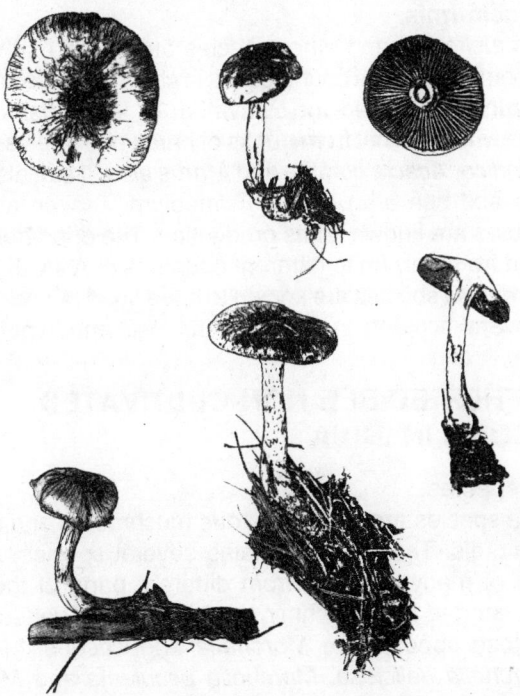

Fig. 4.2 Showing morphological characteristics of edible mushroom – *Flammulina* species.

Flammulina velutipes

This mushroom is commonly cultivated in Japan, Taiwan and Europe. It is called as winter mushroom. In India, it has been domesticated on experimental basis. The substrate presently in use are saw dust and rice bran. In Japan, it ranks second to *Lentinus edodes* in respect of economic importance.

Auricularia species

Like shiitake, *Auricularia* species are grown popularly in China and other Asian countries like Japan and Philippines. *Auricularia polytricha* is expected to become another popular dried mushroom in the world market. It is delicious and rich in nutrition.

Wooden logs of *Acacia confusa, Ficus retusa, Morus australis, Fagus crenata* and some other species of broad leaved trees are used as substrates for its cultivation.

Tremella fuciformis

Tremalla fuciformis and other species are called as the "white jelly mushroom" in different countries but in china it is called as "silver ear". The substrates used for cultivation of this mushroom are wooden logs which are cut from trunks of hardwood trees especially *Mangifera indica, Acacia corfusa* and *Morus alba.* It can also fruitify on sawdust and rice bran (1:3 v/ v) medium. Taiwan and other Asian countries are known for its production. The dried fruit bodies are exported from Taiwan to different countries of Asia, Japan and America. *Tremella* species are known to have good medicinal value in curing several ailments such as tuberculosis and hypertension.

SOME OTHER EDIBLE NON-CULTIVATED MUSHROOMS IN INDIA

Morchella species

Morchella species are ascomycetous mushrooms and are also known as morels. The genus contains several species. About 5 species out of many reported from different parts of the world, have been reported from Kashmir and Himanchal Pradesh in our country. These species are *Morchella angusticeps, Morchella conica, Morchella deliciosa, Morchella esculenta* and *Morchella hybrida.*

Distinguishing characteristics

The species of *Morchella* have a very characteristic shape and can be easily recognised. The stipe is thick, hollow and dirty white in contrast to dark brown conical or cylindrical pileus which is pitted and looks like a sponge. The size varies from 2 to 10 centimeters. The asci form a palisade layer all over the surface of the pileus.

Phellorinia inguinans

It is a gasteromycetous mushroom which is known to produce its spores in a closed structure (stomach) and not in gills like many other edible mushrooms. Commonly known as *khumbi,* this wild mushroom is very much popular in Haryana and Rajasthan. It usually grows in sandy places.

Distinguishing characteristics

This mushroom consists of a stipe and an obclavate to semi pyriform head. Its coat has two layers—the outer and the inner.

The outer layer is slightly yellowish covered with coarse over lapping scales arranged irregularly. The inner layer is white or cream, smooth, membranous, continuous with stipe and rupturing irregularly at the apex. The stalk has the bulbous base, measuring 4–7 centimeters in length and 1–2 centimeters in width. The stalk is solid and composed of an outer fibrilose scaby layer and an inner light yellow, tough and woody core. It grows and is collected from the nature. Immature fruit bodies are mostly preferred. It is also dehydrated and sold dry.

Hydnum repandum

Hydnum repandum is a spreading type of mushroom and is also known as spreading hydnum. It is edible and belongs to family Hydnaceae in which spores are borne on the surface of spines. No poisonous species are known.

Distinguishing Characteristics

Pileus of the the genus Hydnum is convex to plane in morphology. It is irregular, very brittle, varying greatly in size, measuring 2 to 16 cms in width. The surface is dry and smooth in texture and white to buff or brown in colour. Margin remains wavy, cotext white or whitish with tender straight spines. These spines are white or yellowish in colour. The stipe is eccentric, usually clavate, measuring about 2–10 cms X 1–2 cm in size.

Economic importance

The species are widely distributed, occurring during late summer among moss or leaves in woods. It is too tender. It should be sliced and steeped for 20 minutes in a water before cooking. The flavour seems to be improved. Some of the species of this genus are bitter, they should be boiled for a short time before cooking.

Hydnum Caputursi Fries

This mushroom is also known as Bear's head or Hydnum. It is an edible mushroom and is eaten by mushroom lovers in different countries.

Distinguishing characteristics

Large fleshy, tuberculi form, pendulous rarely erect, white in colour, 7–15 cms or more in thickness, somewhat tough, mild flavour, spores are globose in shape and hyaline in colour, measuring about 5–6 cms in diameter.

Economic importance
This species occurs in temperate regions of the world. During summer and autumn, this species is commonly found on dead or dying trunks of deciduous trees especially beech and birch. Being some what tough, it can be made very attractive in appearance and taste by proper cooking.

Polyporus frondosus (Dicks) Fries
It is an edible variety and is also known as Frondose polypore. It is a large and branched species which grows commonly at the base of oak trees. It also arises from their roots on which it feeds. It also attacks the roots of chestnut trees.

Economic importance
It is collected when young and become too tough. It is used with butter after boiling for about 20 minutes.

Polyporus sulphureus Fries
It is called as sulphur coloured edible polypore mushroom. It looks a bit larger in morphology and known to be widely distributed in different countries. It is commonly found in conspicuous yellow clusters on dead spots on the trunk of the oak and various other trees.

Distinguishing characteristics
Hymenophore multiplex, 30–60 cms broad; pileus cheesy not becoming rigid, reniform, very broad, more or less stipitate, 5–15 × 7–20 × 0.5–1 cms in size; surface rugose, varying from lemon yellow to orange in colour, colour fading out with the advancement of age; spores ovoid, smooth or finely papillate, hyaline in colour, measuring 6–8 cms × 3–5 cms in size.

Economic importance
It was used for food and is good in taste and flavour after boiling.

Boletus castaneus
It is chestnut coloured edible mushroom. This species is common in Europe and United States on sandy soil and at the edges of woods.

Distinguishing characteristics

Pileus of this species looks convex to sub expanded, slightly depressed, measuring 3–7 cms broad. The surface remains smooth, dry, orange brown in colour with thin margin. In colour, it is usually paler, convex white and firm. It is nutty in flavour. Colour unchanging when wounded. Spores are ellipsoid, smooth, hyaline to pale yellowish, measuring 8–9 × 4.5–5–5 microns in size. Stipe is cylindrical or somewhat flattened, bright brown in colour, light coloured at the apex, measuring 4–5 cm × 6–10 cm in thickness.

Economic importance

The fresh is white and edible. Colour unchanging when wounded. It is mild in flavour.

Boletus edulis Bull

This species is abundant, well known and widely distributed in thin woods through out temperate regions of the world.

Distinguishing characteristics

The sporophore is large and usually yellowish brown. The stipe is more or less reticulate especially above. The pileus is thick, broadly convex, surface smooth, globrous, dry, slight viscid when moistened and varying in colour from brown to reddish brown, sometimes pale. The colour usually unchanging, white or yellowish and sometimes reddish beneath the cuticle. It tastes sweet and nutty. The stipe remains unequal or enlarged. Below the stout, it remains considerably pale becoming bluish or discoloured when wounded. The stipe is wholly or partly reticulate.

Economic importance

This species is commonly used in Europe and is often sliced and dried for winter use. It is baked in a covered dish for an hour after removing the tubes and stipe and cutting it into pieces.

Boletus scaber Bull

This mushroom is most abundant on the grounds in woods or groves.

Distinguishing characteristic

Pileus convex, 3–12 cm board; surface very variable in colour, white-red or brown, context white becoming slightly darker when fresh and coloured when bruised; spores oblong, smooth, brown,

13–16 µ long; stipe firm, solid, tapering upward, whitish with rough end; numerous reddish or brownish dots are seen on scales.

Economic importance
It is rough-stemmed edible species and is very handsome in appearance.

Boletus granulatus L.
It is abundant and widely distributed in occurrence. It is collected chiefly in mid summer in open ground under or near the conifers in Europe.

Distinguishing characteristics
Pileus is subhemispheric to nearly plane in appearance; 4–10 cms broad and 1–1.5 cms thick; surface very variable in colour usually pinkish-grey to reddish brown fading to yellowish and often obscurely spotted especially in centre; spores fusiform, pale yellowish brown, 7.5–9.5 × 2.5–5.5 µ in size; stipe short, thick, enlarged below, white or pale yellow, dotted with pinkish brown droplets which becomes darker on drying.

Economic importance
It is granulated edible species.

Boletus luteus L.
Commonly found in sandy soil in coniferous or mixed woods.

Distinguishing characteristics
Pileus convex, solitary, 5–10 cms broads; surface, smooth, glabrous, very viscid, yellowish brown, greyish brown or reddish brown in colour; some-times streaks becoming darker and duller in old age; spores oblong to fusiform, smooth and yellowish-brown in colour, 6–9 × 2.5–4 µ in size; stipe slightly tapering downwards, pale yellow to reddish brown in colour; annulus large, membranous, white to slightly brownish, glandular-dotted and persistent.

Economic importance
It is egg-yellowish edible species.

Chanterel chantarellus (L) Murill
Commonly found through out the temperate regions in deciduous coniferous woods of Europe.

Distinguishing characteristics

Pileus fleshy, firm, turbinate, nearly plane, sometimes depressed, 13–8 cms broad; surface glabrous, rarely paler yellow; context white and nutty; lamellae thick, narrow; spores ellipsoid, some white irregular, smooth, 8–10 × 4–5 microns in size; stipe attenuate below, measuring 2.5–5 cms × 6–12 mm in size.

Economic importance

It is seasoned with butter. It is an excellent addition to meat, stews and omelets.

Lactaria deliciosa (L) Fries

It is considered as one of the best mushrooms and is readily recognised by its orange-red milky juice.

Distinguishing characteristics

Pileus fleshy, 5–12 cms broad; surface orange, yellow orange or paler, zoned with deep orange becoming paler with age; margin involute then arched and at length upturned, glabrous, context firm, yellow stipe of the same colour as the pileus, spotted with brighter orange; spores yellow, subglobose to ellipsoid, slightly echinulate, more or less hyaline, 8–8.5 μ × 8–11 μ in size.

Economic importance

It is also recognized as delicious edible lactaria. It should be cooked slowly for nearly an hour. It is not so delicious but rather coarse.

Lactaria lactiflua (L) Barl.

It is also recognized as orange brown edible species. It is very common in occurrence in woods and groves.

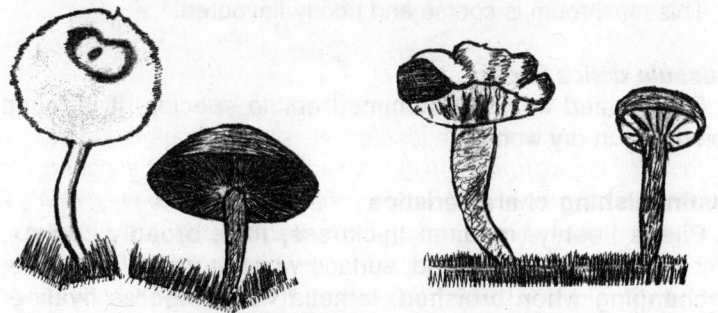

Fig. 4.3 Showing two edible species of *Lactaria*.

Distinguishing characteristics

Pileus fleshy, convex then nearly plane or slightly depressed, 5–13 cms broad; surface fulvous, buff in colour, sometimes much paler, dry, smooth, context firm, thick, whitish, changing brown when exposed to air; lamellae creamy white or tinged with some colour as pileus, becoming darker with age, changing brownish when injured; stipe solid, sometimes becoming hollow, 2–10 cms long and 1–2 cms thick; spores white, echinulate, measuring 7–10 μ in diameter.

Economic importance

The flavour of this species is somewhat unpleasant and astringent. It is fairly good when cooked slowly for 40 minutes.

***Lactaria piperata* (L.) Pers**

Also known as peppery edible lactaria, chiefly found in great abundance in oak woods thoughtout temperate regions of the world. It contains an acid as a resin 'Piperon' which is extremely acrid in fresh state but becomes disorganised by heat and harmless when cooked.

Distinguishing characteristics

Pileus fleshly, convex, 4–12 cms in diameter, surface white, dry and glabrous; context compact, latex white, unchanging, very acrid, abundant; lamellae white or creamy white; stripe white, equal, dry, solid and firm; spores white, subglobose, nearly smooth, 8–9 μ in diameter.

Economic importance

This mushroom is coarse and poorly flavoured.

***Russula delica* Fries**

Recognized as short stemmed edible species. It is found commonly in dry woods.

Distinguishing characteristics

Pileus fleshly, medium thickness, firm, broadly convex, umbilicate, 8–16 cms broad; surface white; context firm, white; unchanging when bruised; lamella white; spores hyaline, subglobose, tuberculate, 10 × 9 min sizes; stripe white, sometimes

Fig. 4.4 Showing morphological characteristics of mushroom – *Russula virescens.*

with a glaucous-green ring at the apex, measuring 2–5 cms long and one to two cms. thick.

Economic importance

It is excellent when fried in better before use.

Russula virescens (Schaett) Fries

Fig. 4.5 Morphological characteristics of other *Russula* species.

This beautiful green *Russula* species has long been enjoyed as a reputed mushroom for edibility and taste.

Distinguishing characteristics

Pileus fleshy, globose becoming convex, centrally depressed, 5–12 cms broad, surface green or greyish green; stripe white, firm, 1.5 cms long; context white; lamella white; spores sub globose; echinulate, hyaline, 7 × 8 microns in size.

Economic importance

It is an edible mushroom well recognized for edibility and taste.

Russula flava Romell

It is found in mixed woods and recognized as yellow *Russula* species. This species is rare in occurrence.

Distinguishing characteristics

Pileus fleshy, convex, becoming slightly depressed in the centre, 5–8 cms broad; stripe white becoming more or less gray with age and in drying; spores are pale yellow, globose, echinulate, measuring 8–9 m in diameter.

Tricholoma personatum (Fries) Quel

Fig. 4.6 Morphological characteristics of mushroom – *Tricholoma nudum*.

Fig. 4.7 Showing morphological characteristics of Edible mushroom – *Tricholoma personatum*.

It may be found in open woods or among weeds or long grass in rich field. Its large size and violet tint of all its parts distinguishes it from most of the other species.

Distinguishing characterises

Pileus thick, firm, convex, 5–12 cms broad, surface moist, glabrous, purple coloured, fading to greyish, margin in rolled; spores ellipsoid, smooth, dull pinkish in mass, 7–10 m in length; stripe short, often bulbous at the base, 3–6 cms long 1.5–3.0 cms thick.

Economic importance

This is the valuable edible species known for excellent flavour.

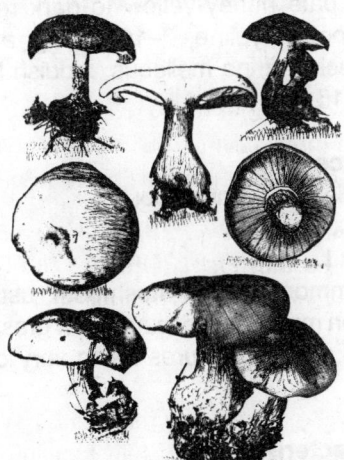

Fig. 4.8 Showing morphological characteristics of different parts of *Tricholoma* species.

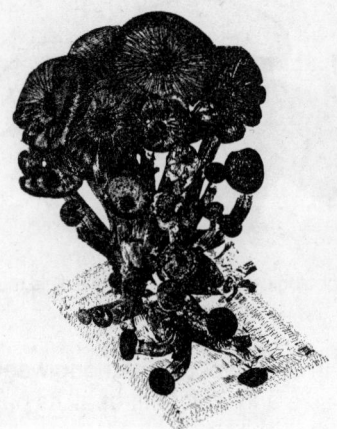

Fig. 4.9 Showing general morphology of mushroom – *Armillaria mellea.*

Armillaria mellea (vahl) Quel

This species is very widely distributed and very abundant on stumps and buried roots of both deciduous and evergreen trees on which it grows as a parasite.

Distinguishing characteristic

Pileus convex to expended, very variable, 4–12 cms broad, surface usually dry, pale honey-yellow to dark reddish-brown; spores ellipsoid, smooth, hyaline, 7–10 m long; annulus white, cottony with dark specks; stripe melleous, reddish brown or dirty brown, measuring 5–15 mm thick.

Economic importance

It is known as edible honey mushroom.

Agaricus campester L

It is known as common pasture mushroom, usually found in pastures. This common mushroom occurs in low grass in meadows or on rich, moist and upland pastures being very common after rains.

Distinguishing characteristics

Pileus convex to expanded, 5–9 cms broad; surface dry, silky and white and light reddish-brown, the colour being chiefly in the scale; context white, thick, solid, mild flavour, sometimes becoming reddish when broken; lamellae free, rounded behind, white when young; spores ellipsoid, smooth, dark brown, 10–12 m in size; annulus delicate; stipe smooth, white, cylindrical, nearly equal, 3–6 cms long, 1.5 to 2 cms thick.

Economic importance

The spawn 'or vegetative portion remain hidden in the soil and it feeds upon the dead organic matter found therein. This is the mushroom usually found in market.

Agaricus arvensis Schaieff

This mushroom is also known as horse mushroom or field mushroom. This species usually grows in rich soil in pastures, fields and wood borders.

Distinguishing characteristics

It resembles with the common mushroom and is larger with longer stipe, stipe long white often enlarged at base; lamellae paler with a peculiar double annulus; pileus large convex, 6–15 cms broad; surface white, thick, highly flavoured and easily digested.

Podaxis pistillaris

It is a gasteromycetous mushroom and has some resemblance with *Phellorinia inquinans*. It is usually distinguished by its stalk. In this mushroom, the coat splits at the base of the head whereas in *Phellorinia inquinans* it ruptures irregularly at the top. This mushroom grows in sandy soil, rich in organic matter. It is seen in nature mostly after rains in July and August. It is found mostly in Haryana, Punjab, Rajasthan and some parts of Uttar Pradesh.

Distinguishing characteristics

This mushroom has also not been cultivated so far in our country. The fruit body is 5–10 centimeters in length and 2–4 centimeters in width.

SOME CRITICAL EDIBLE MUSHROOMS

Polypores that are sufficiently tender in texture, are edible. Avoid certain *Boletus* species not listed so far.

1. *Boletus* species that have been tested, are edible. Avoid all

species with red tube-mouths and bitter or peppery taste and also those species that turn blue quickly when handled.

2. Species of *Russula* and *Lactaria* with pleasant odor and flavour are edible. Avoid such species like *Lactaria rufa, L. torminosa, Russula foetens* and *R. emetica*.

3. Several species of *Lepiota* are edible. Avoid *L. morgani* with green spores.

4. Common species of *Clitocybe*, Tricholoma and *Collybia* are usually edible.

POISONOUS MUSHROOMS

Frankly speaking, very little is known about the subject of poisonous mushrooms and the statements and opinions about the poisonous mushrooms are so conflicting that one often does not know what to believe regarding the commonest and best known forms.

Characteristics of Poisonous Mushrooms

1. Two species of mushrooms namely *Venenarius muscarius* and *Venenarius phalloides*, which owing to their abundance, wide distribution, conspicuous appearance and deadly qualities are known to be poisonous. They had been the chief cause of death from mushroom eating all over the world years earlier.

2. The poisons occurring in flowering plants belong chiefly to two classes of substances known as alkaloids and glucosides. The former, are known bases such as aconitine from aconite, atropine from belladona, nicotine from tobacco and morphine from poppy plant. Glucosides are sugar derivatives of complex, unstable and often unknown composition like poisons found in digitalis, hellebore, wistaria and several other plants.

3. The more important poisons of mushrooms also belong to the same classes—one represented by the alkaloid as found in *Venenarius muscarinus* and the other, the glucoside which is the deadly principle found in *Venenarius phalloides*, is known mainly through its effects.

4. There are various other minor poisons, which usually manifest its toxic effects to the taste or smell that cause local irritation. Such poisons are more or less damaging to the health. They usually function adversely according to the body constitution of the individual.

5. In some cases in olden days, poisonous species were used in committing murder. The annual number of deaths due to mistaking poisonous species for edible ones were probably as more as many hundreds.

6. The tests used to distinguish poisonous mushrooms are most varied and curious. They are usually mixed with queer traditions and superstitions. Therefore, the only safe rule is to know each species accurately before eating it. Mushrooms grown by the reputed mushroom farms should only be taken for safety in all respects.

7. The chief poisonous species listed by ancient mushroom eaters were—*Venenarius phalloides, V. muscarius, V. cothurnatus, V. solitarius, Clitocybe illudens, Inocybe infida, Panaeolus venenosus, Panus stypticus* and *chlorophyllum molybdites.*

KINDS OF MUSHROOM POISONING

There are about 24 genera splitted into many species and out of that more than 100 cultivated species/forms are presently domesticated either on a small or large scale. The fruit bodies of hundred of other species of edible mushrooms cannot be easily grown under controlled conditions because of their biological and ecological speciality. Besides these edible species, there are so many fleshy fungi, which are deadly poisonous, are called as toadstools. Most of the people ignorantly use to say mushroom to these poisonous toadstools. Due to lack of knowledge about such poisonous species or almost frequent carelessness on the part of mushroom collector, mushroom poisoning is usually observed. With adequate knowledge and familiarity with these fungi and with due care during collection, troubles resulted from eating of such poisonous mushrooms can easily be avoided. One should not eat any mushroom unknown to him and must be sure that the collected specimens are safe to eat.

Different types of mushroom poisoning

There are different kinds of mushroom poisoning, which may be classified under five major types as under:

1. Gastro-intestinal type, 2. Nerve affecting type, 3. Blood dissolving type, 4. Cholerifrom type and 5. Cerebral type

1. **Gastro-intestinal type** of poisoning may be characterized by the symptoms of nausea, vomiting and diarrhoea. The symptoms terminate rapidly and usually spontaneously. The patients recovers to normal health in a day or two. This type of poisoning may be suspected to be caused by *Russula emetica, Lactarius torminosus* and *Entoloma levidum*.

2. **Nerve affecting type** of poisoning is usually caused by eating of *Amanita muscaria, Inocybe infelix* and *Clitocybe illudens*. The symptoms produced in this type of poisoning include convulsions, coma and often death. The active principle of such poisoning is 'muscarin'. Its antidote is atropine sulphate.

3. **Blood-dissolving type** of poisoning is manifested by the abdominal stress with jaundice developing in 4 to 5 days. It may cause death in some cases. Transfusion of blood may be desirable in such type of poisoning. Causative toadstools include *Gyromitra esculenta*.

4. **Choleriform type** of poisoning usually develops in 10 to 15 hours after eating of poisonos mushroom species followed by rapid loss of strength and weight. The causative toadstools include *Amanita plzalloides* and *A. virosa*. The death rate is high

5. **Cerebral type** of poisoning manifests symptoms like exhilaration and disturbance of vision. The patients recover the health after some time. The causative toadstools are species of *Panaeolus*.

CATEGORIES OF MUSHROOM POISONING

There are not general rules or methods by which deadly poisonous mushrooms may be recognised. One of the most important precautions is not to tough any mushroom for consumption that has a volva (cup) at the base. Generally, the poisonous varieties are attractive to the eyes. The most deadly ones are the death cap- *Amanita phalloides*, destroying angels-*Amanita virosa*, the fool's cap-*Amanita verna* and the fly agaric-*Amanita muscaria*. The toxic principle in these species is the mixture of a and b -*amanitin* and *phalloidin*. Both of these are complex cyclic polypeptides containing sulphur. Cooking does not destroy toxins nor these are affected by the human digestive juices. Symptoms of poisoning appears only after 8–24 hours of ingestion and by that time the toxin is absorved by the body and neither vomiting nor a stomach pump can help.

There are more than 7 species of poisonous *Amanita* which are responsible for poisoning. Poisoning based on organs affected may be of different categories as given below:

1. Cyclopeptide poisoning
This is the most dangerous type of poisoning and is responsible for most deaths caused by mushroom poisoning especially in Europe and America. Symptoms may obscure liver and kidney damage.

2. Haemolytic poisoning
The patient of such kind of poisoning shows the symptoms of anaemia after eating raw or under cooked mushrooms especially belonging to *Amanita rubescens* and *Amanita vaginata*.

3. Muscarine poisoning
This type of poisoning is known to be caused by the eating of *Amanita muscaria* and *Amanita pantherina*. The symptoms include increased perspiration, salivation, nausea, vomiting, abdominal pain, thirst and mucous with bloody stool. Death usually results from respiratory arrestation.

4. Coprine (Antabuse-like) poisoning
This type of poisoning is usually caused by the eating of *Coprinus attramentarius*. The nervous system is adversely affected in this kind of poisoning.

5. Gastero-enteric irritants
Mushrooms responsible for such kinds of poisoning are *Agaricus xanthodermus*, *Boletus satanus*, *Paxillus involutus* and some of the species of *Tricholoma*, *Lactarius* and *Russula*. In this poisoning, gastro-intestinal irritation is the most important symptom to be experienced. The symptoms appears usually after 30 minutes to 3 hours after ingestion.

6. Psychotropic poisoning
Poisonous mushrooms affect nervous system in such a way that the man perceives non existent sights and sounds or has hallucinations and delirism 2 to 4 hours after ingestion of the

Table 4.2

Keys to some most common poisonous species of mushrooms with their distinguishing characteristics.

Name	Distribution	Distinguishing characters	Remarks
Panus Stypticus (bull.) Fries **(Astringent panes)**	This small inconspicuous species is common through out the temperate regions. Usually found on stumps of deciduous trees in thick woods.	Pileus tough, spatulate to reniform, 1–3 cms broad; context thin firm, rather tough, waterwhite, astringent; lamellae narrow; spores globose, smooth, hyaline, 2–4 × 1–3 min size; stipe lateral, short, swollen, dull white above and darker below.	It is phosphorescent and poisonous possessing a strongly acrid and astringent taste.
Clitocybe sudorifica peck **(Sweet producing clitocybe)**	Usually found in open grass places. When eaten, this varity causes profuse perspiration and has been used to break a cold.	Pileus fleshly, thin, slightly depressed in the centre; context watery when moist, white when dry, taste mild, odor none; spores subglobose, 4 – 5mx 3 – 4m in size; stipe short.	Disagreeable and persistent taste; causes sickness and discomfort.
Amanita phalloides Fries **(Deadly amanita/ destroying angel)**	Occurs widely distributed in many forms and colours. It is usually distinguished by the presence of a distinct volva or death cap.	Pileus convex, 3–15 cms broad; surface smooth; context extremely Poisonous white, not objectionable to taste but somewhat disagreeable odor; lamellae white; spores globose, smooth, hyaline, 7–10 min diameter; stipe sub equal and bulbous.	The effect of poison is slow from 6 to 15 hours; sudden and severe pain in abdomen, no antidote is known so far.
Amanita muscaria (L) Pers. **(Fly amanita/Fly Agaric/ Fly poison)**	Widely distributed in woods, wood borders and thick forests through out temperate regions. It is a beautiful plant and area abundant especially near pine trees.	Pileus globose to convex; surface slightly viscid when fresh, red or orange to yellow; cortex white, yellow under pellicle, extremely poisono⸱ ⸱ spores subglucose to ellipsoid, ₋10 × 7–8 min size; stripe subequal, white or pale yellowish.	It contains alkaloid-muscarin poison. It affects the ganglia controlling the nerve of heart, stops the heart beating.

Table 4.2 *(contd.)*

Name	Distribution	Distinguishing characters	Remarks
Amanita cothurnate Atk. **(Booted amanita)**	Found in woods of New York to Alabama and Pennsylvania. It is known to be important poisonous mushroom of Japan.	Pileus globose, 3–7 cms broad, surface quite viscid; cortex white without odor; spores glucose, smooth, hyaline, measuring 7–9 min diameter; stripe cylindrical; volva white.	Intoxication similar to *Amanita muscaria*. It contains muscarin and cholin as poisons, not known to be fatal.
Amanita spreta Peck **(Sheathed Venenarius)**	Found in open and bushy places.	Pileus subovoid to convex, 7–10 cms broad; surface white or pale greyish brown; lamellae subcrowded; spores ellipsoid smooth, hyaline; annuals membranous, persistent; volva thim.	The species is poisonous. Sheath of this species is much similar to edible species *Vaginata plumbea*.
Panaeolus venenosus Murr **(Poisonous panaeolus)**	Usually occur in manure rich soil in open places.	Pileus thick, fleshly; surface moist; context white or slightly yellowish, very thick at centre; spores ellipsoid or ovoid, measuring 11–13 mx 7–8.5 m stipe thick, fleshly.	It produces hilarity and a mild form of intoxication in man.
Dictyophora duplicata Bose. Ed Fisch **(Veiled stink horn)**	Usually found near stumps in field and in edges of woods. It is easily recognised by its veil.	Pileus campanulate, 5 cms long; veil white, reticulate, variable in length; spores oblong, ellipsoid, 4x2 min size, involved in mucus at maturity; stripe fusifrom, cylindrical, tapering at each end.	Extremely fetid, attractive to flies which probably disseminate the spores.

poisonous mushroom. The symptoms include sleep, torpidity or coma in extreme cases. Isoxazole derivatives and indole group derivatives are the important poisons responsible for this kind of poisoning. *Psilcybe mexicana, P. strichfer, Amanita muscaria* and species of *Panaeolus* and *Stropharia* are the mushrooms responsible for such kind of poisoning.

IDENTIFICATION OF POISONOUS MUSHROOMS

There are no clear cut visible signs on any mushroom that can differentiate edible from poisonous species. Similarly, there are no thumb rules to distinguish edible and poisonous species. These species may be differentiated among them on the basis of experience as there are certain characteristics of poisonous species. However, no generalized characteristics are possible.

Nature of Poisonous Mushrooms

1. Some people have common belief that wild mushroom species, which have been nibbed by insects, squirrels and rabits are edible. Such kind of belief does not hold any scientific explaination and is not sure to be edible in actual practice.
2. Some mushrooms are poisonous when raw but becomes harmless when cooked. Example—*Clitocybe nuda.*
3. Some mushrooms are poisonous before they are boiled. After boiling, they are safe to eat after cooking properly. Example—*Gyromitra esenlenta.*
4. Some mushrooms are poisonous regardless to the manner of preparation. Example—*Amanita phalloides.*
5. Some mushrooms are poisonous only under certain conditions such as when consumed with alcoholic beverages, such as *Coprinus atramentarius.*
6. Some mushrooms are poisonous only when eaten in large quantities, such as *Verpa bohemica.*
7. Some mushrooms for reasons unknown are deadly poisonous in some geographical areas but edible in others, such as *Paxillus involutus.*
8. Some mushrooms are poisonous when they are old, decayed or damaged by frost and are edible when fresh and young such as *Armillariella mellea.*

GUIDELINES TO AVOID POISONOUS SPECIES

1. There are many poisonous species among little brown mushrooms, that defy identification. They should be avoided.
2. Never eat any white-capped mushroom species because most of them are deadly poisonous.
3. Beware of any new mushroom with a ring on its stalk as found on *Amanita virosa.*
4. Mushroom with a sac or cup around the base of its stalk may be *Amanita fulva.* This is an edible species. It may be confused with poisonous *Amanita phalloides.*
5. Many edible mushrooms have a pronounced swelling at the base of their stalk as observed in *Armillariella mellea.* Many poisonous species like *Amanita muscaria* also have swollen stalk base. A critical observation is must before picking such mushrooms.
6. Mushrooms with warts, scales or raised projections on its cap, should be avoided. The poisonous species with warts, scales or raised projections on its cap include *chlorophyllum molybdites* and *Amanita muscaria.* Some edible mushrooms also have similar scales on its cap such as *Lapiota procera.* Critical identification in such cases is desirable.
7. Avoid all species of *Boletus*–fleshly mushrooms with pores instead of gills on the under side of their caps which stain blue on bruising.
8. Avoid brain like *(Gyromitra),* saddle shaped fungi or deformed morels. Some of these species are edible but most of them are poisonous.
9. Always cut all puffballs in half and examine the contents. Do not use any species whose inside is not pure white. One that is discoloured or black within can be poisonous earth ball such as *Scleroderma aurantium.*
10. Never eat any mushroom found growing on or near dung that you have not positively identified. Some poisonous species also grow on dung.

Chapter 5

Cultivation System & Farm Design

> *Fundamentals of cultivation system, small village unit, larger commercial unit, mushroom farm layout, location of the building plot, design of the farm, bulk chamber, equipments and facilities, pasteurization room, growing room, installation of the warming and steam unit, mushroom research laboratory.*

Mushroom cultivation is of recent origin in India. Years ago, mushroom cultivation began experimentally in Solan in Himanchal Pradesh in an ordinary room. The compost was prepared in open space outdoor on a small scale. Mushroom growing rooms in winter, had to be heated to increase the temperature to the desired level in those days. In J & K, mushroom farms on above pattern were established in large numbers but due to lack of expert guidance, growers suffered losses frequently. However, with the import of knowledge and advanced technology in our country, mushroom growing became a profitable business gradually. FAO experts visited to our country some years earlier and suggested short method of composting for profitable production of mushroom. The short method of composting was successfully tried and many other modifications were made. Such modifications resulted in increased yield up to 16–18 kgs of mushroom form 100 kgs of compost as against 6–8 kgs of mushroom obtained from 100 kgs of compost prepared by long method of composting. Both small village units and larger commercial units now do cultivation of mushroom successfully.

MUSHROOM GROWING IN SMALL VILLAGE UNIT

Years earlier in Kashmir, mushroom-growing houses were constructed. These were constructed with Kucha/Pucca bricks.

121

Mushroom houses consisted of shelves made of woods. Ventilators were provided on walls for air changes and the roofs were invariably made of galvanised iron sheets. Saw dust stoves were used for heating mushroom houses in winter season. The mushroom growing rooms were kept small and compost was prepared by long method of composting. In such mushroom houses two or three crops were obtained with miner imputes in heating and cooling. In plains of north India, only one crop was possible to be taken in winter months. This activity has now become popular in Jammu, Punjab, Haryana, Weston U.P. and Delhi. The produce so obtained in small village units was sold in local market. In Sonepat (Haryana) mushroom growing has become a permanent activity and large number of farmers have adopted growing mushroom as a source of additional

Fig. 5.1 Showing structure of a low cost *Mushroom growing* room that is composed of walls made from bricks and roof from sarkanda.The roof is supported on bamboo pillars. Forced air circulation facility provided.

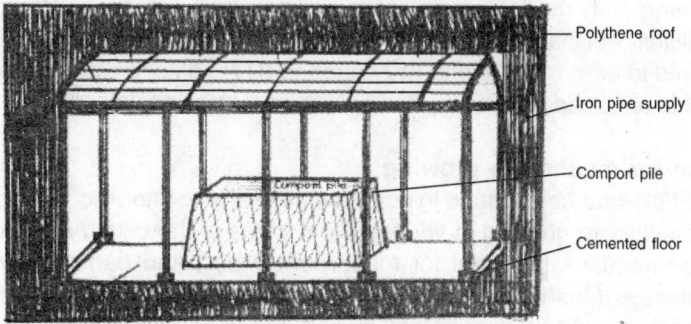

Fig. 5.2 Showing low cost *Composting shed made* from iron pipe support, polythene roof and cemented floor. Compost pile has been shown above the floor.

income. They get raw materials locally and mushroom houses are built of kacha brick preparing shelves with **sarkanda**. The farmers take one crop with ease. Spawn is made available and the government provides market support. These farmers usually construct the shed measuring 70 feet x 30 feet with 4–5 shelves. Approximately 10–15 tons of compost are used at a time. The depth of compost is generally maintained upto 5"–6" and a mixture of FYM and farm soil is used as casing material after formalin treatment. They usually produce 10–15 kgs of mushroom per 100 kgs compost.

MUSHROOM GROWING IN COMMERCIAL UNITS

Modern mushroom houses with facility of making pasteurised compost in bulk have also came up into being in many parts of the country. In Punjab and Maharastra, some cold storages have been converted into mushroom houses. Short method of composting is brought into practise there and phase-I of composting is done outdoor. The compost is then filled into the shelves in modified cold store rooms. The compost is pasteurized and conditioned in these shelves. The spawning, spawn run, casing and cropping are also done on the same shelves. All the rooms are kept properly insulated and provided with facilities for heating, cooling and ventilation. In some districts of Punjab, the cold storages have been converted into mushroom growing rooms with certain modifications. Kishan foods and Ponds India Ltd. have their growing units in hills of ooty (TN). Ponds India Ltd. is growing mushrooms in low cost plastic growing houses/tunnels. In Bangalore, 3–4 big units are running with modern mushroom growing and compost making facilities. At Bhagalpur (Bihar), one commercial mushroom grower is said to earn much profit. At Allahabad (U.P.) also, a commercial unit is engaged in growing mushroom on a large scale.

Plan for mushroom growing

Efforts are being made to popularise the science and technology of mushroom growing in various tribal areas of the country. There is tremendous potential for mushroom export and earn foreign exchange. Mushroom cultivation as cottage industry especially in villages should be popularised in rural areas so that farmers may earn extra income. This idea may be translated into practice by the government by providing desirable facilities through bulk compost preparation, spawn distribution, better marketing support and technical backup to promote this cottage industry at national level.

PRINCIPLES OF MUSHROOM FARM LAY OUT

Mushroom cultivation is usually an indoor horticultural activity and a wide variety of designs and constructional materials have been used for mushroom houses. Mushroom farms comprise a set of buildings constructed in such a way that various operations related to mushroom cultivation may be done continuously and efficiently to get mushroom production all the year around. Mushroom farm should not be constructed near the other mushroom farms or business points because it may adversely affect the consumption of the produce in the market. It is one of the most important conditions for obtaining good mushroom yields at a low cost with profitable marketing. Mushroom farm should be properly designed and well equipped with modern facilities. For obtaining profit, one should start with at least three growing rooms and one-bulk chambers each of about 20 tons capacity with scope of future extension.

Location of the building plot

While selecting plot, one must keep in mind the following precautions for profitable mushroom cultivation:
1. Plot for constructing building should be next to or close to public road / high way, so that raw materials/removing materials and spent compost etc. may be easily delivered.
2. There should be facilities for water, electricity and disposal of sewage etc.
3. The building must be located on the plot in such a way that the compost filling area can be reached in a direct-line from the road. The access road must be about 5 meters broad so that vehicles/trucks may be turned easily.
4. Farm layout should be prepared after drawing plan of the farm and should preferably be constructed in phased manner. For example, if farm is proposed to be of 12 rooms, only three or four rooms should be constructed initially.

An ideal commercial mushroom farm should have about 12 rooms each of 200-m² area having capacity of 20 tons of compost in bags with two bulk chambers or tunnels each of 20 tons capacity. The composting yard with dimensions of 100' × 45' for holding phase I stacks with scope for future extension. The composting yard should be covered and cemented with facilities for water and proper drainage.

Design of farm

There are different types of mushroom farm designs adopted in different parts of the world suiting to the local conditions. The Dutch farm design and construction method is being widely adopted all over the world with some modifications to suit local conditions. There are two systems, which are usually used in mushroom growing farms. These are as under:

I. **Single zone system** – In single zone system, peak heading, spawn run and cropping is done in one room. Each room is insulated properly and equipped in such a way that the highest temperature required can be maintained. In this system, growing is almost done in fixed beds called shelf beds.

II. **Second zone system** – In second zone system, separate rooms for peak healing, spawn run and cropping are maintained. In this system, temperature in the cropping rooms will not rise higher than 16–20 C° and there is no need of heavy insulation. Rooms for peak heating and spawn run are heavily insulated to maintain desired temperature.

In the Netherlands, cropping rooms with 200 m² cultivation surfaces are used. There are two rows of shelves each having five beds one above the other. The room size is kept 6.00m × 17.75m × 3.80m. In the front of room 4m wide passage is provided and in backside of the room, cemented area to facilitate compost filling is provided.

Bulk chamber

Situation of a bulk chamber in a mushroom farm is extremely important. The size of chamber depends on the compost to be loaded. For 20 tons capacity, bulk chamber with dimensions of 36' (Long) × 9' (Wide) × 12' (Height) is best suited under Indian conditions. The wall should be well insulated. The plenum should be 3' deep at lower end and 6' deep on upper end, thus giving a desired slop for run off sufficient space of steam to penetrate the compost mass. about 25–30% of the total floor area should be left in the form of gaps for efficient steam circulation. The walls as well as ceiling of the tunnel should be effectively insulated. Walls are provided with 5.0 cms thick insulating materials between brick wall (9" wide) and inside plaster. The roof should also be insulated and surface be sprayed with specific paint to serve as a vapour barrier. Two vents should be kept, one connected to main re-circulating duct and the other to outside to exhaust extra air/ gases from the chamber. The doors of the chamber should be made airtight by using a rubber gasket on inner side of the door and the door insulated with 5–6 cms thick insulation material should be covered with GI sheets on both inner and outside.

Cornposting platform

It is advisable to have spacious platform consisting of two parts-one at lower level with slop and medium sized tank to collect seepage water and an other part about 3' above the ground level connected with small tank for collection of seepage water. It should be provided with shed. Platform must have road approach for delivery of raw materials. For 10 tons compost, 50' x 25' sized platform can be utilized. For big projects, big platforms should be used.

Equipments and facilities

During pasteurization, airflow of 150–200 m³/hour per ton of fresh compost is required. Compost filling should be 900-1000 kgs/m² floor area with depth of 2.0–2.2 m. There will be a loss of about 25–30% dry matter. Filling in tunnel should always be loose and uniform. There may be about 10% loss in moisture content. In India, small chamber measuring 22' x 8' x 10' with iron door measuring 4' x 6' has been used after providing proper insulation. The boiler of an usual capacity and coal/wood/oil fired will be enough. Oil fired to get temperature should be preferred. The blower is used to introduce and re-circulate hot air. The blower has 24" fan with an opening fresh air from one side with provision to control air by adjusting shutter. The blower is run by 1440 rpm motor and pulling 6" x 3" is used to run blower.

Pasteurisation room

In India, many farms have conventional pasteurisation rooms where compost is filled in trays and stacks in centre of the room. Perforated steam pipe is provided on one side at about 4' (feet)

Fig. 5.3 Showing *Mobile compost turner.*

Fig. 5.4 Showing *Front end loader.*

Fig. 5.5 Showing *Power tiller.*

Fig. 5.6 Showing *Fluidized bed drier.*

Fig. 5.7 Showing *Cabinet air drier.*

Fig. 5.8 Showing *Dehumidified air drier.*

height from the ground. On this side, only fan is provided at about 75 cms away from the vent at ceiling level. The fan should be kept covered with a duct having capsized holes at 30 cms gap at right angle to the wall, so that it may introduce and re-circulate hot air. Trays are stacked in centre leaving 3' gap from ceiling to provide free movement of air from the duct. At 1–2' above the ground level on other end of the duct ventilator with wire mesh is provided for the escape of gases. The size of pasteurisation room should be same as for spawn running and cropping rooms or a little smaller than that. It should be insulated or should be made of hollow cement brick wall.

Growing rooms

Growing rooms should be insulated properly. Generally, ground is not insulated. In Europe, cropping rooms are kept quite big in size but, in India different sizes of such rooms are constructed. These rooms usually measure 15' × 17' × 10–12' or 25' × 15' × 10–12' or 35' × 20' × 12' and 35' × 25' × 12' in size. The racks/shelves in the room should preferably be made of iron with wooden base and sides. The side support of bed should be movable for periodic inspection of the compost texture and quality. If cultivation is to be done in bags, racks can be made of steel with net floors for keeping the compost filled polythene bags. Practically 10–12" deep compost bags are used for optimum utilization of space and compost. The working distance between two shelves should be at about 26–28", in case of bag cultivation as against 18–20" for shelved beds. The growing room should be made in such a way where air exchange in and out of room should be at the will of the grower. The floor of the growing room should have a slight slope to remove run off water and facilitate regular cleaning after various operations. Forced air circulation system should also be arranged.

Low cost bulk chamber and growing rooms

Low cast bulk chamber and growing mushroom rooms can be built with high density polythene sheeting supported by skeleton of iron pipes. In this case, the thickness of insulation has to be increased to 15 cms.

The Casing pasteurisation

The casing pasteurisation chamber is also insulated (both walls and ceiling) as in bulk chamber. The walls can also have simple air space for insulation. The stream pipes are placed in plenum below grated floor. The casing soil is placed in trays and pasteurised for 4–6 hours at 65C°.

INSTALLATION OF THE WARMING AND STEAM UNIT

Two primary components namely, a warming unit based on a boiler or heater and the other steam unit usually based on boiler are installed. For an average farm with 2 tunnels and 12 growing rooms, a boiler with usual capacity may be good enough. In order to control the temperature, the oxygen supply and the removal of gaseous waste products such as carbon-di-oxide (Co_2), it is necessary to change the air of the growing room several times and in compost room when needed.

MUSHROOM RESEARCH LABORATORY

Basic Rules of Research Laboratory

For efficient working, there should be a well-established mushroom research laboratory nearby mushroom cultivation house. Besides these, cultural media room, autoclave room and cool room should also be fully established near the mushroom research laboratory for proper research work. If a large number of students are working in the laboratory, they should be aware what to do and what to not and what are the different apparatus, instruments and equipment present in the laboratory. How do apparatus and instruments are operated and what are their functions? Thus, it is important for fresher including students, teachers, assistants and helpers to follow the fundamental rules and guidelines for efficient and safe working in the laboratory. Some of the important rules and guidelines may be summarized as under :

1. Always maintain aseptic conditions in the laboratory while doing different kinds of laboratory works including media preparation, autoclaving and sterilizing other instruments and glassware.
2. Always wear an apron before entering the laboratory to protect from contamination and laboratory hazards. Apron should always be kept well cleaned and washed.
3. Long hairs and nails etc. should be cut to normal to avoid contamination and chemical hazards and facilitate efficient

working with different instruments, apparatus, chemicals and reagents.

4. Avoid keeping books, purses and bags etc. so as to keep the working bench clean for efficient working.

5. Eating food, drinking water and other drinks as well as smoking and spitting in the working laboratory should be avoided to avoid contamination and infection from microorganisms. Never put pencil, pins, inoculating needle and thread in mouth, nose and ear, so as to avoid infection and adverse effect of chemicals due to contamination and carelessness.

6. Working benches should be cleaned regularly with ethanol (70%) or phenol (1:100) and hands must be washed with soap in running tap water before and after the work performed in the laboratory.

7. Do not put your finger in nose and avoid its contact with lips and eyes and use quality gloves where necessary while handling the chemical solution, stains, reagents, ultra-violet light, sprit lamp and different glassware etc.

8. Always keep the burner at proper distance from the organic solvents and it should be turned off soon after the use so as to avoid fire accidents.

9. Always use flame sterilized inoculation needle/loop, scalpels and knife etc.

10. Keep the chemicals, reagents and stock solutions etc. at their respective places.

11. Ask your teacher or laboratory technician for any difficulty and maintain proper record of the work done day by day.

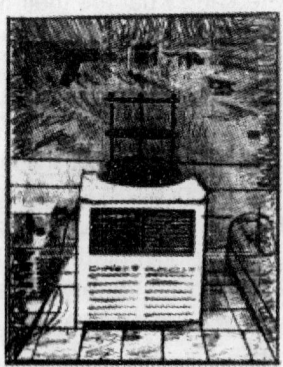

Fig. 5.9 Showing *Freeze dryer.*

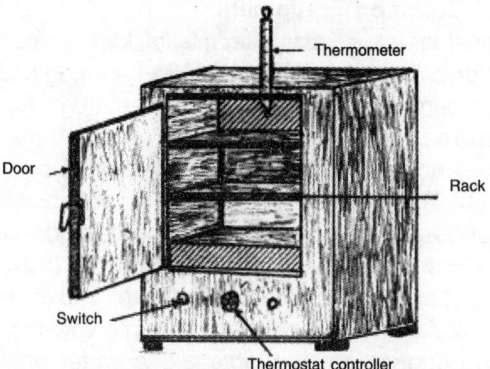

Fig. 5.10 Showing *Incubator*, its switch, thermostat controller, thermometer and inside view have been demonstrated.

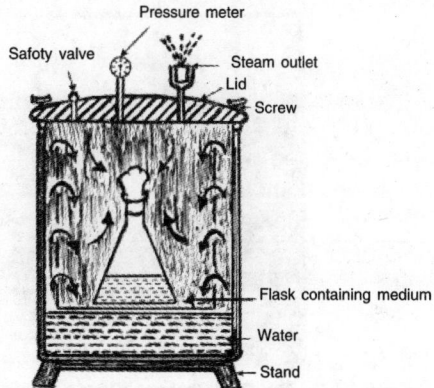

Fig. 5.11 Showing ultra structure of *Autoclave*, commonly used for sterilization of media and glassware etc. In above figure different parts of autoclave have been demonstrated. Inside the autoclave medium containing plugged flask, water and circulating steam have been demonstrated.

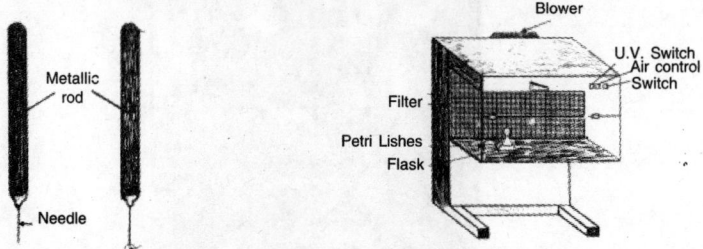

Fig. 5.12 Showing *Inoculating needle* and *inoculating loop* that consisted of metallic rods supporting the needle and loop.

Fig. 5.12a Showing *Laminar air flow* with its different parts like blower, filter, U.V. switch and air control switch.

132

Partial List of Common Equipment

Autoclave; Refrigerator; Rainmaker misting kit, Climate regulator, Balance electronic (micro and macro), Ultra-centrifuge; Distillation Plant, Table top centrifuge, Table top micro-centrifuge, Microfuges-refrigeratred and non-refrigerated, Ultra low freezer (Vertical); Ultra-freezer (–80°C) horigental, Freeze dry system; Deep freezers (–20°C and –80°C); pH meter, Thermo Cycler with power block-II system, Easycycler; Horigental gel electrophoresis unit with electro power pack; Submarine gel electrophoresis set (tray comb of different sizes), Laminar air flow hood, Vortex mixer; Hot plate; Microwave oven; Automatic pipettes of variable volumes; Shaker, incubator with refrigeration; Stirring/shaking water bath, Hot air ovens Power pack, Freeze dryers, ELISA reader; Suction pump and gel dryer.

Fig. 5.13 Showing *Flange rectifier.*

Fig. 5.14 Showing *Steam jacketed kettle.*

Fig. 5.15 Showing *Canning reptort*.

Fig. 5.16 Showing *Lid embossing machine*.

Fig. 5.17 Showing *Double seamer*.

Fig. 5.18 Showing *Exhaust box.*

Fig. 5.19 Showing *Can reformer.*

Fig. 5.20 Showing general view of a mushroom house.

Others
Plastic gloves, syringes; filters, filter holder, magnetic bars, pH paper; pestle and mortar; paper and polythene bags; markers; thread; rubber bands and wax coated labels.

Preparation of Chromic acid for cleaning Glassware
Care should be taken that the glassware to be used in the laboratory are neat and clean. Chromic acid is widely used as cleaning agent for glassware. It is a mixture of sodium dichromate and concentrated sulphuric acid. Chromic acid possesses powerful oxidizing and solvent properties and is suitable for cleaning glassware.

Method of preparation
Weigh 5g of sodium or potassium dichromate ($K_2 Cr_2 O_7$ or $Na_2 Cr_2 O_7$) and dissolve it in 5ml of distilled water in a beaker of 250 ml capacity. Add 100 ml of concentrated sulphuric acid (H_2SO_4) slowly, stirring it constantly. The mixture is allowed to cool at about $4C°$ and now store it in a dry glass stoppered bottle. It is ready to use. Use brush and tap water.

How to use autoclave
Autoclave is usually operated at 15 pounds pressure per square inch (1.1 kg pressure per square centimeters) steam pressure. The killing acting action of heat can be done by using increase in steam in a closed system. The water boils at 100°C and the steam accumulates in a closed container resulting in increase in pressure. The steam passes from below the base. The side walls are heated by the steam jacket. It has a provision to record the pressure and temperature. The water level should be checked and kept to the normal level as desired.

How to use incubator
Incubator is an instrument that consists of copper/steel chamber, around which warm water or air is circulated by electric current by small gas flame. The temperature of the incubator is kept constant and is controlled by thermostat. The incubator is made up of double walled chamber adjusted to a desired temperature. It is done by adjusting the external knob controlling the thermostat system. The door of the incubator should only be opened when necessary.

How to use Electronic Balance

For chemical and biological experiments, accurate amount of chemical should be weighted by using an electronic balance. There are several types of balances according to the requirement and the amount of material to be weighed. Balance may be single pan balance, chemical, analytical and electronic balance. Ultra micro balance can weigh the materials of 0.01mg to 2.0 mg. Electric balance works in presence of electricity that shows digital display of weight. In electronic ultra micro balance, weights of different measurements are not required.

Chapter 6

Compost and Composting

Compost requirement for Agaricus bisporus and Agaricus bitorquis, principles of composting, materials for compost preparation, formulations, determination of moisture content, two phases of composting, methods of composting, long method of composting, short method of composting, important tips for good compost and indicator moulds.

Cultivation of button mushrooms, which include chiefly *Agaricus bisporus* and *Agaricus bitorquis*, require dung or synthetic compost for the growth and development. Compost is the suitable substrate for the development of the mycelium of these fleshy fungi (button mushrooms) which grow gradually and eventually develop to the fleshy forms,—the mushrooms. As known to all of us, mushrooms are heterotrophic organisms and they lack the ability to form organic compounds from the carbon-di-oxide of the atmosphere for their cellular growth. Thus, they fulfil their nutritional requirements by the materials absorbed from the substrate, known as compost. The process of preparing the compost required for the growth and development of these mushrooms, is called composting.

PRINCIPLES OF COMPOSTING

Under natural circumstances, when mushroom spawn is inoculated into raw substrate, the competing microorganisms may quickly gain dominance and prevent the mushroom mycelium for development. The Main purpose of composting is, therefore, to prepare a medium of desirable characteristics that the growth of mushroom mycelium be promoted with the practical exclusion of other organisms. Fundamental principles of composting may be summarized as under:

1. After composting, certain chemical, physical and biological

properties are developed in the compost. All these properties are equally important and are inter-independent on each other. In other words, we can say that changes brought about by composting, result in such a state that food materials are best available to serve the nutritional needs of the mushrooms.

2. The foodstuffs contained in compost, should be converted in such a form that may be easily utilized by the mycelium of the mushrooms. For instance, it would be unsatisfactory if all the nitrogen were changed to nitrate instead of protein since the mushrooms cannot use nitrates.

3. Toxic substances, which inhibit the growth of spawn, should not be produced in compost.

4. The compost must have certain physical qualities, which may support aerobic conditions, hold water without becoming water logged and have proper p^H and good drainage.

5. Biologically, compost must have a population of suitable microorganisms useful to the mushrooms.

MACHINARY REQUIRED FOR COMPOST MAKING

In our country, a medium sized farm would not require unnecessary mechanization owing to availability of cheap labour in the area, the farm is located. At such farm, little quantity of compost at a time (around 10 tons of straw per week) may be handled manually. However, at large and export oriented farms having capacity around 1000 – 3000 TPA, which handles the compost in bulk around 30–40 ton of straw per day, mechanization of the operations becomes necessary to hasten the process for quality compost preparation. Computerization of different activities including process of pasteurization and conditioning inside the tunnels are also essential for an export-oriented unit:

1. **Pre-wetting machine:** It is used tor mixing the compost ingredients such as chicken manure and horse manure and also to turn and restack the pre-wetted compost materials. Compost materials may be stacked in the long and wide heaps by tractor and front loaders before wetting.

2. **Compost turners:** It comes in different capacities ranging from 30–70 tons of compost per hour. It is consisted of a round stainless pick-up drum, one spinner and one forming case. The turner is located on four wheels—two of which are ordinary

wheels and remaining two are powered and large diameter wheels. Turner is usually fitted with a full width water spray pipe mounted at the front of the machine with water outlets over the full input width.

3. **Pile forming case:** This machine is used when the pile is formed for the first time. It is usually supported on four catering wheels and the remains are attached to the front of the compost turner pushed by the turner during pile formation.

4. **Front end loaders:** Bucket type loaders may be used for various composting operations viz., pre-wetting and transportation of the compost during pile formation in combination with compost turner and forming case.

5. **Oscillating head filling machine:** This is made up of two conveyers units mounted upon a self-propelled chassis. The two conveyers are designed in such a way that one feeds directly into the other from above. It is oscillating type, which fills the compost loosely in the tunnel over the entire width. The head filling machines are of different sizes depending upon the size of the tunnels.

6. **Compost feed conveyers (2–3 units):** These are ordinary conveyer systems slightly elevated and can be coupled to form a single conveyer system feeding one to the other during tunnel filling. The length and width of each conveyer is generally 7.5 – 9.0 m and 0.6 m respectively.

7. **Hopper regulator:** This machine is required to feed the compost to the feed conveyers. It accepts the compost from the bucket of the loader and provides regulated output of the compost to these feed conveyers.

8. **Tunnel emptying winch with combination of spawn dosing machine:** This unit is employed for emptying compost tunnel filled with pasteurized or spawned compost by means of a polyethylene glide and pulling of the nets. Spawn discharging unit consists of twin spawn dispensers mounted over the full width of the compost flow on the discharge elevator.

9. **Bag filling machine:** This machine is used for filling the bags with spawned compost.

10. **Other materials and equipment:** Multipurpose digital thermometers, oxygen meters, ammonia measuring equipments and computers are also required for efficient working.

MATERIALS FOR COMPOST PREPARATION

Years ago, partially decomposed horse manure was used for providing desirable nutrient medium for the growth and development of the mushroom. In recent times, other materials are also used successfully with cereal straws forming the major part of the bulk. The nitrogen content of straw is less than 3% and, therefore, it is supplemented with various organic and inorganic sources of nitrogen to bring the nitrogen content ranging from 1.5 to 1.75% on dry weight basis.

The ratio of nitrogen, phosphate and potassium of mushroom mycelium is 6.4: 2.4: 4.4. Each ton of compost assumed to have a moisture content of 70 %, should contain NPK ratio of 13: 4: 10 and converts to 1.98% N, 0.62% P and 1.5% K on a dry weight basis. This ratio is still useful as guide in preparation of compost. Composting materials used in compost making is classified into following categories:

1. **Vegetable based materials:** These include cereal straws which provide cellulose, hemicelluloses and lignin. Vegetable-based materials used are usually straw of wheat, paddy, barley, rye, oat, hay, maize stalk and vegetable plant wastes. These materials also provide physical structure in heap which facilitates air exchange for aerobic microbes.

2. **Supplements to activate fermentation:** There are several materials which are added to the base materials in order to prepare balanced compost. These supplements are sources of nitrogen and carbon compounds. Supplements used in compost making may be divided into following four categories on the basis of their nutritional contents.

    *   **Category–1:** Animal manures (horse, chicken and pig, sheep, mule, yak, goat, cow, bullock and elephant manures). They provide 1.0 to 5.0% nitrogen. Carbohydrates are also present. Both nitrogen and carbohydrates should be released slowly.
    *   **Category–2:** Carbohydrate rich molasses, brewer's grain, malt sprouts, potato, apple and grape wastes and wastes rumen contents from slaughter houses.
    *   **Category–3:** Nitrogen rich fertilizers such as urea, ammonium sulphate and ammonium nitrate.
    *   **Category–4:** These include supplements to rectify mineral deficiencies. Examples are super phosphate, potash and gypsum.

DIFFERENT FORMULATIONS

As a result of prolonged research, a number of synthetic formulae have been proposed. Long method of composting (LMC) requires about 28–30 days and short method of composting (SMC) takes about 16–17 days for proper compost preparation. Short method of composing (SMC) technique came into being during 1974–75. Short method of composing is improved method in many respects for the profitable cultivation of mushroom under Indian conditions. The mushroom production was doubled with the adoption of this technique. The purpose of composting is to make the raw materials specifically suitable to mushroom mycelium for its growth.

Selection of composting materials

Following points must be kept in mind while selecting materials for compost preparation:
1. The base materials and their chemical and physical characteristics particularly their nitrogen contents should be known.
2. Initial total nitrogen content should be between 1.40–2.00 % of dry matter. This may be achieved by adding animal manure and other nitrogenous supplements like urea, brewer's grain, cotton seed and bran etc.
3. The material should be readily available to growers at a price competitive with that of horse manure or wheat straw.

COMMONLY USED FORMULATIONS

Several formulations have been evolved in our country and abroad. These may be adopted at different locations. Some important formulations are as under:

LONG METHOD OF COMPOSTING (LMC)
Natural compost – Basic formula (IARI)

Horse dung	1000 Kg
Wheat straw	350 Kg
Urea	3 Kg
Gypsum (hydrated calcium sulphate)	30–40 Kg

Urea can be replaced with 100–110 Kg of poultry manure. With the development of the technology, synthetic compost is most commonly used. Some important synthetic compost and their formulae are being given as under:

Synthetic compost and its advantages
Synthetic compost is more advantageous than natural compost. Advantages of synthetic compost may be summarized as under:
1. Synthetic compost usually produces more yield than the natural compost in most cases because of the better aeration within the bed.
2. Horse manure compost although being cheaper, it has drawback as its quality varies which results in inconsistent yields.
3. Natural compost if not pasteurized as per requirement, pests and diseases become active in such natural compost.
4. Synthetic compost is uniform in quality and texture. It supports better spawn run, since the bed is better aerated.
5. Synthetic compost is known to have more desirable physical properties including texture and yielding quality.

Synthetic compost formulae
Different synthetic formulae commonly used by mushroom growers in India and abroad are as under:
1. Solan formula-I (LMC)

Wheat straw	300.0 Kg
Calcium ammonium nitrate	9.0 Kg
Urea	3.6 kg
Muriate of potash	3.0 kg
Super phophate	9.0 kg
Wheat bran or spent brewer's grain	30.0 kg
Gypsum	30.0 kg
Nemagon (60%) or Furaden	40 ml/150 ml
Lindane or BHC	250.0 g
Molasses	5.0 g

Schedule – 0, +6, +10, +13, +16, +19, +22, +25, and +28 day. This quantity of ingredients is sufficient for 18–20 wooden trays of 0.5 square meters.
2. Solan Formula-II (LMC)

Wheat straw	300.0 kg
Calcium ammonium nitrate	9.0 kg
Urea	3.6 kg
Muriate of potash	3.0 kg
Super phosphate	3.0 kg

Other ingredients and schedule to be adopted, remain the same as is given in Solan formula no. 1.

3. Solan Formula-III (LMC)

Paddy straw	300.0 kg
Horse manure	100.0 kg
Calcium ammonium nitrate	9.0 kg
Urea	3.6 kg
Muriate of potash	3.0 kg
Super phosphate	2.5 kg

Other ingredients and schedule remain the same as for Solan formula-I except that gypsum is added at the time of second turning.

SHORT METHOD OF COMPOSTING (SMC)

Formula-I

Wheat straw	1000.0 kg
Chicken manure	400.0 kg
Brewers grain or	72.0 kg
Wheat bran	100.0 kg
Urea	14.5 kg
Gypsum	30.0 kg

Formula-II

Horse manure	1000.0 kg
Wheat straw	500.0 kg
Chicken manure or	300.0 kg
Wheat born	70.0 kg
Urea	7.0 kg
Gypsum	30.0 kg

Formula-III

Paddy straw	1000.0 kg
Chicken manure	400.0 kg
Molasses	40.0 kg
Wheat bran	100.0 kg
Urea	6.6 kg
Gypsum	35.0 kg

Schedule = −5, −3, −0, +2, +4, +6, +8 and +10 day.

FORMULATIONS AS USED IN FOREIGN COUNTRIES

Darlington's (U.K.) formula

Horse manure	1000.0 kg
Chicken manure	200.0 kg
Sugar beach pulp	7.2 kg
Cotton seed meal	7.0 kg
Gypsum	17.0 kg

Japan formula

Air dry rice straw	1000.0 kg
Ammonium sulphate	22.5 kg
Urea	7.5 kg
Mushgen	20.0 kg

Taiwan formula

Rice straw	30.30 kg
Ammonium sulphate	0.60 kg
Urea	0.15 Kg
Super phosphate	0.60 kg
Calcium carbonate	0.90 kg

DETERMINATION OF MOISTURE CONTENT

Natural products such as wheat straw, rice straw, wheat bran and cotton seed meal etc. varies in moisture and nitrogen content from place to place and sample to sample. These samples should be analysed frequently on dry weight basis. Moisture content of compost can be determined by weighing overnight oven dried 100 g. of compost. Moisture percentage is calculated by following formula:

$$\text{Moisture percent (\%)} = \frac{\text{Wet weight of compost } - \text{ Dry weight of compost}}{\text{Wet weight of compost}}$$

Moisture content and its level is adjusted by adding more water in case of less moisture content and by evaporation if it is more than the normal.

Table 6.1
Moisture and nitrogen contents in different composting materials commonly used for computation.

Intgredients	Fresh wt. Kg.	Moisture (%)	Dry weight Kg.	N (%)	Kg N
Wheat straw	300.0	10	270.0	0.4	1.08
Wheat bran	15.0	10	13.5	2.0	0.27
Chicken manure	125.0	10	112.5	2.6	2.94
Urea	5.5		5.5	46.0	2.53
Gypsum	20.0		20.0		
		Total	421.5		6.82
		N% =	1.61		

TWO DIFFERENT PHASES OF COMPOSTING

The process of composting has two distinct phases:
1. The establishment stage and
2. The maturation stage

The establishment stage
The establishment stage is the initial stage of composting with appearance of mesophils. Bacterial population *(Bacillus* species*)* dominates this stage and coincides with maximum heat generation. Consequently, temperature builds up and the thermophilic microflora takes over. This condition usually takes place only in central aerobic zone. Both outer most and inner most anaerobic zones are devoid of this activity. To overcome this, the compost is turned at regular intervals to bring the inner zone out and outer zone to inner side.

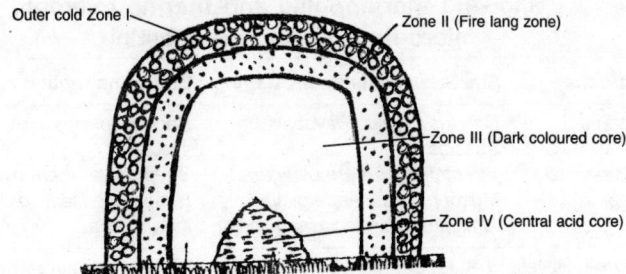

Fig. 6.1 Showing different heat zones in compost heap during composting.

Different zones may be represented as under.

Zone I - Temp. approximately upto 35C° well aerated and dry;

Zone II - Temp. 55C°–60C°, aerated and decomposed;

Zone-III - Temp. 70C°–80C°, aeration restricted;

Zone-IV - Temperature approximately 35C°, yellow coloured, foul smelling and anaerobic

The maturation stage

This stage remains for 4–5 days and is dominated by thermophilic micro flora. Population of some bacteria declines during this stage and population of Actinomycetes including *Streptomyces thermovulgaris* and *Streptomyces rectus* increases. After some time, there is decline in population of Actinomycetes and thermophilic fungi namely, *Torula thermophila, Mucor pusillus, Aspergillus fumigatus, Humicola griseus* and *Humicola languinosa*. The temperature of compost at this time usually ranges between 50–36C° which towards the end of this stage comes down and reaches between 30–35C°. It is the end of this stage and the compost is now ready for spawning.

BIOCHEMICAL CHANGES IN COMPOST

The process of composting is also called as biodegradation process. Micro organisms present in the compost, breakdown the complex substances to such a form which are suitable to be utilized from the raw materials and as such they produce vitamins, amino acids,

Table 6.2
Showing thermophilic and thermo tolerant
micro-flora during composting.

Micro flora	Start of establishment stage	End of maturation stage
Bacteria	*Bacillus subtilis, Flavobactereum* Species	*Bacillus* species, *Pseudomonas* species
Actinomycetes	*Streptomyces thermovulgaris*	*Streptomyes thermovulgaris*
Fungi	*Mucor pusillus, Aspergillus fumigatus, Humicola languinosa*	*Humicola grisea, Torula thermophila.*

Source: Hayes, W A. (1968) Microbiological changes in composting wheat straw/ horse manure mixtures. *Mushroom Science*, VII, 173–186.

enzymes and proteins of unique nature for utilization of the mushroom. Compounds of high energy are usually converted into low energy compounds and there is production of much heat. During the start of establishment stage and in maturation stage certain micro flora increases and decrease as shown in the table given below.

TWO DIFFERENT METHODS OF COMPOSTING

There are two methods of composting.
   (a) Long method of composting, and
   (b) Short method of composting

Long method of composting (LMC)
   Long method of composting may be summarized as under:
1. Composting yard where the compost is to be made should have concrete floor, covered roof and must be spacious enough to accommodate the maximum number of stacks. It should be cleaned and disinfected with 2% formalin.
2. Vegetable waste material–the straw is first wetted in a heap for 48 hours so that every portion of straw may absorb enough water. The heap is now pressed and left as it is for about 24 hours.
3. All other ingredients excluding gypsum and pesticides are mixed together by sprinkling water.
4. After 24 hours of mixing the ingredients, an aerobic stack measuring 3–5 feet × 3–5 feet having desired length should be made (0 day).
5. Turning is given to the compost heap so that the inner portion may come out and *vice versa* for uniform fomentation.
6. On sixth day, the first turning should be given and water should be sprinkled in desired quantity. The turning should be given so as to bring inner portion of compost out and *vice versa* as stated earlier (+6 day).
7. Second turning on 10th day and 3rd turning on 13th day are given. During the 3rd turning gypsum is added in recommended quantity (+10 and + 13 day).
8. Fourth turning is given on 16th day, 5th turning on 19th day and so on up to 6th turning (+16 +19 and 22 day) on 22 day.

9. On 7th turning suitable insecticidal dust is added to the compost in recommended dose (+25 day).
10. After 28 days, the compost is checked for smell of ammonia. If there is no free ammonia, compost is allowed to cool to about 25 C° (+28 day).
11. The compost made in such way, is now ready for spawning.

Short method of composting (SMC)

Sinden (1950) first introduced the so-called short method of composting consisting of phase I and II. The early part of the process is carried out doors, is called phase-I. This phase is of 7–14 days. In phase I, the compost is given 3–4 turnings on alternate days with addition of gypsum at third turning. No pesticide is required to be added in this method. After fourth turning, the compost is filled in pasteurization chamber where aerobic conditions and a temperature of 52–56 C° are maintained with introduction of air and steam.

Air is re-circulated so as to have concentration of ammonia in re-circulating air at or less than 10 ppm. This process is called conditioning which goes for 2–3 days and is followed by raising the air temperature to 57–59C° for 6 hours (pasteurization). Pasteurization can also be done in beginning followed by conditioning. Gradual cooling of compost by introduction of fresh air, normally takes 36–48 hours, follows this process. In phase II, insect pests, nematodes and competitive moulds are killed. In this method, period of composting is reduced to 14–18 days and therefore, more compost is produced per unit wheat straw.

Advantages of short method of composting

Although high capital cost is involved in the preparation of compost by short method of composting, still compost prepared by this method has some distinct advantages over long method of composting as under:
1. Composting time is shortened from 28 days to 14–15 days.
2. More compost per unit weight of straw is produced. Yield per unit weight of compost is almost double.
3. Compost prepared by this method is highly selective with least chances for diseases and pests.
4. Labour requirement is less.

Requirements for short method of composting

Composting yard, Phase-1 tunnels and Phase-two tunnels are pre-requisites for short method of composting. Procedural requirements are as under:

1. Selection and mixing of different ingredients.
2. Selection of raw materials is very critical and the raw materials selected should have qualities like high bulk density, good structure and texture, perfectly mixed materials, well-balanced chemical composition and high level of desirable nutrients.
3. To obtain these qualities ingredients like straw, hay, cobs, chicken manure, horse manure and gypsum etc. are mechanically treated so as to provide high bulk density, good water holding capacity and thorough mixing of raw materials.
4. Pre-composting operations should be done properly. These operations include analysis of raw materials, mechanical pre-treatment, water addition and mixing, use of special additives and specific biomass etc.

Summary of short method of composting (SMC)

Short method of composting is different from that of long method of composting as described above. SMC may be summarized as under following the most common schedule.

The schedule to be followed is −4D, −2D, +0D, +4D, +6D, +8D, +10D and 12D (compost filling in trays for pasteurization).

Phase I-Outdoor composting Process

Phase-I : It is also called as outdoor composting and includes the process of mixing raw materials on a platform and turning according to the schedule. Before four days of composting, poultry manure and brewer's grains are consolidated by trampling to initiate uptake of moisture and anaerobic fermentation. Before two days of phase I (outdoor composting), the whole mass is turned into slightly smaller stack and much water is added in it. The standard stack is prepared as prepared in case of long method of composting. For this purpose, all vegetable waste materials are wetted and all other ingredients excluding gypsum and pesticides are mixed with it by sprinkling of water. In such mixture, urea is also mixed. On fourth day of making mixture as above first turning is given. On 6th day, second turning is given and gypsum is added to it. On 8th day and 10th day, third and fourth turnings are recommended. On the 12th day, such mixture is filled into trays for processing of phase II.

Phase II-Indoor-composting process

Phase-II process includes pasteurisation of compost either by employing hot air or the live steam. Indoor composting process is usually started on 12th day. Trays evenly filled with compost are stacked in a pre-warmed room as quickly as possible. Sufficient space is kept between trays to allow hot air to move in between and across the trays. Ratio of compost volume and air volume is maintained to 1:6 and 1:8. All ventilators and doors are kept closed. Hot air (between 35–40C°) is supplied to the room. Such temperature is desirable to be maintained for about 12 hours. The fresh air is introduced slowly and gradually through controlled ventilation so that the temperature attained may not drop down for 24 hours. Live steam is injected after closing all the doors and ventilators in order to raise the air and compost temperature to 60±1 C° in order to pasteurize the compost. This temperature is maintained for 4 hours with ventilation system. Introduction of live steam is stopped and air temperature (35–40 C°) and compost temperature (52–56C°) are maintained for 48 hours or until complete absence of ammonia smell is observed. The sure test for absence of ammonia is to measure the pH of compost, which should be around 7.0 to 7.5. When compost is free from ammonia, full fresh air is introduced to bring the compost temperature of 25±1C° in general. Now the compost is ready for spawning.

Advantages of indoor composting
1. Indoor composting does not require costly machine.
2. Requirement for composting yard is reduced to 1/3.
3. Number of labour and cost of production is reduced.
4. There is no emission of foul smell.
5. Duration of composting is greatly reduced.
6. Higher yields of mushrooms are obtained.

TWO METHODS OF INDOOR COMPOSTING

Two methods of indoor composting are generally followed throughout the world. These are (1) INRA method and (2) Anglo Dutch method.
1. **INRA method** – This method is also called as double phase high temperature process. In this method entire compost mass in tunnel is subjected to two different temperature phases –

- First, the high temperature phase which is carried out at 80C°. At this temperature partial sterilization of compost mass occurs, ammonia production is observed to be very high, bulk density of the compost mass increases, compost becomes dark brown to black in colour due to various chemical reactions.
- Second, the lower temperature phase is carried out at 46C°. During this phase, temperature of compost mass is raised to 58–60C° for few hours to affect the pasteurization.

This process of composting is followed in Italy and France. This method requires 13–14 days for composting with dry matter loss of around 25%. Yield has been reported to be 36–40 kg mushroom per 100 kg compost.

FLOW CHART OF INRA METHOD

(Total duration — 13–14 days)
Pre-soaking, turning + mixing of ingredients for 2–3 days including horse and chicken manure.
-
Addition of ammonium sulphate
-
Filling of tunnels
-
Ventilation from plenum and from both the doors for 3 days (Temp. 40 C° bottom and 80 C° in centre)
-
Empty the tunnel, remix the ingredients again, and add water if required and fill into other tunnel
-
Keep the entire mass at 45 – 50C° and raise the temperature at 57 C° for few hours and again maintain 45–50 C° for 5–6 days.
-
Cool the compost and spawn

It has been reported that indoor composting through INRA method may yield 36 to 46kgs of mushrooms/100kgs of compost.

2. Andlo Dutch method

This is also called as single stage process where compost is kept in the tunnel between 45–50°C. Total length of composting cycle is 6 to 9 days.

FLOW CHART OF ANGLO-DUTCH METHOD

(Total duration in the tunnel-6–9 days)
Mix and soak the ingredients
-
Make a heap/pile of about 6 feet width. Daily turning,
There should be aerated floor.
Keep the compost out doors for 4 to 5 days.
-
Filling in the tunnels fitted with the nets.
Maintain low temperature 45–50°C.
-
Pasteurize at 56–57°C for four-five hours.
-
Cooling the compost
-
Spawning

HOW TO CALCULATE NITROGEN CONTENT

Nitrogen content may be calculated on dry weight basis. Some important ingredients with their fresh weight, dry weight, percentage of water and nitrogen percentage are as under.

Table 6.3
Showing fresh weight, dry weight, percentage of water and nitrogen percentage of different ingredients.

Ingredients	Fresh weight (kg.)	Percentage of water	Dry weight (kg.)	Nitrogen %	Weight of Nitrogen
Wheat straw	1000.0	10.0	900.0	0.4	3.60
Chicken manure	400.0	20.0	320.0	2.6	8.30
Brewers grain	72.0	78.0	15.8	5.0	0.79
Urea	14.5	0	14.5	46.0	6.67
Gypsum	30.0	0	30.0	0	0

Total dry weight   = 1280.30 kgs.
Total weight of nitrogen   = 19.36 kgs.
Percentage of nitrogen in dry weight   = 1.51%

Characteristics of good compost

1. Compost should be soft in texture.
2. Colour should be dark brown and odour should be pleasant.
3. Compost should consists of dark brown colour along with profuse fire fangs-Actinomycetes.
4. Compost should not remain sticky or greasy.
5. Compost should have moisture content of about 68-70 percent.

Chapter 7

Spawn & Spawning

What is spawn?, different kinds of spawn, preparation of spawn substrate, pure grain spawn, characteristics of good spawn, preparation of pure culture, facilities required for spawn preparation, raising mycelia culture, culture maintenance, precaution in spawn preparation, precaution during transit, storage of spawn, spawning methods and limitations in commercial spawn production.

The world 'spawn' is derived from an old French verb 'espandre' and Latin word 'expaner'. Both these words mean as "to spread". Spawn has also been defined in Webster's Dictionary as 'the mycelium of fungi especially of mushrooms used for propagation. In the *Agaricus* mushroom industry, term spawn is used for the substrate into which mushroom mycelium has been impregnated and which will be used as seed. In addition, the verb to spawn is used to mean inoculation of a substrate with mushroom spawn. In other words, spawn could be regarded as analogous to the seeds of the higher plant. In mushroom industry, spawn means the planting material and such planting materials usually consist of the vegetative body (mycelium) and its substrate. Dagger in 1905 made the significant discovery that a piece of inner growing tissue of mushroom is capable of producing mycelium. Since then, the potential of this method for isolating pure cultures has been utilized. Ferguson (1902) first discovered the use of germinating basidiospores of *Agaricus* for making spawn. Although the use of basidiospores is a better and safer method of making spawn but tissue culture due to easy in handling, had laid the foundation of today's spawn industry.

DIFFERENT KINDS OF SPAWN

Initially small masses of infected manure from naturally infected beds were used as spawn. Subsequently, more reliable forms of spawn such as French flake and English brick spawns were developed. Different kinds of spawns were used earlier as summarized below :

1. **Flake spawn** – Flake spawn is dried mycelium filled in compost. French flake spawn was most common in use.

2. **Brick spawn** – Brick spawn consisted of compressed bricks of horse, cow manure, loam soil and leaves colonised mushroom mycelium. Like natural spawn, however, flake and bricks spawns were not pure cultures. In flake and brick spawn neither the identity of mushroom species nor the absence of diseases and pests were assured.

3. **Natural virgin spawn** – This kind of spawn was recognised as the spontaneous appearance of spawn. It occurs in nature wherever any mushroom species germinates and produces a mycelium. Such mycelium rich soil was used as spawn for further production of mushroom. Ordinarily, such spontaneous appearance of spawn may be anticipated in compost heaps, rich garden beds and pastures near the feeding places of animals etc.

4. **Pure culture spawn** – Pure culture spawn was produced by inoculating a bottle of horse manure/any other suitable substrate with tissue cultures from a quantity mushroom or spores germinated under sterile conditions. Production of bottle spawn had led to the development of various types of pure culture spawn.

5. **Liquid spawn** – All the mushroom spawns stated above are prepared on solid substrate. However, under certain conditions liquid medium is inoculated with mushroom spawn. Such spawn is suitable for effective spawning of a bed, bottle or bag of compost on which mushroom can grow.

Now a days, following three kinds of spawn are commonly used for mushroom production. These are as under—

1. Manure spawn, 2. Grain spawn, and 3. Perlite spawn

In **Manure spawn**, composted horse dung or synthetic compost are used. The composted manure is taken and washed thoroughly in order to remove such substances, which are thought to retard the growth. The excess water is squeezed out and moisture content is adjusted to 60%. The manure is packed in half-litre milk bottles or heat resistant polypropylene bags of suitable size. The bottles or bags are plugged with non-absorbant cotton-wool and sterilized in an autoclave at usual temperature and pressure for 2 hour or on two consecutive days for one hour each. After this, they are inoculated with a bit of agar containing mycelium. After inoculation under aseptic conditions, these are incubated at 22–24 C° in a dark place for two weeks or more. The spawn becomes ready for use usually after two weeks. The prepared spawn can also be used to inoculate fresh bottles or bags to obtain more spawn.

In **Grain spawn**, 10 kilograms of wheat grains are taken, cleaned properly and boiled for 15 minutes in about 15 litres of water. Such boiled grains are allowed to soak for another 15 minutes without heating. The excess water is drained off and the grains are cooled in sieves. Now 120 g gypsum ($CaSo^4$ $2H_2O$) and 30g calcium carbonate are mixed with the cooled grains. The gypsum prevents the grains to stick with each other and calcium carbonate is necessary to maintain the desired pH. The prepared grains are now filled into half-litre milk bottles or polypropylene bags at the rate of 150–200 g per bottle or bag. These bottles or bags are autoclaved for 2 hours as above. After sterilization and maintenance of pH at 6.5 to 6.7, the bottles are inoculated with grain spawn or with the bit of agar containing mycelium. After inoculation under aseptic conditions, bottles are incubated at 22 to 24 C° in dark place. In about 2 weeks, the spawn is ready to use. Sorghum and pearl millet are also used commonly for spawn preparation. Kodo grains when used, poor quality spawn is prepared.

In **Perlite spawn**, ingredients used for preparation are Perlite 1,450 g; wheat bran 1,650 g; gypsum 200 g; calcium carbonate 50 g and water 665 ml. These ingredients are mixed properly, filled in bottles and sterilized in autoclave. Thereafter, the process is similar to that of grain spawn. Perlite spawn is thought to be cheaper and easy to disperse. Besides, this spawn can be stored for a longer period. In our country, this is not in practice.

PREPARATION OF SPAWN SUBSTRATE

A number of materials, alone and in different combinations are used as spawn substrate. Materials used usually vary from country to country and place to place depending on availability of waste materials to be utilized as substrate and its cost benefit ratio. Some of the commonly used substrates may be summarized as under:

Mother spawn's substrate

Pond mud manure was usually used for preparation of mother

spawn in ancient times. Earlier, barley straw and swine manure were used as raw materials. These two raw materials were used in ratio of 8:5. The straw was first moistened and 3 days later, it was mixed with manure. The mixture was composted for 30 days with three turnings. After removing the residual clumps of manure, the composted straw was dried and cut into pieces of 2.5 cm. long. These pieces were then mixed with 10% composted cattle manure and 1% gypsum and moistened moistened with limewater until the moisture content is maintained around 60%. The p^H value was maintained about 9.0. After further composting for 12 hours, the substrate was bottled, sterilized and inoculated with pure mushroom mycelium. This substrate was used for mother spawn preparation. Such substrate of mother spawn was used in China years ago:

Substrate for the culture spawns
The substrates for culture spawn as was used in China contained pond mud and dry cattle (swine) manure in 1:1 ratio by volume. First dry manure with a small quantity of paddy straw was composted for 20 days with 2–3 turnings. It is then mixed thoroughly with pond mud and fermented for 10–15 days. This substrate is then air dried and stored. When spawn was to be made the substrate was moistened with limewater. Final moisture content should be around 45%. One bottle of mother spawn can inoculate about 60 bottles of cultural spawn substrate. Each bottle may contain about 0.5 to 0.6 kg of the manure and pond-mud spawn compost.
Different kinds of substrates with different materials are used in different countries. Some of the important types of substrates for culture spawn may be summarized as under:

1. Straw manure spawn
The raw materials of the substrate contained paddy straw 45.5%, dry cattle manure 45.5%, peanut bran 1.7%, gypsum 0.9%, ammonium sulphate 0.5%, urea 0.5%, calcium super phosphate 4.5%, and lime 0.9%, All materials were mixed thoroughly with water to give a water content of about 70–75% and then the mixture is composted for 16 days with four turnings.

2. Cotton waste spawn
The card fly grade of cotton waste was usually chosen. It was washed and 2% calcium carbonate was added to adjust p^H.

3. Used tea leaves spawn

Used tea leaves were washed, drained and 2% calcium carbonate may be added to adjust the p^H. The substrate was mixed thoroughly and put in bottles, plugged and sterilized.

4. Grain manure spawn

The grain manure spawn was made by using wheat grain. Wheat grain amounting 40–42 kgs, dry cattle manure 4–5 kgs, rich hulls 1.5–2.5 kgs, calcium carbonate 1kg and calcium hydroxide 0.8 kg are used to prepare grain manure spawn. Wheat grains were first washed and then soaked for 18–24 hours. Before cooking, the grains were rinsed several times and boiled for 15 minutes. The grains should be well cooked but should not be broken. It should be mixed with other ingredients. Moisture content should be around 52%–55%. Before sterilization, the p^H value should be in range of 11–12 and after sterilization should be around 7.0. The grain manure spawn was widely used especially in Guangdong province of China. In most western countries, manure spawn has completely been replaced in the market by pure grain spawn.

5. Lotus seed husks and horse manure spawn

In Thailand, spawn substrate was made by mixing fresh horse manure and lotus seed husks in equal amounts after they have been steeped in water until they have swelled. Enough moisture was maintained to prevent drying out of the spawn.

6. Coffee pulp spawn

In Philippines, fresh coffee pulp was used to prepare spawn to give uniform mycelial growth on both outer and inner surfaces of pulp.

7. Ipil-ipil leaves spawn

In Philippines, leguminous leaves of dried ipil ipil (*Seucauraglauca* species) leaflets and coir dust or sawdust were used to prepare spawn. Coir dust or sawdust was soaked in water and fermented for 3–4 days. The fermented mixture was washed with three changes of water. In it, 15% rice bran was added and then the mixture was bottled for use.

8. Pure Grain spawn

Grain as substrate for spawn production is the most popular and most widely used method. At present most of the mushroom growing countries use pure grain for spawn preparation.

Advantages of pure grain spawn

The advantages of pure grain spawn are as follows:
1. Pure grain spawn contains more nutrients and more initial growing points.
2. By using grain in spawn preparation, spawning can be handled more quickly.
3. Grain spawn can be distributed more easily over the compost.
4. The mycelium from grain spawn can colonize the compost rapidly and can form the fruiting bodies early.
5. Much yield ranging from 17.3 to 33.1% can be obtained from pure grain spawn as compared to straw manure spawn and other spawn substrates used so far.

CHARACTERISTICS OF GOOD SPAWN

Quality of spawn is mainly determined by the biological value of the strain used and the technology involved at different steps of spawn production. Chief characteristics of good spawn may be summarized as under:
1. The spawn should be fast growing in the compost.
2. There should be early cropping after casing.
3. It should give high yield of the crop.
4. It should produce better quality mushrooms.
5. Spawn prepared with jowar (*Sorghum vulgare*) or wheat grain gives more yields than the spawn prepared on bajra, barley or Kodo grains.
6. Proper coating of mycelium around the grains used as substrate is essential.
7. The growth of the mycelium in the spawn bottles should be of silky type. It should not be cottony type.
8. The growth of the fresh spawn is more or less white and as the spawn grows, brown colouration develops.
9. Fresh spawn is better than old spawn. Spawn should not be more than one month old.

Precaution in using spawn

1. No loose grains should be seen in the bottle and no grains without mycelial coating should be left over. Under such circumstances, contamination may occur in the compost during spawn running period.
2. · The growth of the mycelium on the spawn grain should not be cottony type.
3. If there is any slimy growth in spawn, it may be the indication of bacterial contamination.
4. There should not be any green or black spot in spawn bottles. Such spots are suspected to be of moulds.

Facilities required for spawn preparation

Different laboratory facilities are required for producing quality spawn. A partial list of important items/equipments may be given as under:

1. Spawn preparation and autoclaving room.
2. Inoculation chamber 5' × 6' × 7' (fitted with ultraviolet tube 3' in length) provided with one table and double door entrance.
3. Chamber for spawn growth.
4. Autoclave.
5. Facilities to boil grain. These include hot plate, gas and containers for boiling.
6. Milk or glucose bottles.
7. Non-absorbent cotton.
8. Sprit lamp.
9. Rectified sprit
10. Inoculation needle.
11. Jowar or wheat grains
12. Chalk power
13. Gypsum
14. All other material required tor preparation of culture medium.

PREPARATION OF PURE CULTURE

The preliminary requirement for marking spawn is to make a pure culture of the desired mushroom species on suitable medium. Such pure culture can be used for making the spawn bottles. Mushroom culture should be pure and without contamination. The whole process should therefore be carried out under strict aseptic conditions.

The pure culture is prepared by two methods.

1. By germinating the spores of the desired mushroom species, or,

2. By growing pieces of inner tissue of desired mushroom species on suitable culture medium.

The pure culture thus obtained should be inoculated onto some sterilized spawn substrate. When the spawn substrate is completely impregnated with the growing mycelia, it is ready for use as spawn in mushroom production.

Raising of pure spore culture

In raising spore culture, spores are collected from a large sized healthy and good-looking mushroom with veil intact under sterile conditions. The sporophore (mushroom) is mounted on a wire stand over a particle under sterilized glass beaker after the surface disinfection process. The spores are discharged on to the petridish on the opening of the veil in 1–2 days by itself in a thick mass. The spore print is stored under sterile conditions in a refrigerator for future use. These spores are used for direct inoculation of wheat extract agar medium or Lambert's medium.

COLLECTION OF SPORES FOR PURE CULTURE

Selection and identification of desired mushroom species may be done through spore print method. There are several criteria used in identification of mushrooms, one of them is the spore colour. Mushroom spores are of several colours. e.g. white, green orange, brown and cream etc. which are the genetic features. These colours may be the diagnostic criteria for selection of desirable mushroom species and strain. Spores of *Agaricus* and *Amanita* usually look alike from the outer appearance, but the spores of *Agaricus* are chocolate brown and that of *Amanita* are white to pale. These spores are produced on basidia formed in gills of the basidiocarp.

The spore print is a simple method used for selection, identification and collection of pure spore culture. This method is most frequently used in gilled fungi. When the cap of mushroom is held stationary on a paper in a cooled chamber for a long period, the impression of pattern of gills is printed and the spores are accumulated onto the paper and invisible spores appear coloured.

Table 7.1
Showing different kinds of mushrooms and some important genera with their characteristics colour

Mushroom type/Genus	Spore colour
Gilled mushroom	
Amanita	White to pale
Chlorophyllum	Green
Clitocybe	Fleshy colour
Hebeloma	Rusty to yellow brown
Hygropharus	Cream
Inocybe	Brown or cinnamon
Lepiota	Green
Naematoloma	Purple brown
Panaeolus	Black
Pleurotus	Lavender colour
Russula	White, cream or yellow
Schizophyllum	Pink, salmon or flesh
Tubed mushrooms	
Boletus	Yellow to olive brown
Cyrodon	Yellow to yellow brown
Suillus	Yellow brown to cinnamon
Puffball mushroom	
Scleroderma	Purple black

Single spore (mono-spore) culture method

Single spore cultures are prepared by employing the following process.

1. One ml of spore suspension containing about 15–20 spores is transferred with the help of sterilized pipette in a 9 cm sterilized petridish.
2. Thin layer of agar medium is poured in each petridish and stirred clockwise slowly to distribute the spores evenly on the petridish surface.
3. Turn the plated Petri dishes upside down and place some grain spawn in the lid.
4. About 10 days after it the mycelium of germinated spores will become visible. The lid containing spawn is exchanged with a sterilized lid at this stage.
5. The mono-spore is cut out with very little medium and transferred to the fresh sterilized medium filled in tubes. It is also possible to isolate germinating spores with a well established technique.

6. The screening of single spore culture is further done after 2–3 weeks for fluffy oppressed or strandy types. It is best for multiplication.

Precaution

It must be kept in mind that all the mono-sporous cultures of mushrooms of heterothallic nature (*Agaricus bitorquis* and *Lentinus edodes*) are sterile. In secondary homothallic fungus (*Agaricus bisporus*) 30% of the mono-sporous cultures are sterile.

MEDIA USED IN RAISING PURE CULTURE

Different kinds of media are used for raising pure culture.

Wheat agar medium

32 gr of wheat grains are boiled with one litre of distilled water for about 2 hours and filtered after 24 hours. 20 g agar is then added to a litre of filtrate. The p^H of the medium is adjusted at 6.5 and sterilized in autoclave.

Lambert's medium

10 g glucose, 0.5 g magnesium sulphate (Mg $SO_2.7H_2O$, 1.9 gr. KH_2PO_4) and 20g. agar are added to 1 litre distilled water. The remaining process is similar to that of wheat agar medium as stared above.

Spore suspension

Spore suspension is prepared in the sterilized distilled water. Liquid agar medium (45C°) is poured in culture tubes (9 ml) and spore suspension prepared separately in sterilized distilled water is mixed (1 ml) in each tube and slants are prepared. The slants are then incubated at 28C° for spore germination for about 2 weeks. The mycelial threads will become visible on slants surface.

Mushroom culture preparation

The vegetative mycelium of a mushroom grown on a culture medium is known as a mushroom culture. It is required for preparation of spawn (seed). Each mushroom variety has its own culture and from one type of culture, only the particular mushroom

variety will be produced.
There are three steps in culture preparation.
1. Preparation of media
2. Culture inoculation
3. Incubation

1. Preparation of media

To maintain the mycelial cultures and multiply them, a suitable medium that can provide sufficient nutrients to growing mycelium is needed. A partial list of media normally used for maintenance, multiplication and preservation of mushroom cultures is given below. For *Agaricus bisporus*, compost agar and malt extract are the best media. For *Pleurotus* species, malt extract agar, yeast potato dextrose agar and potato dextrose agar are most suitable.

(a) Potato dextrose agar (PDA)

Potatoes are boiled in water for 15–20 minutes till they are soft. Mixture is filtered to remove the potatoes and volume is made to one litre by adding water. All ingredients are taken in quantity listed below:

Peeled and sliced potato	250 gr
Dextrose	20 gr
Agar-agar powder	20 gr
Distilled water	1000 ml

(b) Yeast potato dextrose agar (YPDA)

Yeast extract @ 1.0 gr is added to PDA

(c) Malt extract agar

Malt extracts	25 gr
Agar-agar powder	25 gr
Water	1000 ml

(d) Compost agar

Pasteurised compost	150 ml
Agar-agar powder	20 g
Distilled water	1000 ml

Compost is boiled in 2 litres of water for 2 hours or till half of the liquid is evaporated. It is strained after 24 hours to get the supernatant. The volume is made to one litre. Agar is added and medium is sterilized.

(e) Wheat extract agar

Wheat grain   32 g

Agar-agar powder   20 g

Wheat grains are boiled in water for 2 hours, strained after 24 hours and the volume of supernatant is made to one litre with water. Agar-agar is added to this supernatant and then sterilized.

(f) Oatmeal agar

Oatmeal flakes   30 g

Agar-agar   20 g

Oatmeal flakes are wrapped in cheese cloth and boiled in water for 2 hours. Now the cheese cloth is removed, volume of water is made to one litre. Agar-agar is added and the medium is sterilized.

(g) Rice bran decoction medium

Rice bran   200 g

Gelatine   20 g

Rice bran is boiled in water for 10 minutes, filtered, gelatine is added to broth and this is used as medium.

Sterilization of the media

The medium is filled in test tubes @ 10 ml per tube. These tubes are plugged with non-absorbent cotton and sterilized in autoclave at 121C° (15 lb/sq. inch pressure) for 15–30 minutes. Another method of sterilization is that in which the medium is sterilized at normal pressure for three consecutive days, each day for one hour. After the sterilization, the tubes are taken out and kept in a slanted position to increase the surface area of the medium in each tube. In no case, the medium should touch the cotton plug, as this will invite contamination. For Petri-plate cultures, the medium is sterilized in conical flask and poured in melted state in oven-sterilized petri-plates (180C° for 2–3 hours) under aseptic condition.

Culture-inoculation

Wheat or Jowar grains are washed well in water and boiled in such away that grains are not broken. Excess of water is drained off and boiled grains are spread on a fine wire mesh for about one hour. Chalk powder (6%) and Gypsum (2%) are mixed in boiled grains. These grains are now filled in milk or glucose bottles up to 2/3 of a bottle. Mouth of the bottles are cleaned and plugged with non-absorbent cotton. Plugs are wrapped with paper and bottles are sterilized at 15 lbs pressure in autoclave for 2 hours. For inoculation, first of all, two percent formaldehyde is sprayed inside the inoculation chamber and next day ultraviolet tube is put on for half an hour prior to inoculation. Ultraviolet light should be switched off before entering the chamber for inoculation. Now a bit of culture is taken out from a culture tube having pure culture and is put it into the sterilized bottles with the help of inoculation needle by sterilizing it over the flame of the sprit lamp. After inoculation, these sterilized bottles are transferred to inoculation chamber.

Raising mycelial cultures

For production of spawn, pure mycelial cultures are raised. The pure mycelial culture of a mushroom is vegetatively propagated mycelial culture that can be obtained from a healthy fresh mushroom showing all the desirable attributes of that species/ stain in following ways:

I. **Tissue culture** – Young and vigorous mycelium can be obtained from a fruiting body by tissue on a solidified medium. During the process of taking the tissue culture, the fruit body is cleaned with a clean cotton swab to remove dust/straw particles adhered to it.

II. **Sub culturing** – After a pure culture has been established, the cultures are maintained and multiplied on test tube slants. For sub-culturing a small bit of agar from pure culture tube is cut under aseptic conditions and put in sterilized tubes. The pure culture tube is opened over flame; plug removed and a bit is taken out with the help of a flame sterilized needle. Another tube is opened by the same way, the bit is transferred to the new tube, and the tube is plugged. The newly inoculated slants are incubated at 25C° expect for *Volvariella* which is incubated at 35C°. After complete mycelium growth, the cultures can be stored in refrigerator at temperature around 5C° expect for *Volvariella* which is stored at 15C°.

III. **Culture maintenance** – If a strain is cultivated continuously, it may eventually loose some of its desirable genetic traits. A tissue culture of such a degenerated strain will give rise to the degenerated culture. Degeneration in fungi can be caused by lack of nutrients, oxygen, change in p^H of the substrate, accumulations of toxic metabolites or by the infection of the viruses. Maintenance of vigour and genetic characteristics of pure mycelium is the main objective of strain preservation. Various techniques have been used to maintain mushroom strains. These include storage on agar medium or compost in tubes. Such cultures can be stored for 1–2 years. Immersion in liquefied nitrogen is the other best method for long-term storage of non-speculating mushroom species such as *Agaricus*. Liquid nitrogen has very low temperature (-196 C°) and there are reports of storage of mushroom cultures for up to 10 years without loss of genetic stability.

The preparation and maintenance of cultures require expert technical knowledge in different fields such as taxonomy, microbiology and mycology. Therefore, it is not possible for a small sized mushroom farm to keep and maintain its own cultures. Therefore, such small growers must procure cultures of spawn from reliable government, semi-government or voluntary organisations or spawn makers.

TECHNIQUE FOR CULTURE PRESERVATION

1. Storage on compost

Agaricus cultures can be best stored on compost for two years. For preparing compost substrate, 300 g of dried compost is taken from well-prepared pasteurised compost. The compost is moistened with 1 litre of tap water, washed three times with hot water to remove undesirable gases and metabolites. The tubes filled with such compost up to 1/3rd of their capacity are sterilized at usual pressure and temperature for 2 hours. The sterilization process is repeated next two days to kill heat resistant bacteria. Storage on such compost is done at temperature as below as 5C°. Cultures of *Volvariella* are highly unstable and stored best at 15C°. Cultures maintained in this way should be transferred after every two months by changing the medium from paddy straw to agar medium and *vice versa*. The cultures should be strictly protected from mites. If mites invade the cultures, these will carry all kinds of contaminations. Therefore, to avoid mite infestation, the pure culture tubes should preferably be covered with aluminium foil.

2. Storage in mineral oils

The cultures immerged under mineral oil can be stored at room temperature or refrigeration, as the mineral oil above the cultures does not allow mites to invade. It also prevents agar from drying out. Mineral oil of specific gravity 0.865 to 0.89 is used for this purpose. The oil is sterilized for half on hour, cooled and poured above the cultures aseptically. Tubes for mineral oil storage should preferably be screw-capped.

3. Storage in demineralised water

The cultures are grown on agar medium and after full growth, small bits of colonized agar are transferred aseptically into sterilized bottles containing demineralised water. The bottles containing demineralised water are sterilized for 2 hours and on cooling, agar bits of 0.5 cm diameter are put in these bottles aseptically at the rate of 2–3 pieces per bottle. All mushroom cultures except *Volvarieila volvacea* can be stored by this method.

4. Lyophilization of freeze drying

This is a method suitable for storing sporulating fungi. Mushroom cultures cannot be stored by this method. However, spores collected from a young and healthy mushroom aseptically can be stored for more than 20 years by this method.

5. Cryogenic freezing

Mycelium cultures are kept in liquid nitrogen at temperature of $-196C°$ or nitrogen vapours at -150 to -180 C°. At these temperatures, there is no growth of mushroom mycelium but it can be revived with all its genetic characters intact. This method is very costly, involves technology at its best, and is not suitable for smaller laboratories.

ROLE OF MUSHROOM BANKS

There are various research laboratories/institutes/stations in various states working for mushroom production. They are maintaining mushroom culture banks. One can obtain pure cultures trom there for making spawn.

Piece of culture thus maintained is inoculated in the bottles with the help of inoculation needle. The culture should be preferably transferred in the middle towards wall side so that the growth can be noticed. Inoculation should be done over the burning spirit lamp to avoid contamination. After inoculation, bottles are transferred inside spawn growing chamber where temperature at 25 ± 1 C° should be maintained. All bottles should be checked at least once a week and contaminated bottles should be removed.

The spawn prepared from the culture can be further used to multiply spawn @ 1 bottle for 30–35 bottles by transferring few grains (2 spoonfuls) of spawn. This helps in faster multiplication of the spawn.

Precaution in spawn preparation

Quality control in spawn making usually consists of inspection of the spawn units and prevents contaminations. Such contamination can be observed by the observation of unacceptable differences in colour, appearance, odour and growth of the spawn. Care should be taken that spawn is free from viruses also. For this purpose, stock cultures should be raised from virus free mushrooms. Following precautions should be taken for better spawn production:

1. Unbroken and intact boiled grains should be used for spawn production.
2. Boiled grains mixed with lime and gypsum should not be kept un-sterilized for more than 10 hours.
3. Bottles should be plugged and sterilized properly.
4. Sterilized bottles should be inoculated after 10–12 hours of sterilization.
5. The bottles should be kept in ultraviolet rays for 30–60 min. before inoculation.
6. The whole process should be carried out in a double closed airtight inoculation chamber.
7. The inoculation should always be done facing the burner.
8. Give minimum time for removing and placing the plugs.
9. Shake the bottles thoroughly after inoculation to get early and uniform growth.
10. Inoculation bottles should be kept at 25 ± 1C° after inoculation.
11. Store bottles at a temperature of 4C° after complete growth.

Precaution during transit of spawn

Care must be taken during transit. Spawn bottles are not exposed to a temperature higher than 35C°. Spawn bottles exposed to 40C° for 48 hours have been found fatal to the spawn mycelium. However, the spawn exposed to 35C° remains alive for 14 days. To avoid such risk, spawn bottles should be packed in thermocal boxes containing ice cubes during transit.

Always use fresh spawn and its storage should be avoided. However, the spawn can be stored and used efficiently between 5–10C° for one month.

DIFFERENT METHODS OF SPAWNING

A simple definition of spawning is the planting of mushroom spawn on the prepared suitable substratum/compost. Along with the advancement in spawn making, the methods of spawning have also been continuously developed and improved.

There are many methods of spawning. Four important types of spawning are as under:

1. **Mixed or thorough spawning** – In this method of spawning, compost is mixed with the spawn properly. The spawn is thoroughly mixed with the compost and then pressed with hand in bags or in wooden trays.

2. **Single layer spawning** – In this method, the grain spawn is scattered uniformly all over the compost/substrate surface and it is then covered with a thin layer of compost. This method is known as single layer spawning.

3. **Double layer spawning** – In this method, the trays are at first half filled and the grain spawn is scattered over it smoothly. The trays are now completely filled and grain spawn is again scattered over it as before. A very thin layer of compost is usually sprayed after spawning. This method of spawning is called double spawning.

4. **Spot spawning** – In this method of spawning, trays are filled according to its capacity and compost surface is labelled properly. Now holes measuring 2.5–5.0 cm deep are made with the finger about 8–12 cm apart in rows.

Mixed or thorough spawning is the best and most popular method and is generally followed by almost all the growers. One bottle of spawn per 40 kg of pasteurised compost is the standard rate to seed the compost. The spawn is generally available in bags or bottles.

RESPONSIBILITIES OF COMMERCIAL SPAWN PRODUCERS

Commercial spawn laboratories should employ intelligent people who are careful and skilful in carrying out their jobs. The workers must have some background and experience in mushroom technology, mycology and microbiology so that they may use those methods in economic mushroom production. Commercial spawn should be produced under facilities that can ensure sterilization of the spawn substrate or media, inoculation under aseptic conditions, incubation and storage in optimally controlled conditions, safe packaging and delivery and presarvation of the original quality of the spawn.

Chapter 8

Casing Materials and Case Running

What is casing mixture? importance of casing mixture, quality parameters of casing soil, different types of casing mixtures, commonly used materials, adjustment of pH, pasteurization of casing mixture, time and depth of casing.

Because of the process of spawn run, mushroom mycelium grows to its maximum extent on the compost. In order to induce fruiting and get higher yield, the compost is covered with a thin layer of a special kind of soil known as casing soil or casing mixture. The process of covering the compost with such casing soil is called as casing or casing of mushroom beds. In other words, *'covering the top of mushroom beds after spawn run with an appropriate soil mixture is known as casing. Casing is applied when the compost is fully impregnated by the mycelium'*.

IMPORTANCE OF CASING

The various functions of the casing layer may be summarized as under:

1. The casing layer promotes the factors responsible for pinhead formation.
2. It protects compost layer against drying out and assists in fast disappearance of metabolites.
3. It provides suitable environment, conductive for the growth of both mushroom mycelium and certain bacteria known to be useful for fructification.
4. It allows toxic gases including carbon dioxide to escape.
5. It provides physical support to fruiting bodies.
6. Besides providing a firm substratum for the fruit bodies, it

regulates the flow of nutrients from compost to the young cells of the mushrooms.

7. The casing layer acts as a reservoir of water.
8. It keeps the compost fully grown through with good mycelium.

QUALITY PARAMETERS OF CASING MIXTURE

A good casing mixture must have the following properties:

1. Casing material must have high water holding capacity and high porosity.
2. It should be capable to release harmful gases during cropping.
3. It should protect compost layer against drying out and fast disappearance of harmful metabolites.
4. It should be free from harmful microorganisms.
5. The optimum pH of the casing soil/mixture should be about 7.5 to 8.
6. Texture of the casing soil should be light, open and properly decomposed.
7. Casing mixture should be free from heavy metals and ions.

Different types of casing mixture

Although different materials are capable of supporting fruit bodies; however, their importance for obtaining a good crop has not been studied well. The way a casing material is made and managed after application has a considerable bearing on its performance in terms of quality and yield. Mushroom growers in different countries have been using different types of casing materials depending upon their availability. Some of these casing materials commonly used are being given as under:

Table 8.1
Showing different casing materials commonly used in different countries

Name of the country	Types of casing materials used
France	Local sub soil mixture
India	FYM + loam soil + calcium carbonate
Korea	Clay loam + spent compost + calcium carbonate
Taiwan	Clay loam sub soil + chalk
U.K.	Moss peat + chalk
U.S.A.	Local sub soil + peat + chalk

COMMONLY USED MATERIALS

In foreign countries, mixtures based on neutralized peat are usually used in the mushroom industry for casing mushroom beds. In Europe, variations occur in the type and quality of materials added to peat, such as sand, gravel, spent compost and also the type of peat used. Fern peat, sphagnum peat and iris sphagnum peat are most widely used in U.K. and Ireland. In our country, because of non availability of peat, following mixtures are usually used as casing mixtures:

1. Garden loam soil and sand mixture (4:1).
2. Decomposed cow dung manure and loam soil (1:1).
3. Spent compost (2 years old), sand and lime.

In addition to the above, various other substrates like cattle manure, paper mulch, tree bark, rice husk, ash, forest litter and sugarcane leaves etc. have also been used. Some of these mixtures have proved promising.

Adjustment of pH

Adjustment of pH of the casing material should be done after getting it tested with a pH meter. If F Y M has been used as a component, its pH is adjusted to 8.0. F Y M itself has a good buffering capacity. In order to raise the pH level, add calcium carbonate to maintain desired pH level.

PASTEURIZATION OF CASING MIXTURE

Casing soil needs pasteurization at 65 C° for four hours with steam. Pasteurization is done to eliminate harmful microbes and insect pests from casing material. There are two different methods of pasteurization.

1. *Steam pasteurization*

Moist casing material is filled in wooden trays (6–7 inches deep) with two legs and stacked in the centre of casing pasteurization chamber in tiers leaving gap between walls and trays. Lay the perforated pipes at ground level. The trays are stacked at about 2 feet above the ground with brick support, which should not block steam movement. The door is closed and steam is released to maintain casing material's temperature at 65 C° for 4 to 6 hours. Steam pasteurization should be done 24 hours in advance of casing. This method is the most efficient way of pasteurization.

2. *Chemical pasteurization*

Chemical pasteurization is done where facilities for steam pasteurization are not available. Formaldehyde, methyl bromide and chloropicrin are the important chemicals commonly used for pasteurization. Formaldehyde is most popular among them. In case of methyl bromide, closed chamber should be used and care must be taken to avoid inhaling this gas. This gas is odourless and poisonous. In formaldehyde pasteurization, moist casing material is spread on cement floor and is drenched with 5% formaldehyde solution at the rate of 50 ml per litre of water. About 2 buckets (15 litres) of solution is used for ½ cubic meter of casing soil. Solution should be poured after making channels and covered with removed casing soil. After chemical treatment, it should be covered with polythene sheet. After two days, soil is turned and such turning is repeated every alternate day until casing material is used. Chemical pasteurization is done two weeks in advance of casing as it takes time for getting casing material free from formaldehyde smell.

Time and depth of casing

The best time of casing is when the compost is fully covered with mushroom mycelium. However, time taken for such conditions usually depend upon the quality of compost, spawn rate and environmental conditions. At the time of casing, compost should be uniform. Casing layer should be 1.0 to 1.5 inches in thickness in case of casing soil and 1.0 to 2.0 inches in thickness in case of peat, spent compost and F Y M. Even and recommended thickness of casing layer is considered to be important factor for good cropping.

The water content of the casing and amount of water sprayed affect the mycelial growth and subsequently the yield. When moisture in casing is low, it results in the growth of the fine hyphae; however, higher moisture content encourages thick strands but slow growth. A casing, which has been kept moist from the start, may present a little problem. Excessive watering should be avoided in early stage of casing, as it may not allow the mycelium to come on the top surface due to crust formation. It should be preferred to bring the casing material to its moisture saturation point gradually. Some growers reshuffle the casing layer after 6 to 8 days of casing. It helps in uniform distribution of mushroom mycelium in casing layer resulting in uniform crop.

Chapter 9

Breeding for Quality Mushroom

Importance of breeding, precaution in commercial spawn production, breeding for quality mushroom production, techniques for breeding, techniques for strain development, essentials for mushroom breeding, programme and future breeding prospects.

There are several reports that some of the most widespread strains show signs of degeneration in several countries. It was because of the fact that spawn producing laboratories do not preserve the viability and vigour of the strains. Different precautions are advised to be taken for the commercial spawn production:

1. Any change in morphological, physiological and genetical nature, should be observed seriously. Spawn producers must be able to keep the strains in viable conditions and to detect any change well in time.

2. Certain kinds of mycelium which is weak and is growing slowly on agar medium and grows slowly on the spawn substrate and on the compost should be avoided.

3. Spawn producing fluffy cottony mycelium and forming white patches on the compost bed usually yields low and poor quality mushroom. Such spawn should be discarded.

4. The simplest way to maintain vigour and productively of the strains, is to subculture them from time to time on suitable nutrient agar media and to store them in refrigerator at 3–5C°.

5. Performance of the strain should be checked carefully and periodically. No spawn should be sold to the growers until it has been thoroughly pre-tested for its good quality.

BREEDING FOR QUALITY MUSHROOM PRODUCTION

The taste and texture of the mushroom variety/ species are the important characteristics for consumer's acceptability. Besides these two characteristics, there are many other desirable characteristics, which may be summarized as under:

1. Nutritional value of the mushroom is known to attract the mind of the purchaser of mushroom. The public is becoming aware of the good nutritional value of mushroom day by day. Thus, breeding for better nutritional values is a worthy objective.

2. Increase in yield is reflected as greater profit. Therefore, the breeder must keep in mind to improve the quality of strains, that may yield better.

3. Breeders should improve the quality of the spawn, which may be stored for longer period. There should be stability about mutation and degeneration.

4. Extension of temperature range for mycelia growth and good fruiting is desirable; therefore, breeding to obtain such characteristics is essential.

5. Breeding work should be done for developing such a strain, which may be easier to grow on different agricultural, industrial and household waste materials. A breeding programme that selects stocks with better enzyme activity for the substrate polysaccharides has the potential for increasing yield. The possibility also exists of inoculating the compost with thermophilic micro-organisms that have been selected or even 'bio-engineered' to break down particular substrates of compost efficiently.

6. Sporeless fruiting bodies are desirable because fruiting bodies of *Pleurotus* species shed spores at early stage during the development of the mushroom and continue to do so up to harvesting. Under such circumstances, spore density in the air in mushroom growing houses can become very heavy. Mushroom workers at big mushroom farms, have been found with respiratory tract problems and allergic reactions to spores of *Pleurotus* species. For this reason, great interest should be taken by the breeders to develop sporeless mutants. Whole fruiting body of such species should have qualities equivalent to those of accepted commercial spore forming stocks.

7. Two sporesless cultures of *Pleurotus ostreatus* are now commercially available in Germany. There are reports of sporeless mutants in other species like *Pleurotus pulmonarius, Coprinus macrorhizus, Schizophyllum commune* and *Pleurotus florida.*

TECHNIQUES FOR STRAIN DEVELOPMENT

Following breeding techniques are used for strain development: Biological knowledge of the species to be improved is essential. If the life cycle is not well known, the opportunity for strain development is limited to the selection of mutant varieties. The breeder must know whether the species is homothallic, heterothallic or secondarily homothallic. In homothallic species, the mycelium from a single type of basidiospore that will lead to the completion of life cycle with the formation of mushroom and its basidiospores, but in heterothallic species, the mycelia from single spore are sterile and for the completion of the life cycle and formation of the mushroom, compatible mycelia must be brought together.

In secondary homothalism, some of the single basidiospores complete the life cycle while others are self-sterile. When their mycelia are brought together in compatible communication, mushroom may be produced. Genetic manipulation for breeding obviously requires complete detail of the life cycle. Besides life cycle, knowledge of the habitat, the substrate, the temperature range, the relationship with other organism, the nutritional and environmental requirements for both mycelia and fruiting are desirable for breeding programme for strain improvement.

The goal of the mushroom breeder, no matter what the species, is to bring together the best possible combination of genes that control characteristics of commercial importance.

ESSENTIALS FOR MUSHROOM BREEDING PROGRAMME

For successful breeding programme, following points are important to be kept in mind by the breeders interested in strain development of mushrooms:

1. Provision of wide genetic base

A large number of pure cultures should be obtained to provide a wide genetic base and variation in agronomical important traits. Therefore, fruiting bodies should be collected from wide spread geographical areas and diverse ecological situations.

2. Maintenances of cultures

The cultures established for breeding work should be maintained in a manner that will maintain genetic stability to the greatest possible extent. The most effective means of maintaining cultures in this way is by storing them in liquid nitrogen.

3. Characterization of monosporous mycelia

If monosporous mycelia (i.e. mycelia derived from single spore) are to be used in recombination experiments, their mating types must be known. Mating types are determined by the determination of compatible or non-compatible reactions when different monosporous mycelia are confronted in pairs.

4. Selection of recombinants

Since the gaol of a breeding programme is to bring together genes controlling characteristics that are desirable in commercial mushroom production. The selection of recombinants from the mating between different strains, each of which has certain desirable trails, is a reasonable approach. Certain techniques are available to facilitate the selection of recombinants.

Desirable traits for which the mushroom breeder may wish to select mutants usually include such things like taste, colour, nutritive value, odour, temperature, tolerance for both mycelia growth and fruiting, yield, a shortened time from spawning to cropping and disease resistance.

FUTURE BREEDING PROSPECTS

Use of modern techniques of genetic engineering to develop improved strains of edible mushroom remains a difficult problem since the mushroom is a complex organism with a range of specific characteristics. Many of such specific characteristics are certainly under mutagenic control. Therefore, natural breeding system, supplemented by means like para sexuality and protoplast fusion techniques should be brought into practice.

Chapter 10

Button mushroom Cultivation

General morphology, distinguishing characteristics, spore germination and life cycle, crop management, selection and maintenance of strain, composting, spawning and spawn run; casing and case run, pinning, cropping and picking; harvesting, grading and packing, cultivation of summer button mushroom.

Button mushroom has derived its name from its shape, which looks like button during a passing development stage and becomes umbrella shaped on maturity. This mushroom has a pleasing taste and aroma. The vegetative body of the mushroom consists of hyphae originated from uni-nucleated cells containing vacuolated cytoplasm and oil globules. Uni-nucleated mycelia twist together forming thick root like cords known as rhizomorphs. During twisting, both plus (+) and minus (-) strains come in contact and fuse. A nucleus from one hyphae passes into the adjacent cell of the other hyphae, forming a bi-nucleate mycelium.

GENERAL MORPHOLOGY

Most commonly cultivated genus *Agaricus* is well-known, belonging to family Agaricaceae with about 200 species known to be very common in occurrence. Most of the species grow on ground in pastures. Some of these such as *Agaricus bisporus* are a well-known table delicacy in many parts of the world. The characteristic features of the genus are the presence of deep purplish brown free gills. All the species of *Agaricus* are edible except a few such as *Agaricus placomycesan* and *Agaricus silvaticus*. These species are poisonous and may cause gastro intestinal disturbances in some individuals. *Agaricus bisporus* is the cultivated mushroom and is characterized by two - spored basidia. The plant is usually more robust and the flesh is thicker and firmer than the wild field mushroom *Agaricus campestris*. In nature this grows on manure heaps, road scrapping and on manured soil in gardens.

Recent taxonomic position

Agaricus bisporus has been classified in Ainsworth & Bisby's "Dictionary of fungi" (1995) under Kingdom - mycota, phylium Basidiomycota, subclass - Basidiomycetes, order - Agaricales, family - Agaricaceae, genus - *Agaricus*, species - *bisporus*.

Distinguishing characteristics

Distinguishing characteristics of *Agaricus bisporus* may be summarized as under:

Morphologically, the fruiting body or the mushroom as it is called, usually consists of a stem known as stipe, which supports the expanded umbrella - shaped cap - the pileus. Stipe of the *Agaricus bisporus* is centrally situated. It is white, annulated, solid when young becoming hollow below the annulus at maturity. Stipe measures 30–120 mm in length and 10–15 mm in width. It is thicker at the base and slightly tapering upwards. Important characteristics may be summarized as under:

1. *Pileus*

It is usually separable from the stipe. The shape of the pileus may vary from conical to flatten and the centre of the pileus may have a knob or pit in different species of *Agaricus*. It is fleshy in structure and measures 5–10 cm in width. Its colour is white, cream or brown. Apparently, it is smooth to finely scaly and dry. It looks convex with flat centre or entirely flat and white when young and becoming reddish on bruising or prolonged exposure. It has pleasant odour when fresh.

2. *Lamellae-or-gills*

On the underside of the pileus, gills also known as lamellae, are found. These are free, crowded, narrow and usually pinkish at first turning dark brown with age. Gills are enclosed by a membrane that extends from the margin of the pileus to the stipe. The gills are generally strips of tissue radiating from the margin of the pileus toward the stipe. The membrane that encloses the gills is known as partial veil and it usually tears around the margin of the pileus.

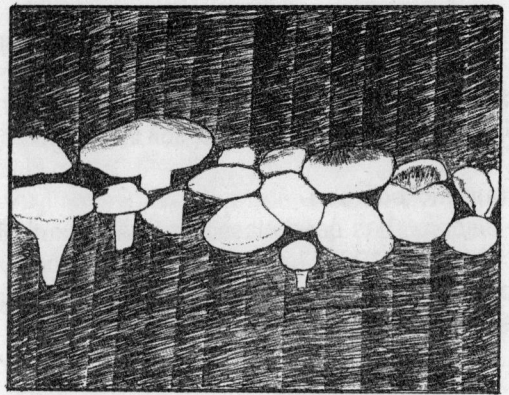

**Fig. 10.1 Showing general appearance of mushroom–*Agaricus bisporus*
in growing bed.**

3. *Basidia*

Basidia are invariably 2-spored with spore print sepia to mummy brown coloured.

4. *Spores*

Spores are broadly ellipsoidal in shape and measure 6 – 7.5 nm × 4.5 – 5.5 nm in size.

5. *Colony characteristics*

In pure culture, colony characteristics are observed as circular colony on agar medium. Apical growth of hyphae and repeated branching is observed. The hymenium or the fertile layer is found beneath the pileus. It lines lamellae (gills) that hang below the pileus. The hymenium is composed of palisade like layer of ripe basidia. On the basidia, spores are produced. The basidia are the cells on which the spores are produced. Each one has little two apical projections called as sterigmata and a spore develops on the tip of each sterigma. The spores are too small and are purplish-brown to sepia in colour when seen in mass or observed from spore print. When a spore germinates, it puts forth a germ tube. This thread like germ tube grows rapidly, develops cross wall or septa and becomes many celled and as such producing a mat of hyphae termed the mycelium. This is the vegetative part of the fungus which produces the fruiting body known as mushroom. The germination is best at temperature ranging from 22–25C°. The most suitable pH for germination has been observed to be 6.0–7.0. Each cell of the mycelium usually has two nuclei. The vegetative mycelium may produce secondary spores, which may be thin walled or thick walled.

In the beginning the young basidia has two nuclei, which fuse to form a diploid fusion nucleus. Meiosis follows and results in four haploid nuclei. A pair of nuclei passes through the sterigma to the developing spore. The mature spore has thus two nuclei. The two nuclei in each basidiospore may be of one sex only or of different sexes. They may be non-compatible or may be of opposite sexes and compatible. Mycelium derived from the spores having non-compatible nuclei remains sterile and no fruiting bodies are produced. In other case, mycelium from a single spore may be self-fertile and it readily produces fruiting bodies and is technically called secondary homothallic. Most of the spores may contain non-sister nuclei, which are compatible. The cultures derived from them are self-fertile.

CROP MANAGEMENT

In India, white button mushroom is grown on hills all the year round and in northern plains, it is grown in winter under seasonal growing conditions. With the increased understanding of the various environmental parameters and technologies available to create such environment for mushroom growth, it is now possible to grow white button mushroom at any place at any elevation. The cultivation of white button mushroom can be divided in to following parts

1. Selection and maintenance of strain
2. The composting
3. Spawning and spawn run
4. Casing and case run
5. Pinning/Cropping
6. Picking/Harvesting
7. Grading and packing
8. Processing

All the operations other than composting are included in crop management.

SELECTION AND MAINTENANCE OF STRAIN

Selection of best and quality strain should be done for successful mushroom production. Strain should be high yielding and visually attractive in performance. Presently, there are many strains of white, cream and brown varieties available in the market. The brown variety is the natural mushroom and is considered most vigorous. It has more capacity of tolerance to different adverse conditions as compared to white variety. Brown variety mushroom should be grown where growing conditions trend to be on the dry side and humidity cannot be perfectly controlled. In our country S 11, S 649 and S 791 are the suitable strains available for cultivation. Superior strains may be obtained through selection, hybridization, and induced mutation by research laboratories and commercial spawn makers.

Three methods namely multi-spore culture, tissue culture and mycelia transfer are known by which strains can be propagated. By periodic sub-culturing of the mycelium on a suitable agar medium, the spawn strains can be kept for many years in a good state. In the tissue culture, small pieces of fruit bodies are cut under aseptic conditions and inoculated on a nutrient medium. Mycelium growing out of these tissues can provide the starting point for subsequent spawn production. Mycelia transfer is the most reliable method but its performance is desirable to be checked continually to detect any degeneration.

THE COMPOST AND COMPOSTING

White button mushroom is grown on a selected substrate which provides adequate nutrients to support the crop. Compost is prepared by short method or long method as described under the chapter entitled 'Compost and composting' of the text. The compost should be free from smell of ammonia at the time of spawning. It is preferable to use the compost as soon as it is ready. At the time of spawning nitrogen, percentage of 2.2 to 2.3% and moisture of 70–72 per cent are desirable. When the compost substrate is ready, beds are prepared and it is seeded (spawned) with the spawn made from pure culture of the desired strain of the fungus.

SPAWNING AND SPAWN RUN

The spawn is prepared by inoculating fungal mycelium on wheat or bajra grains as described under the chapter entitled spawn and spawning. Following precautions must be taken for successful spawning and spawn run.

1. Spawn so prepared is mixed with the compost under most hygienic conditions at the rate of 0.5% of the compost weight.

2. There are several methods of spawning. Any one method of spawning should be followed. All the methods are equally effective and are at par as far as yield is concerned. Generally, spawn is mixed with the compost and the compost is then compressed and levelled in the bed, tray or bag.

3. The moisture content of compost at spawning for tray and bed growing should preferably be maintained between 68–72C° but for bag growing the moisture content should be kept 65–66 C°. Excess of moisture will invite moulds infection and dry compost will not be supportive to healthy spawn run.

4. Bed temperature should be maintained at 24 ± 1 C°. The heat needs to be removed if growing is done in insulated and environment controlled cropping rooms. It has been observed that approximately 4–5 thousand Kcal of heat have to be removed per hour from an insulated room containing 20 tons of compost during spawn run and first few weeks of cropping.

5. Under seasonal growing conditions, the heat is removed through air in the cropping room without any use of cooling aids. There is no need of air changes or fresh oxygen intake into the room during spawn run.

6. Spawn run is quicker and more effective at higher concentrations of carbon dioxide (1,000 to 15,000 ppm) inside the spawn running room.

7. If cultivation is done in trays and shelves, the compost bed should preferably be covered with old newspaper sheets during spawn run. It needs to be wetted once or twice a day to avoid compost from drying. The water should not percolate into compost. If the cultivation is done in polythene bags, the mouth of the bag should partially be folded and there is no need of water spray in polythene bags.

8. Relative humidity in the cropping room during spawn run should be 90 to 95%. It prevents drying of compost beds and supports good spawn run.

9. Carbon-dioxide production and its requirement at various stages of growth is always strain dependant. It has been observed that carbon-dioxide production is highest during first two flushes. Carbon-dioxide production in strain U-3 has been observed as

186

under:

- Start of spawn run   30 g/hour/ton of compost
- At complete spawn run   65 g/hour/ton of compost
- One day after casing   100 g/hour/ton of compost
- 5–6 days after casing   80 g/hour/ton of compost
- Just before venting   50 g/hour/ton of compost
  (Fresh air entry)

10. The carbon-dioxide requirement at spawn run /case run is about 10,000–15,000 ppm and for cropping, it should be between 800–1500 ppm. The concentration of carbon dioxide can be maintained at different stages of growth in the cropping room by closing and opening of the fresh air vent.

11. The spawn run takes about 12–15 days. Compost made through long method of composting, usually requires a little more time that may be as much as 3 weeks.

CASING AND CASE RUN

Much has been described about casing and case run. Traditionally beds are cased when spawn has penetrated the compost bed sufficiently. Depending upon the kind and quantity of spawn used, the quality of compost and the prevailing atmosphere, it normally takes 12 to 14 days. Therefore, the beds are cased usually after 14 days of spawning. Casing is an essential process in button mushroom cultivation. It is done when vegetative growth has stopped after spawning. Casing induces the fruiting. Casing is very useful for proper cropping and high yield of mushroom.

Observance of effect of casing

Following qualities may be observed on application of casing mixture.

1. It exhibits good water holding capacity and prevents percolation of the water.
2. It allows enough aeration and no crust is formed on the surface.
3. It is neutral or slightly alkaline which is very suitable for good cropping.
4. No harmful moulds, insects and disease causing microorganisms develop on the surface of the cased layer.

Selection of casing materials

The use of casing is important and pre-requisite for pinning and healthy crop growth. Peat (dead organic matter of an aquatic lower plant called moss) is used in forein countries as an excellent casing medium. It works as a good reservoir of water for mushroom growth. In our country, peat is not easily available; therefore, farm yard manure (FYM) and spent compost are used. Farm yard manure and spent compost must be well rotten and at least of 2 years old. FYM alone or in combination of 50:50 (V/V) with spent compost has been found to be an effective casing medium in absence of peat. A mixture of clay loam and humus soil with a good structure having pore space of about 50% of the total volume of the soil, may also be recommended to the growers as casing mixture. The used compost generally weathered for at least a year, sieved and mixed with about 20 to 30% clay loam soil may also be used as casing mixture. In case, the casing mixture is acidic in nature, ground limestone should be used as neutralizing material to maintain right pH that should be pH 7 to 7.5. It has been found that when this material is stored for a week or two, pH level automatically falls to desired level pH 7.5.

Different Steps

Different steps related with the casing mixture and case run desired for better crop yield may be summarized as under:

1. The pH of casing medium should be between 7.0–7.5. It should be water leached for 6–8 hours before steam pasteurization for removing soluble ions.
2. Casing material should be wetted and steam pasteurized at 65–70 C° for 6–8 hours before use. Formalin can also be used as a fumigant for treatment of casing medium. Formalin should be used undiluted at the rate of 1 litre per cubic meter of casing. It should be allowed to fumigate at 20–25 C° for 48 to 72 hours for effective treatment.
3. Before applying the casing material, light water spraying over the spawn run compost should be done. It facilitates wet contact between casing medium and spawn run compost, resulting in quicker case run.
4. Uniform layer of casing should be about 3–4 cm thick. Immediately after casing, water is sprayed over the casing material to bring its water holding capacity to 100%.
5. Care should be taken to prevent the percolation of water into spawn run compost.

6. For complete case run, beds/trays/bags should be maintained at 24 ± 1 C° for next 7 days. During case run, no air changes are required because higher concentration of carbon dioxide inside the room usually initiates quick case run.
7. The relative humidity of the room should be maintained at 95% at this stage.
8. Thicker strands and not fine silky threads of mycelium should develop through the casing. Silky thread like structures of mycelium through casing indicates inappropriate conditions for case run and pinning.

Crust formation

It has been observed that there is frequent cake formation (crust formation) on the top of the casing due to some reasons as under :
1. One of such reasons is the accumulation of carbon-di-oxide around crop because of the insufficient air circulation.
2. Second reason of cake formation (crust formation) is due to the application of dry casing material and delay in watering of the same.

Precautions

In such cases, it is advised to rake the spawn run casing deep up to compost level and level it again followed by repeated light water sprays. It results in healthy flush appearance and crop growth. It has become a common practice to rake the spawn run casing for uniform flush break in cropping rooms with controlled environment.

PINNING AND CROPPING

After completion of case run stage, we have to provide suitable conditions for reproductive growth. Following precautions are taken for successful cropping.
1. When more than 80% of the casing is colonized with the mushroom mycelium, it is advisable to open ventilation so as to intake fresh air.
2. Removal of carbon dioxide and lowering of bed temperature should be done for proper cropping. At this stage, requirement for oxygen is more for switching over of reproductive phase. The carbon-dioxide (CO_2) concentration at this stage should be lowered to 800 to 1500 ppm depending upon the strain

used because CO_2 concentration in cropping room is strain dependent.

3. During the first two flushes, continuous air changes are required.

4. Temperature required during pinning should range between 17 to 19 C° in the bed. It can be brought about by opening of ventilation of the cropping room for introduction of the fresh air.

5. Combined effect of cool temperature, lower concentration of carbon dioxide, higher concentration of oxygen and relative humidity of more than 85% in the growing room usually results in pinning in 10–14 days. Too much oxygen concentration at this stage usually sets in profuse pinning, which is not considered to be good.

6. In another 3–4 days, the pinheads will develop into button-sized mushrooms.

7. For maintenance of desirable temperature and relative humidity in side the cropping rooms under seasonal growing conditions, the rooms are frequently ventilated in the mornings and evenings to remove CO_2 and bring in fresh air. Forced air circulating system can also be installed in the cropping rooms for effective air exchange in the growing rooms. This can be done by using an exhaust fan facing inwards connected to a perforated polythene duct running across the room. Two vents are kept open for exhaust of inside air at backside of the room.

8. Regular water spraying should be done to maintain the moisture content of the casing medium because the mushrooms get 80 to 85% of the water from the casing layer. It has been observed that on an average, one litre of water is added to the casing medium on harvest of every kilogram of mushroom. Watering is an important job, which needs regular monitoring.

9. Different factors such as external temperature, existing season, casing medium and other such factors usually determine the frequency of water spraying and its requirement. It is important to note that water spraying is a vital operation and should always be done by the most experienced worker.

PICKING AND HARVESTING

Mushrooms are picked just before the cap expands and the gills are exposed. When the caps develop 3–4 cm in diameter and attain button stage, individual mushroom should be picked by holding it between forefingers and thumb. Now rotate gently to disconnect it from the base and finally remove it from the bed. Remove the dirt by cutting off the soiled stem portion with a knife and clean mushroom should be collected in collecting baskets. After harvesting, fresh casing soil must be applied at respective places from where mushrooms have been harvested. The yields are highly variable and depend upon the quality of the compost, the strain of the spawn used and the proper management of the crop. In mushroom growing countries where technology is highly advanced, average yield of 20 to 25 Kg per square meter is obtained. In India, the average yield varies from eight to 10 kg, in Taiwan and Korea it ranges from 10 to 12 Kg per square meter. The yields are expressed in terms of fresh mushroom weight per kilogram of dry compost. The total cropping time usually varies from six to 8 weeks depending on the climate, the quality of compost and the strain of the mushroom used. Yield decreases substantially in the subsequent flushes.

GRADING AND PACKING

Mushrooms are very delicate, therefore, they have to be handled with proper care due to the reasons described as under:
- Bruising during harvesting period should be avoided.
- They should be gently placed in the collecting basket and should not be heaped to avoid injury due to mutual pressure.
- It is advisable to case and water the beds after picking and not before to avoid soil sticking to the caps.
- Mushrooms should be sold after proper grading and packing.

Grading of fresh mushrooms

Grading of fresh mushrooms should be done according to the internationally accepted standards as under:
1. *Buttons* – Characteristically, the membranes remain closed, cap measuring 3–6 cm across and stem length not exceeding two cm. Buttons are considered to be the best grade mushrooms and are preferred by most of the consumers.
2. *Cups* – Mushrooms with membrane well developed or just opening with cap. It retains a pronounced cup shape. Stem length does not exceed 2.5 to 7.0 cm.

3. *Opens* – The cup forms the shape of the letter 'T' with the stalk. The cup diameter may vary from 5–7 cm and stem length does not exceed from 2.5 to 3.0 cm. These mushrooms are also called as 'flats'

Button mushrooms have very short shelf life. At the temperature of 20 ± 1C°, this mushroom deteriorates in 1 or 2 days. In cool stores maintained at 1 to 2 C°, button mushrooms deteriorates in 3–4 days. Deterioration includes browning, toughening and desiccation resulting from unfavourable atmospheric conditions and bacterial contamination. In order to maintain the keeping quality of such mushrooms for comparatively longer period, mushrooms should be packed in transparent polythene sheet bags by perforating the bags to permit evaporation of excess moisture that would trend to accumulate in the bags. The mushroom growers in our country usually follow this practice. In western countries, mushrooms are packed in thin cardboard cartons with compartments in such a way that each mushroom remains separate from each other.

Flow chart for button mushroom cultivation
Collection of raw materials
–

Compost preparation
(By short method/ Long method)
–

Filling of compost in beds/ trays
Maintenance of temperature 22–24 C° and humidity at 85%
(Spawning, 12 to 15 days)
–

Casing of casing soil on spawned compost
(Casing after 15 days of spawing)
–

Maintenance of temperature 17–19 C° and humidity at 85%
(Pinning of mushroom from compost after case run)
–

Picking of mushroom
(Mushroom production continued for 60 to 90 days)
–

Mushroom marketing/ consumption/ preservation
(Mushroom preservation maximum 2 years)

Cultivation of summer button mushroom
(Agaricus bitorguis)

In literature this species of mushroom has been referred under various names such as *Psalliota bitorquis* Ouel., *Agaricus rodmanii* Peck, *Agaricus campestris* var. edulis vitt., *Psalliota edulis* (Vitt.) Schaffer & Moller, *Agaricus peronatus* Richon & Roze, *Psalliota bivela* vel., *Chitonia edulis* (Vitt.) Hurrfurth. This species is closely related with *Agaricus bisporus*. *Agaricus bitorquis* is most popular in Netherlands and other European countries and some growers take a summer crop in rotation with *A. bisporus* in those countries with reduced cost of cultivation.

This species of mushroom is also known as summer white button mushroom. It is a high temperature tolerant white button mushroom and it differs from *Agaricus bisporus* as it has different optimum temperature ranging from 6–8 C° for vegetative growth and fruiting. It is a 4–spored, uni-factorial, heterothallic species of *Agaricus* and single spore isolates are homokaryotic and non self fertile. Whereas in *Agaricus bisporus*, single spore isolates are predominantly hetero-karyotic and self fertile. Difference in *Agaricus bitorquis* and *A. bisporus* may be summarized as under.

Recent taxonomic position

In Ainsworth & Bisby's Dictionary of fungi (1995) this mushroom has been classified under kingdom – mycota, phylum –

Table 10.1
Showing difference between *Agaricus bisporus* and *Agaricus bitorquis*

S.N.	Agaricus bisporus	Agaricus bitorquis
1.	*Agaricus bisporus* is not high temprature tolerant.	*Agaricus bitorquis* is high temperature tolerant.
2.	*Agaricus bisparus* is 2-spored species.	It is a 4-spored, uni-factorial, heterothallic species of *Agaricus*.
3.	Single spore isolates are predominantly hetero-karyotic and self fertile.	Single spore isolates are homokaryotic and non self fertile.
4.	It is not so resistant to viruses.	It is highly resistant to viruses.
5.	It does not tolerate higher concentration of CO_2 in the cropping room.	It tolerates higher concentration of CO_2 in cropping room.
6.	It does not has long shelf life.	It has superior shelf life.

Basidiomycota, subclass – Basidiomycetes, order – Agaricales, family – Agaricaceae, genus – *Agaricus*, species – *bitorquis*.

CULTIVATION TECHNOLOGY

In India, trials for profitable cultivation of *Agaricus bitorquis* on a large scale were successfully undertaken from 1988 at National Research Center for Mushroom, Solan (Himanchal Pradesh). In 1995–96 a complete package of cultivation technology was developed at the centre for commercial cultivation of this mushroom (Technical Bulletin No. 8). It was observed that this mushroom can be grown in summer months on hills and during spring/autumn seasons in sub-tropical areas of our country. Two crops were raised successfully under seasonal growing conditions in summer months at Solan (H.P.). An average mushroom yield of 15 kg was obtained from 100 kg. of compost in 8 weeks of cropping from two different strains namely, NCB-6 and NCB-13 which were the best yielding strains identified.

Compost and composting

This mushroom necessarily has to be grown on pasteurized compost for ensuring economic returns. Compost should be prepared by short method and be pasteurized properly. Wheat straw may be used as base material, supplemented with chicken manure, brewer's grain and inorganic source of nitrogen. Pre-wetting takes 5–6 days for pasteurization and conditioning. Pasteurization is done at air temperature 57–58 C° for 4–6 hours followed by conditioning at 48–53C° for 4–5 days depending upon the raw materials used. The compost should be free from ammonia smell at the time of spawning. There should be nitrogen percentage of 2.2 to 2.3% and moisture content of 70–72 per cent.

Spawn and spawning

The spawn should be prepared following standard procedure of spawn preparation and the culture should be maintained and propagated on malt extract-agar medium. Wheat grain spawn has been found to be the best for spawning. For spawning, the spawn should be mixed with the compost at the rate of 0.5 per cent by popular spawning method. Cultivation has been found most economical in polythene bags. The spawn run should be done at temperature 28–30 C° which may take 15–16 days. During spawn run there is no need of air changes in the spawn running room. Although no air changes are desirable to be done during spawn run but CO_2 concentration is desirable to be raised in the room by closing all inlets.

Casing and case run

The bags should be cased with 4 cm. thick steam pasteurized (65 C° for 4 hours) casing material consisting of FYM and spent compost (50: 50 V/V) both 2 years old. No water spraying should be given prior to casing. Water spraying may be given immediately after casing and spawned bags are desirable to be maintained at 26–28 C° for another 7 days so that mycelium may impregnate the casing layer. At this stage, adequate ventilation should be provided. Only completely spawn run bags should be cased. Immediately after casing, a light spray of 0.5 per cent formalin solution should be applied on the top of casing layer to kill spores of harmful moulds that might have lodged on casing surface. It also helps in lowering the temperature to 24–26° C. The pin heads usually start appearing after 18 days of casing.

CROPING AND CROP MANAGEMENT

Maintenance of the crop

The floor of the cropping rooms should be washed with 1–2 per cent formalin solution. During cropping, utmost care should be taken to maintain absolute cleanliness in the cropping room. Frequent air changes and proper ventilation should be given during entire period of cropping. Ventilators should be provided with fly nets to prevent entry of flies and other insects. Clean tap water should be used for water spraying. The incubation temperature for vegetative growth of this species is 28–30 C° and for fructification is 24–26 C°. The beds should be water-sprayed once or twice a day, depending upon the atmospheric temperature. The floor and walls of the cropping rooms should also be sprayed with water to maintain about 85% relative humidity in the growing rooms.

Crop protection

False truffle *Diehliomyces microsporus* is a serious competitor-cum-mycoparasite causing serious crop losses if it appears on the beds. In such case, the entire bag so affected should be destroyed. Use of fungicides should be avoided as far as possible. However, Nuvan (DDVP) can be used for control of mushroom flies during cropping. The stumps should not be left on the bed and fresh casing soil should be poured over from where mushroom has been picked. This species of mushroom needs more suitable conditions for its growth. Due to its high temperature requirement and slower growth as compared to A. bisporus, the mould competitors and insect-pests are always a serious problem if proper care is not taken during its cultivation. Considerable damage to this crop (A. bitorquis) by Verticillum fungicola var aleophilum and isolates of V. psalliotae have also been reported.

Picking and packing

Mushrooms measuring 3–3.5 cm. diameter are ready for picking after 3–4 days of pinhead formation. The stipe in this mushroom is shorter as compared to Agaricus bisporus. This species of mushroom (Agaricus bitorquis) is comparatively heavier and tough and do not open on beds if allowed to stand for a day or more. This mushroom can be stored in a non-perforated polythene bag unwashed at temperature up to 15C° for several days without any deterioration in its quality. However, one small hole in the polythene bag (1–2 mm. diameters) is necessary to prevent deterioration and increase longer storage capacity.

Fig. 10.2 Showing suitable method of irrigation in which flow of water spray is kept far from the bed to avoid damage to the mushroom beds.

BREEDING TECHNIQUES

Breeding techniques in *Agaricus* species

Mushrooms are known to be delicious, nutritionally rich and medicinally invaluable non-conventional source of human food. Amongst various cultivated mushrooms, button mushrooms are commercially important and account for nearly half of total world production. The yield and quality of mushrooms obtained by the grower depends on the genetic make up of the variety / hybrid of mushroom and the environmental conditions in which it is grown. The character, behavior and overall performance of a variety/hybrid depends on the genetic make up, environmental conditions and the interaction between these two factors. Thus, the yield performance of a cultivar depends upon the following equation.

Performance (*Phenotype*) = *Genotype+Environmental conditions+ interactions between genotype and environment.* Thus, lesser the interaction between genotype and environment component; more will be the phenotypic stability. In this way, manipulation of genotype using traditional and advanced techniques of breeding provides an opportunity for the genotype of the variety consisting of desired genes or gene combinations resulting in improvement of yield and quality. The essential feature of any breeding programme is to bring together the desired traits possessed by two different individuals into one. To accomplish this, the breeder must have a thorough knowledge of the basic biology and breeding system of the mushroom species, he is trying to improve it genetically.

Methods of genetic improvement in button mushroom

In order to develope high yielding and quality strains/hybrid, breeder have to use hybrid breeding through the application of molecular genetics. The term 'molecular breeding' has been used to describe breeding programmes that are supported by the use of DNA-based technology, use of molecular markers, applications of RFLPs, ITS (*Internal Transcribed Spacers*), RAPDs and AFLP for quick and reliable assessment of genetic diversity, homokaryon isolation and confirmation of hybridizations in *Agaricus* breeding programmes. The application of molecular markers in *Agaricus* breeding has hastened the development of strains and hybrids in commercially important *Agaricus* mushrooms.

DIFFERENT METHODS USED TO IMPROVE BUTTON MUSHROOM

(1) Introduction

Introduction of improved mushroom cultivars of a country may be introduced in another country is the easiest and quickest method of crop improvement. The introduction provides opportunity for isolation and selection of superior types as genetic base for future breeding programmes. However, extensive care should be exercised to prevent the introduction of new pests and pathogens that may result with the introduction of such improved mushroom strains.

Cultivation of white button mushroom *Agaricus bisporus* was introduced in our country years earlier as an exotic crop and since then different commercial strains have been introduced on various substrates under varied environmental conditions. However, the performances of certain strains were not satisfactory because of the interaction between the genotype of the strain and the environmental conditions. Therefore, such exotic strains should be put to rigorous testing under local climatic and environmental conditions before recommending for commercial cultivation.

Partial list of button mushroom hybrids and cultivars introduced from abroad.

Agaricus bisporus
1. Cultivar S-11- It has been introduced from Germany and is characterized by long stiped structure with wider adaptability. It is suitable for cultivation through long method of composting.
2. *Agaricus bisporus* cultivar S-310- It has been introduced from USA and is characterized by light fruiting bodies.
3. *Agaricus bisporus* cultivar S-791-It has been introduced from UK and is characterized by large and stout fruiting bodies.
4. Hybrid Horst UI (Horronda)-It was introduced from Holland and is suitable for canning.
5. Hybrid Horst U3 (Horwitu) – It was introduced from Holland and is known for high yield performance.

Agaricus bitorquis
6. Hybrid NCB-1(K-32) and Hybrid-NCB-3 (K-26) were introduced from Holland. Both the hybrids have good qualities.
7. Cultivars -NCB-6 (RAB-50) and NCB-13 (PDAB-55) have been

introduced from USA and are high yielding with large fruiting bodies.

(2) Selection

Selection is another method of obtaining cultivars of good performance. Selection may be explained as the process of retention of desired genotypes and elimination of undesirable ones within a strain. Its success depends upon the presence of high additive genetic variance and minimal influence of genotype x environment interaction on the expression of trait to be selected. Selection is also useful to improve the agronomic qualities of the existing cultivars. In button mushrooms, selection can be made from multispore, single spore or tissue culture. This method in commonly used by commercial spawn produces. In this method, a spore print is collected from the healthy looking fruit body and a mass of spores is germinated together on a suitable culture medium. Selection amongst monospore culture is done only in homothallic species such as *Agaricus bisporus*. However, in the heterothallic species like *A. bitorquis*, selection is performed amongst multispore or tissue cultures.

(3) Hybridization

It is one of the most efficient methods of creating variability by combining desirable traits from genetically diverse strains into a new heterokaryon. It usually involves mating of self sterile and compatible homokaryotic lines. Development of hybrids may consist of selection of parental lines, isolation of homokaryons, identification of hybrids and evaluation of hybrids.

Identification of hybrids

In button mushrooms – *Agaricus bisporus* and *A. bitorquis*, the hybrids may be recognized by the different tests such as fructification tests, auxotrophic markers, resistance markers, allozyme markers and DNA markers including *Restriction Fragment Length Polymorphisms* (RFLP) markers and *Random Amplified Polymorphic DNAs* (RAPD) markers.

(4) Mutation breeding

Mutagenesis is attempted to create new variability required for selection and hybridization programmes.

(5) Protoplast fusion

Transfer of genes through using protoplasts is a non-conventional method used to breakdown the natural barrier of gene exchange encountered in conventional breeding system. This technology involves different steps such as isolation of protoplasts using cell wall digestive enzymes with osmotic stabilizers, fusion of protoplasts with polyethylene glycol and $CaCl_2$, regeneration and evaluation of somatic hybrids. Now the fusion of protoplasts can be achieved using electric pulsation (electro fusion). Protoplasts of two strains are mixed and subjected to a high frequency alternating current as a result of which protoplasts are charged. These are now attracted to each other - and make firm contact with each other. There after actual fusion takes place under direct current pulses

Besides production of inter-specific and inter-generic somatic hybrids, protoplast fusion can also be of help in transfer of extra nuclear genetic material. Mitochondrial DNA has been reported to possess genes for resistance.

(6) Genetic engineering

It involves the isolation, cloning and insertion of desirable genes into the genome of target mushroom strain. Successful exploitation of transgenic mushrooms usually depends upon the integration and constitutive expression of engineered gene(s) in the mushroom chromosomes. Besides all above mentioned techniques, marker assisted selection (MAS), back crossing strategy and use of quantitative tait loci have also been suggested.

Chapter 11

Cultivation of Oyster Mushroom

Chief characteristics, physiological requirements, cultivation technology, methods of substrate preparation, spawn and spawning, various types of containers, incubation and fruit body production, management of the crop, harvesting and packing, marketing and storage, other methods of oyster mushroom cultivation, log culture of oyster mushroom, cube culture method of oyster mushroom cultivation and semi mechanized cultivation.

Oyster mushroom which is popularly known as '*Dhingri*' in India, is a basidiomycetous fungus that belongs to the genus *Pleurotus*. It is a cellulose loving fungus and grows naturally in the temperate and tropical forests on dead and decaying wooden logs or sometimes on dying trunks of deciduous or coniferous woods in different parts of the world. It may also grow on decaying organic matter. The fruit bodies of this mushroom are distinctly shell or spatula shaped with different shades of white, cream, grey, yellow, pink or light brown depending upon the species. However, the colour of the sporophore is characteristically extremely variable usually influenced by the temperature, light intensity and nature of the substrate. The oyster mushroom is one of the most suitable fungal organisms for producing protein rich food from various agro wastes without composting it. It is cultivated in about twenty five countries of East Asia, Europe and America. Out of total annual production, about 88% is produced in China, South Korea, Taiwan, Thailand, and Philippines. There has been a significant increase in world production of this mushroom. During 1986, its production was I, 69,000 tones and it occupied the fourth position among all the cultivated mushrooms. In 1989–90 its production jumped upto second position just after the white button mushroom with its global production touching about 9,09,000 tones. China is its largest producer which produces about 80% of total oyster production in the world.

Due to its high biological efficiency and wider adaptability, the future of this mushroom is bright. The possibility of its cultivation in India is unlimited, because of the varied topography, agro-climate, vast quantity of agro-wastes and a large number of *Pleurotus* species occurring in the country.

Fig. 11.1 General morphology of Oyster mushroom (*Pleurotus* species).

Recent taxonomis position

Pleurotus has been classified in Ainsworth & Bisby's Dictionary of Fungi (1995) as under :–

Phylum – Basidiomycota, order – Poriales

Family – Lentnaceae

(Hymenophore lamellate, basidiome centrally to laterally stipitate, sometimes sessile, hyphal system monomitic or dimitic with skeletal or scleto-ligative hyphae, basidiospores cylindrical).

Genus – Pleurotus.

Morphological characteristics

1. The 'Dhingri' mushroom (*Pleurotus sajor-caju*) is soft and white when the weather is hot and looks grayish in cold weather.
2. The stipe is very short and matches with the colour of the pileus. The pileus is depressed.

3. Four basidiospores are formed at the tip of the basidia. The mushroom at maturity produces a number of spores which are released at intervals. These spores are disseminated by wind and germinate on a suitable substrate producing primary mycelium.

4. This mushroom is heterothallic and mating of mycelia from two different compatible spores is essential for fruit formation. Therefore, fusion between primary mycelia of the two compatible spores results in the formation of secondary mycelium.

5. The secondary mycelium develops rapidly and forms primordial which develop into fully formed mushrooms.

Distinguishing characteristics

The genus *Pleurotus* contains more than 50 species and the white or pigmented large fruit bodies of these species are a familiar sight in most parts of the world. The species are usually encountered growing on woods, more rarely on other plant tissues and on dead or living hosts. Some of the important characteristics are as under:

1. Oyster mushrooms (*Pleurotus* species) grow naturally in the temperate and tropical forests on dead and decaying wooden logs or sometimes on outer bark of the living trees in such regions.

2. About two dozen species of *Pleurotus* have been described from India and half of which are already under cultivation. Many species of *Pleurotus* are known to be cultivated are *Pleurotus ostreatus, Pleurotus eryngii, Pleurotus cystidiosus, Pleurotus flabellatus, Pleurotus sajor-caju, Pleurotus cornucopiae* and *Pleurotus sapidus. Pleurotus sajor-caju* is recognized as excellent mushroom and is relatively easier to grow. It has an excellent flavour and texture, therefore, it is being preferred for cultivation on a commercial scale in many countries

3. The fruit body of this mushroom is distinctly shell or oyster shaped with different shades of colour including white, cream, grey, yellow, pink or light brown depending upon the species. Its colour is known to be extremely variable and is influenced by temperature, light intensity and nature of the substrate.

4. This mushroom is easy to cultivate on a variety of crop residues and wastes without composting for producing protein rich oyster fruit-bodies.

5. Artificial cultivation of *Pleurotus* has been known for century.

In India Bano and Srivastava (1962) were the first to standardize the cultivation of *Pleurotus flabellatus* on paddy straw. Later on, a number of agro-wastes have been tried successfully for *P. sajor-caju*. Saw dust, wood shavings, cereal straw, cut logs of broad leaf trees and a number of fodder grasses and residues of mustard, soybean, maize and wheat are commonly used.

6. Various containers have been tried for its cultivation. Important among them are earthen pots, wooden trays, bamboo basket, gunny bags and polythene bags etc.

Physiological requirements

Mycelial growth of all the species of 'Dhingri' mushroom (*Pleurotus* species) is stimulated by high carbon-dioxide concentration in the air. Mycelial growth of *Pleurotus sajor-caju* is usually favoured by the temperature of 25 ± 1 C° and spawn run temperature requirement is 20–30 C°. Formation of fruit bodies are initiated at temperatures ranging from 15 – 25 C°. In *Pleurotus ostreatus*, the optimum temperature for fruit body formation has been observed to be around 16 ± 1 C°.

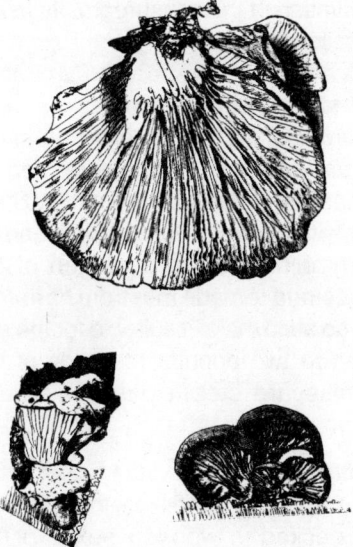

Fig. 11.2 Showing morphological characteristics of oyster mushroom (*Pleurotus ostreatus*), also known as Dhingri mushroom.

CULTIVATION TECHNOLOGY

Selection of suitable substrates

As mentioned earlier, *Pleurotus* species can grow on most of the plant waste materials containing lignin, cellulose and hemicellulose. The substrate should be fresh, dry and free from moulds and diseases. Cereal straw of wheat, paddy and ragi; stalks and leaves of maize, jowar, bajra and cotton; cotton cobs, sugarcane wastes, banana leaves and waste papers; jute and cotton wastes; pseudo stems; pea nut shells and haulms; dried grasses, sun flower stalks and used tea leaf waste, *Brassica* haulms, Jerusalem artichoke and synthetic compost of white button mushroom etc. are conveniently used as substrate. Substrates exposed to rains and immature substrate materials harvested with green chlorophyll patches usually inhibit the growth of *Pleurotus* mycelium due to the presence of several competitor moulds. It can also be cultivated using industrial wastes like paper mill sludge, coffee by-products and tobacco and apple wastes. As a result of higher nitrogen content and other toxic materials present in the industrial wastes, such materials require alteration in the technology of substrate preparation. However, paddy straw is most commonly used substrate for cultivation of this mushroom. Its use involves simplest substrate preparation technology.

Methods of substrate preparation

Although *Pleurotus* species can grow on simple water soaked straw but there are chances of complete crop failure due to the presence of competitor moulds on the straw. Such moulds usually act as competitor with *Pleurotus* for nutrients and sometimes restrict the growth of mycelium due to secretion of toxic metabolites. Therefore, the substrate is made free from harmful micro-organisms before spawning so as to make it suitable for the growth of *Pleurotus* mycelium. There are two popular methods of hygienic substrate preparation. These are steam pasteurization and hot water treatment.

(a) Steam pasteurization

This method commonly sterilizes the substrate partially. Pre wetted straw is packed in wooden boxes or trays and kept in pasteurization room at 60–80 C° for 24 hours. Temperature is manipulated with the help of steam. It is then cooled and spawned.

The entire process takes 2–3 days and requires boiler for steam generation.

(b) Hot water treatment

The substrate is directly put in the hot water or it can be filled in jute bags and then immersed in a container with hot water maintained at 60–80 C° for one hour. The excess water is drained off and substrate is spawned after cooling.

(c) Composting

When synthetic compost is used for growing *Pleurotus* mushroom, some modification in composting technique is desirable. Both aerobic and anaerobic fermentation of the substrate is suitable for *Pleurotus* cultivation. Normally the composting is done in a covered shed to avoid rain. Substrate to be used is chopped into 5–6 cm. long pieces and ammonium sulphate or urea @ 0.5–1% and lime 1% on dry weight basis of the ingredients are added to it. Horse manure or chicken manure @ 10% can also be used instead of nitrogenous fertilizer. Addition of lime improves the physical structure of the compost. After mixing all the above ingredients, sprinkling of water is done till it is completely wet. Now a triangular heap measuring 75–90 cm. but not more than 1 meter high should be prepared. After 2 days of fermentation, turning of pile is done by adding 1% super phosphate and 0.5% lime. The compost will be ready after two days of this turning. It is then filled in polypropylene bags and autoclaved at 15–18 pounds pressure for 2 hours. After cooling, spawning should be done. If sterilization facility is not available, the compost can be used directly for growing the mushroom.

Sterilization of substrate for research

Sterilization of substrate is essential for safe cultivation of the mushroom. For sterilization, substrate may be put into heat resistant polypropylene bags and should be sterilized in an autoclave at 20 pounds pressure for 1–2 hours. Following sterilization of substrate, spawning should be done under aseptic conditions. This method is more suitable for research work rather than for large scale commercial production. It takes more time and is costly. It has been observed that infestation due to various species of *Trichoderma*, *Gliocladium*, *Penicillium* (green mould), *Aspergillus*, *Stysanus* (black mould) and various other fungi are the most common competitors on the straw during oyster mushroom cultivation. Sometimes they do not allow the growth of mushroom mycelium resulting in complete crop failure. In order to avoid moulds infestation. wheat straw should be treated with Bavistin (75 ppm) and formaldehyde (500 ppm) for a period of 16–18 hours. Competitor moulds are either killed or their growth is suppressed for 25–40 days after spawning.

Standardized techniques

The technique as standardized at the National Research Centre for Mushroom (NRCM) may be summarized as under:

1. Ninety liters of water is taken in a rust proof drum (preferably of galvanized sheet) or in a cemented tank of 200 liters capacity.
2. Ten kg of wheat straw is slowly steeped in this water.
3. In another plastic bucket Bavistin (7g) and 125 ml of formaldehyde (37–40%) is dissolved and poured on the already soaked wheat straw. Bavistin tends to settle down in the container and is thoroughly mixed by adding more water.
4. The straw is pressed and then covered with polythene sheet. Bricks or stones are put on the sheet so that it may not blow away with wind.
5. After 15–18 hours on next day, the straw should be taken out and kept on a clean polythene sheet for 2 hours so that the excess water may be drained off in the container and the same solution can be used again for the second time. While using paddy straw 5g instead of 7g Bavistin is desirable. There should not be any trace of formaldehyde in the straw at the time of spawning.
6. Oyster mushroom is usually cultivated on substrates which are poor in nitrogen (0.5–0.8%). It is a common practice to add some food supplements or organic supplements which are rich in nitrogen to the straw substrate while spawning for getting higher yields. Some of the popular supplements are: wheat bran, alfalfa hay (*Medicago sativa* L.), gram powder, cotton seed meal, groundnut cake, soybean cake and ammonium nitrate etc. Wheat bran, rice bran and alfalfa hay can safely be used at the rate of 10 percent (100g in 1 kg straw) while gram powder should be used @ 5 percent.

7. The supplements should be properly treated with 25 ppm carbendazim (half gram Bavistin in 10 liters of water) for 12 hours. It is then thoroughly mixed with pre-treated straw substrate while spawning.

8. The supplements like soybean meal, cotton seed meal and other cakes which are very rich in nitrogen generally encourage the growth of *Coprinus* species in the beds due to ammonia formation.

9. After supplementation, bed temperature generally increases by 3–5 C°. It is, therefore, advisable to record daily bed temperatures. In case it rises, the doors and vents should be opened frequently for cooling.

Spawn and spawning

Freshly prepared (20–30 days old) grain spawn is best for spawning. Spawn of more than one month old should be stored at room temperatures (20–30 C°) to retain its viability. Following precautions should be taken in order to retain the viability of the spawn:

*   Old spawn usually forms very thick mat like structures due to mycelium aggregation and sometimes young pinheads and fruits bodies start developing in the spawn bottle itself. Such spawn should be discarded.

*   Spawn stored at 12–16 C° usually gives satisfactory results upto 3 months. In such case, the spawning should be done in a closed pre-fumigated room. Fumigation should be done with 2% formaldehyde about 48 hours before spawning.

*   The spawn should be mixed @ 2% of the wet weight of the substrate. One bottle of (270–300g) spawn is sufficient to seed 4 kg dry substrate or 15–16 kg. of wet substrate. It is either mixed thoroughly (thorough spawning) or put in layers (1st layer at 5 cm. from the bottom and second surface layer).

*   Spawning on the surface or spawning in spots (2 to 3 spots) is not suitable.

*   In case of non-availability of spawn, active mycelium growing on straw from un-opened bags can also be used but it encourages the spread of diseases and pests.

Various types of containers

Various types of containers have been recommended and are being used based on their availability and cost. Most common containers are polythene bags, wooden trays or fruit packing cartons or boxes. At some places bamboo baskets, earthen pots, pressed blocks or polythene sheets, nylon nets and used jute bags are also used. Cylindrical containers are widely used in European countries. Different kinds of containers are used in oyster mushroom cultivation:

1. **Wooden trays or boxes** – Trays for cultivation of white button mushroom or empty fruit packing cartons or boxes may be conveniently used for filling the substrate for oyster mushroom cultivation. The trays or boxes should be properly sterilized prior to filling by dipping in 2% formaldehyde solution for 30–60 minutes or fumigated in a closed chamber for 2–3 days. The trays are covered with a paper to prevent water loss. Wooden trays are not commonly recommended for oyster mushroom cultivation because of their high cost and risk of infection of moulds.

2. **Polythene bags** – Polythene bags are less expensive and easy to handle. Polythene bags measuring 60 x 45cm or 45 x 30cm of 100–200 gauze can be used for filling 8 and 4 kg of substrates respectively. Ten to twenty small holes each measuring 0.5–1.0 cm in diameter on all sides and two holes on both the corners at the bottom for leaching of excess water should be made. Bags perforated in such a way usually give higher yield than non perforated bags because of accumulation of high carbon dioxide concentration in non perforated bags. High carbon dioxide concentration inhibits mycelial growth of the mushroom.

3. **Pressed blocks** – Polythene sheets of 200–300 gauze thickness, measuring 1.25 x 1.25m are spread in rectangular wooden or metal box. Spawned substrate is filled and the polythene sheet is folded from all the four sides. It is tightly pressed and stapled. The polythene sheet along with substrate is taken out from the box and incubated.

4. **Cylindrical container** – In order to optimize the cropping, cylindrical container has been designed, measuring 30 cm in radius and 2 meter in height with a central supporting tube. The substrate is filled into plastic sack or structure with a removable cover. When the substrate is fully colonized, the outer covering is removed to give a cylindrical structure which exposes large surface area.

5. **Other containers** – Containers like earthen pots, bamboo baskets, nylon nets and used gunny bags are also used but all of these have disadvantages.

Incubation and fruit body production

Spawned bags, trays or boxes are arranged in a dark cropping room on raised platforms or shelves for mycelium colonization of the substrate. Although mycelium can grow between the temperature ranging from 10–33 C° but the optimum temperature for mycelial growth lies between 22–26 C°. The optimum temperature being 25 ±1 C°. Higher temperatures (above 33°C) in the cropping room will inhibit the growth and kill the mycelium. Daily maximum and minimum temperature of cropping rooms and bed temperature should be recorded. The bed temperature should be generally 2–4 C° higher than the room temperature. When the mycelium has fully colonized the substrate, the fruiting will start gradually.

Following precautions should be taken when the mycelium has fully colonized the substrate:

1. Contaminated bags with moulds must be discarded while bags with patchy mycelial growth should be left for a few more days to complete mycelial growth.
2. Early opening of bags will encourage contamination. Therefore, in no case the bags should be opened before 16–18 days except in case of *Pleurotus membranaceus* which forms fruit bodies within 10 days even in closed bags usually at 25–30 C°.
3. In case of wooden trays, the paper is removed from the surface while polythene bags are exposed in many ways. Only top surface of such bags should be exposed by rolling down the polythene upto 5cm or 2–3 vertical slits of 3–5 cm broad, may be made from top to bottom. In the pressed blocks the two open sides are exposed.
4. Casing is not required for oyster mushroom as in white button mushroom beds.
5. All the bundles, cubes or blocks should be arranged on wooden platforms or shelves with a minimum distance of 15–20cm between each bag in the tier.

Management of the crop

Different *Pleurotus* species require different environmental conditions like temperature, relative humidity, light and gaseous exchange. Therefore, suitable environmental conditions should be provided to the crop for higher yield. Such conditions may be summarized as under:

1. Good mycelial growth of all *Pleurotus* species takes place between 20–30 C°. Before growing a species, its temperature requirement should be known for getting optimum productivity. Some species require 20–30C° and are called thermo-tolerant species. High temperature is required for *P. flabellatus, P. sajor-caju, P. sapidus* and *P. citrinopileatus.* However, *P. ostreatus, P. florida, P. fossulatus* and *P. eryngii* require low temperature for their growth.

2. Different species of *Pleurotus* require different range of temperature for their growth and fruit formation. *Pleurotus florida* requires a chilling or cold shock of 20 ± 2 C° for 12–15 days during spawn run and subsequent exposure to 25-30C°.

3. *Pleurotus ostreatus* needs a cold shock of 5–10 C° for 1–2 days for better yield.

4. It has been observed that *Pleurotus ostreatus* and *Pleurotus florida* when cultivated during summer months give very poor yields.

5. Temperature not only affects the yields but also the quality of produce. The pileus or cap colour of *Pleurotus florida* has been observed to be light brown when cultivated at low temperature (10–15°C) but it changes to white pale or yellowish at 20–25 C°. Similarly fruit body colour of *Pleurotus sajor-caju* is white to dull white with very high dry matter when cultivated at 15–18 C° while at 25–30 C° it is whitish brown to dark brown in colour with less dry matter.

6. Generally the oyster mushrooms grown at lower temperature contain high dry matter.

7. All the *Pleurotus* species require very high relative humidity (70–85%) during fruiting. Therefore, frequent spraying of water is required in the cropping rooms depending upon the atmospheric humidity. During hot and dry weather (summer) conditions, the spraying should be done 2–3 times while in hot and humid (monsoon) months, light spraying will be sufficient.

8. If the relative humidity is more than 80%, spraying of water is not advised. Spraying of water should be done with a fine nozzle to create a mist on the bags. Walls and floors are also wetted.

9. Mature fruit bodies should be harvested before spraying of

water. Sometimes the fruit bodies give offensive smell due to the growth of saprophytic bacteria on the wet caps. Therefore, ventilators and exhaust fans should be opened for air circulation so that the water droplets which accumulate on the pileus surface may evaporate at the earliest.

10. The fruit bodies produced at high humid conditions (85–90%) are bigger with less dry matter whereas those developed at 65–70% relative humidity are small with high dry matter.

11. The oyster mushroom can tolerate high carbon dioxide concentration during spawn run (upto 20,000 ppm) while it should be less than 600 ppm or 0.6% during cropping. Therefore, sufficient ventilation should be provided during fructification. Poor and insufficient ventilation will produce abnormal fruit bodies. If the stalk is abnormally long and cap (pileus) is very small and funnel shaped resembling the mouth of a trumpet, it indicates that ventilation is insufficient. Very high carbon dioxide conditions will result in deformed fruit bodies with elongated stipe having profuse and repeated branching.

12. Light is required to initiate fruit body formation. Diffused light for 1–2 hours daily is sufficient. Inadequate light conditions . can be judged by long stalk (stipe), small cap and poor yield. The colour of the pileus is also influenced by the intensity and duration of light. Fruit bodies raised in bright light are dark brown whereas grey or blackish coloured and light coloured in diffused light. White fruit bodies have better market acceptability.

13. The optimum pH during substrate colonization should be between 6.0–7.0 while the pH of the water for spraying should be neither too acidic nor too alkaline. It should also not contain harmful salts or substances.

Picking, harvesting and packing

Picking of the mushroom is done by twisting the mushroom gently, so that it is pulled out without leaving any stub and disturbing the fruit bodies. The base of the stipe found within the straw should be removed by cutting off with a sharp knife. A yield of about 800 gm to 1 Kg fresh mushrooms per Kg of the dry substrate may be expected under normal conditions. The right stage for picking can be judged by the shape and size of the fruit body. The fruit bodies should be harvested before spore release, by twisting so that the stubs are not left on the beds (straw). It is advisable to pick all mushrooms at one time from a cube and the next flush will appear at one time. After harvesting, lower portion of the stalk with adhering straw debris should be cut by using a knife. Stipe should be kept short because it is hard and not liked by many consumers. Good ventilation and adequate light during cropping will produce shorter stalks.

Marketing and storage

Fresh mushroom should be packed in perforated polythene bags for marketing. They can also be sun dried by spreading thinly on a cotton cloth in bright sun light or diffused light. It can be mechanically dried in hot air oven at 40–50°C. Mushrooms dried in sun light usually retain colour. The dried produce with 2–4% moisture can be stored without any change in taste for 3–4 months after sealing in pouches properly. The dried produce should be hydrated by dipping it in luke warm water at 40–50 C° for 20–30 minutes. It becomes 80–90% of the original weight and fit for consumption after cooking.

OTHER METHODS OF OYSTER MUSHROOM CULTIVATION

Some other methods of oyster mushroom cultivation are also practised in different countries. These methods are log culture cultivation, cube culture cultivation and semimechanized cultivation methods. These methods may be summarized as under:

(1) LOG CULTURE OF OYSTER CULTIVATION

Different materials are required for log culture cultivation. Materials needed include cut wood pieces measuring about 5–10 cm in diameter which should be non-resinous in composition. About 160 to 170 pieces per bed are usually required. A list of other important materials may include wooden frame (1 m × 1 m × 15 cm), polythene tube /sheet (1m × 1m), water boiling tin/sheet (1m × 1m), bucket or container (2 nos.), mushroom spawn (2 bottles/ bed), sprayer (1 no.), rice bran (1.25 Kg/bed), saw dust (non resinous) (5 Kg/bed), chalk powder (0.25kg/bed), spade and belcha (1 each), nails (1/2" size) (15–20 nos./bed), nail brush (1 no.) and hammer (1 no.). Besides these, fungicide (Bavistin), insecticide

213

(Malathion/Nuvan) and disinfectant (formaldehyde sol.) are also required for log culture cultivatation.

Procedure of cultivation

Procedure for log culture cultivation may be summarized as under:

1. Shady place is thought to be most suitable, therefore, select a shady place and dig out 1m × 1m square deep. Now put the wooden frame in position inside the dug out area. The margins of the frame should be kept a little above the surface.
2. Place the log pieces upright inside the framed area close to each other and gaps if any should be filled up with small wood pieces. Level the logs properly by hammering if so required. Before placing the log pieces inside the frames, suitable fungicide and insecticide should be sprayed inside the framed area.
3. Now mix together the saw dust, rice bran and chalk powder thoroughly and boil the mixture with enough water. Before using it, log surfaces should be cleaned by using a hard nail brush. After brushing, disinfect them either with formaldehyde or any other disinfectant. Now pour the gruel over the log pieces to form a ½" thick layer and allow it to cool down.
4. Break up the spawn of *Pleurotus ostreatus* into individual grains and with the help of a disinfected clean stick spawn grains should be spread over the gruel uniformly.
5. Now cover the bed with polythene sheet of some bigger size so as to cover the bed. Polythene sheet is fixed with nails hammered into the wooden frame. It should be left as such for spawn run.
6. When the surface is completely covered with the white thread like mycelium, polythene covering should be removed.
7. Suitable fungicide and insecticide solutions as per requirement should be sprayed after removal of the covering in order to protect the crop from diseases and insect pests.

(2) CUBE CULTURE OF OYSTER CULTIVATION

This method of cultivation requires chopped paddy straw (1.5–2.0 kg/cube), spawn (1 bottle/cube), polythene sheet (1 m × 1 m), binding thread (2.2 meters in length), wooden frame (50 cm × 25 cm × 18 cm), pressing board (40 cm × 22 cm × 18 cm), water boiling tin/drum with accessories (one), plastic bucket/container (two) and sprayer (one). Besides these materials, fungicide (Indofil Z-78 or Bavistin), insecticide (Cythion or Nuvan) and formaldehyde solution as disinfectant are required for the cultivation by the cube culture method.

Cube culture method of cultivation as suggested by National Research Center for Mushroom (NRCM) may be summarized as under:

1. Leafy portion of good quality paddy straw should be removed and chopped (about 5 cm long) with a hand-chopper or chaff cutter.
2. Paddy straw should be stocked in cold water for a few minutes before putting it into boiling water for 15–20 minutes. Now the straw is removed from the boiling water and is allowed to cool. Squeeze out the excess water.
3. Punch holes at 6" intervals in the polythene sheet and disinfect with hot water formaldehyde solution and spread on a table or a clean platform. Sterilize the wooden frame and the pressing board also. Place the frame in the centre of the polythene sheet.
4. Break the spawn into small bits with a clean stick and put some bits on the polythene within the wooden frame.
5. Put about one kg of boiled straw and make it uniform. Now press it slightly with hand. Some spawn bits are uniformly distributed over the straw to complete the first layer of spawning. Put another one kg of straw and make it uniform. Press it hard with the pressing board and distribute the spawn bits uniformly over the second layer. Repeat the process 6 to 7 times ensuring that there is proper pressing for every two layers. One bottle of spawn is sufficient for one cube.
6. Remove the frame slowly and carefully by pulling upwards and pressing the straw downwards in such a way that the shape of the cube is not disturbed. Wrap the cube with the polythene and bind it with the thread. Then keep it properly in warm place, safe from rats and insects.
7. White thread-like growth emerging from the spawn-grains will be visible through the polythene which will cover the straw fully within 10–15 days. There after, the polythene cover is carefully removed and the cube is placed on a bamboo shelf in a ventilated room, safe from rats.
8. Spray water regularly and spray Cythion and Indofil Z-78 or

Benlate in recommended strength till pinheads are visible. After 5 to 7 days, the fruits will be ready for harvesting.

9. Harvest the matured fruits carefully and gently without breaking the cube. Use a perforated polythene bag for marketing or storing for 2 to 3 days. Otherwise dry the fruits fully in sun and store in sealed polythene bags.

10. The cube will again come to fruiting after about a week. 3 to 4 flushes of fruits may be harvested from a single cube. Then use the spent straw as manure in kitchen garden or in field.

(3) SEMI MECHANIZED CULTIVATIN OF OYSTER CULTIVATION

There has been very little improvement in the cultivation technology of this potential tropical mushroom. The present method of poly-bag cultivation in India is basically suited to its domestic cultivation. The method is neither labour efficient nor fast enough to attract commercial cultivation of oyster mushroom. An attempt was, therefore, made to work out a semi mechanized production technology of oyster mushroom suiting to Indian conditions and requirement so that large scale commercial cultivation of oyster mushroom could be encouraged by way of efficient use of the cheap labour-force available in the country.

Production Technology

Production technology includes preparation of low cost straw blocks. The preparation and crop management of this semi mechanized method of oyster cultivation may be summarized as under :

Preparation of low cost straw blocks

For this, any cereal straw is first cut into small bits and then dipped in hot water about 90 C° for 10 minutes. The straw is then allowed to cool down before it is used to prepare straw blocks measuring 50 x 25 x 18 cm in dimensions. Method of preparation of such blocks is as described below:

1. These blocks could be made either manually with the help of a wooden mould or with a cube (block) making machine designed and developed for the purpose. The cube making machine primarily consists of an iron mould with a perforated base and a perforated pressing device. It is made by using pasteurized straw which is mixed with mushroom spawn.

2. A known quantity of the spawned substrate is filled up in the

mould and is pressed hard with the help of the pressing device.

3. The cube thus prepared is subsequently transferred on the platform lying underneath the mould. This is achieved by raising the platform up by pressing the paddle provided for the purpose and by gently pulling out the perforated base of the mould. This operation helps to place the cube gently on the platform, on which a polythene sheet has already been put in place.

4. The whole operation takes about 2 minutes. The cube making machine also helps to squeeze the excess water from the straw and makes good compact blocks of uniform shape and size within minutes.

5. With the help of specified boiler, a wire-mesh straw container and some small accessories, an efficient straw pasteurization method was developed which could handle pasteurization of large quantities of straw quite efficiently.

6. The cubes are now wrapped in 1 x 1 meter square polythene sheets and are allowed to incubate and undergo mycelial run in a warm place before these are opened and placed in growing rooms.

7. The cubes are placed on bamboo shelves in erect position resting on one of their longer sides to accommodate large number of cubes. It allows fruiting on their five faces and facilitate easy harvesting.

Economy in use of good quality grain spawns

Good quality grain spawn is the major requirement for mushroom culture. In *Pleurotus* cultivation, the requirement of spawn is more than the button mushroom. The optimum rate of spawn for *Pleurotus* cultivation has been reported to be 10% on dry weight basis. Different rates (3% to 15%) of grain spawn have also been tried. Higher rate of spawning has also been correlated with the higher yield by some of the scientists.

In order to save grain spawn, some of the cubes showing mycelial run and free from moulds and other infestations were tried for making new generation cubes at the rate of 2 & 3 new cubes from each old cube. For large scale cultivation, such spawn cycling might help to curtail appreciably the requirement of grain spawn.

Growing in low cost bamboo houses

The oyster mushroom can be grown in low cost bamboo houses with thatched grass roofing. The growing areas can also be made of bamboo racks in 4 tiers. On the floor of the house, a layer of 3–4 cm thick sand is spread which helps to keep the rim humid and cool.

Environmental conditions

Different environmental factors are required for the quality crop production. Such requirements should be provided by the following methods:

1. The ventilation should be assured through windows provided on opposite sides, fitted with insect proof nets.
2. Spraying of water should be done on the floor, gunny sheets hung on the walls and doors. It helps to maintain the humidity between 75–90%.
3. Temperature around 25 C° is required for *Pleurotus ostreatus* and 28–30 C° for *Pleurotus flabellatus* and *Pleurotus sajor-caju*.
4. During the mycelia run the windows are kept closed to enhance the CO_2 concentration in the room to prevent development of moulds and competitors.

Advantage of semi mechanized cultivation technology

It is apparent from the above that adoption of semi mechanized system of cultivation with the help of cube making machine and hot water pasteurization line are desirable for the large scale commercial cultivation of the oyster mushroom in developing countries like India. Semi mechanized cultivation technology is advantageous because of the following reasons:

1. It could help to reduce the requirement of labour, time and energy.
2. Improved method described above avoids the use of many chemicals, poly bags as well as wooden trays and is obviously more eco-friendly and ecologically sound.
3. The savings of time and labour make the technology more competitive, economical and commercially profitable.

Chapter 12

Straw Mushroom Cultivation

> *Introduction, distinguishing characteristics, life cycle, nutritional and dietary importance, paddy straw mushroom cultivation, substrate preparation, spawn preparation, spawing, bed preparation, other methods of straw mushroom cultivation, Hong Kong method, Malaysia method, Thailand method, modern cotton waste method and improved caged cultivation of straw mushroom.*

Straw mushroom (*Volvariella* species) is another common edible mushroom usually known as Chinese mushroom. It is widely cultivated in some parts of South-East Asian countries like China, Thailand and Philippines. In India, it was brought under cultivation as early as in 1943 in Madras but commercial cultivation is yet to become a reality in our country. This mushroom is highly perishable and has a very short shelf-life, therefore, it creates great difficulties in marketing.

The genus *Volvariella* is characterized by the brownish pink coloured gills and cup shaped volva. It is one of the most important genera and a large number of species of this genus have been described from all over the world. More than 12 species of *Volvariella* have been recorded so far from India and eight of which are economically important and are cultivated in different parts of the country. These species are *Volvariella bombycina, Volvariella diplasia, Volvariella masseci, Volvariella heimii, Volvariella esculenta, Volvariella speciosa., Volvariella terastius* and *Volvariella volvacea*. They are usually known as paddy straw mushroom.

Recent taxonomic position
Phylum – Basidiomycota.
Subclass – Basidiomycetes.
order – Agaricales

Family – Pleuteaceae.
(Characterized by the spore print white to cream or dull pink, hymenophoral trama bilateral with convergent lateral strata).
Genus – *Volvariella.*

(Ainsworth & Bisby's Dictionary of fungi, 1995).

Fig. 12.1 General morphology of straw mushroom (*Volvariella* species).

Distinguishing Characteristics

This genus takes its name from 'volva' which means a wrapper that completely envelops the main fruiting body during the young stage. The fruit bodies of this mushroom first appear as grayish white buttons resembling as bird's eggs. At maturity the buttons enlarge and umbrella-like fruit bodies emerge after the rupture of the volva. Distinguishing characteristics of straw mushroom may be summarized as under:

1. A mature fruit body can be distinguished into the pileus, the stipe, the gills, the volva and the spores.
2. The pileus is initially bell-shaped but later becomes convex to umbonate. It is the umbrella–like fleshy structure attached to the stipe. Morphologically, it looks broad and measures 5-10 centimeters. It is ovoid in shape, fleshy, soft in texture and white in colour when young.
3. Gills are found underside of the pileus which are flesh coloured and wavy. Surface of the cap is soft and smooth in texture. The colour of the fully grown pileus is grayish white with a reddish tinge. The gray colour has been found to be dominant in the centre of the cap.

4. The stipe is whitish, smooth and cylindrical stem which supports the umbrella shaped pileus. Stipe is long, measuring 5–12 centimeters in length and 7–10 millimeters in thickness. It tapers upwards and is more or less bulbous at the base. Wrapper-like covering known as volva covers the base of the stipe. Annulus or ring-like structure on the stipe remains absent in this mushroom. The stipe (stem) tapers from the base to the apex and is solid, smooth and white in colour. The stipe is easily separable from the pileus at its junction. The gills are also free from stipe.

5. Spores measure about 8–10 nm x 6 nm in size. They are more or less ellipsoidal to ovoid in shape. Spore print looks reddish cinnamon in colour. Each basidium produces 4-spores. Clamp connections are absent in hyphae.

6. Carbon, nitrogen, vitamins and other growth substances are desirable for the growth and fruiting of this mushroom. It has been observed that *Volvariella volvacea* grows well on waste cotton substrate which is pure cellulose being the important carbon source. Mannose and starch are also known to support the growth of this mushroom. The fungus does not consume lignin. Organic matter containing nitrogen is necessary to be added to the straw, cotton and other cellulose substances for better growth and yield of this mushroom. Similarly, L-amino benzoic acid, ascorbic acid, pyridoxine, riboflavin and thiamine increase the yield significantly. Among the growth substances gibberellic acid is known to be capable of promoting growth.

7. The optimum temperature for mycelia growth is 30–35 C° and the mycelia growth rate falls at temperature 20 C° and also at 40 C°. It has also been observed that most of the species of straw mushroom does not survive below 5C°. The fruiting occurs in this mushroom between 26–35 C°.

8. In straw mushroom, light is essential but its requirement is not photoperiodic. No fruiting has been obtained in complete darkness.

9. The moisture content of the substrate should be between 70 to 80% and relative humidity is appropriate to be between 75 to 85%. Besides these, pH between 6 to 7 and exchange of air are desirable for growth and fruit formation of this mushroom.

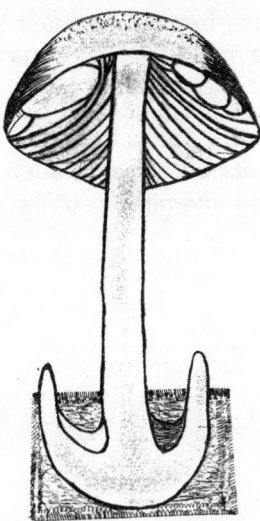

Fig. 12.2 Morphological characteristics showing different parts of
Volvariella volvacea.

Life cycle

The life cycle of this mushroom begins with the germination of
the basidiospores. The basidiospore germinates by producing germ
tube that produces haploid monocaryotic mycelium. It produces
chlamydospores as a result of asexual reproduction. Sexual
reproduction takes place by mating between two adjacent hyphae
resulting in plasmogamy. It gives rise to di-karyotic mycelium.
Karyogamy between the two nuclei takes place in the developing
basidia. The diploid nucleus undergoes meiosis and each nucleus
passes into a developing basidiospore. In such a way, the
basidiospore has only one nucleus.

Primary homothalism is represented by this cultivated subtropical
mushroom *Volvariella volvacea* (Fr.) sing. In addition to presumed
sexual cycle *Volvariella volvacea* has an asexual cycle via
multinucleate chlamydospores as stated earlier. The vegetative
spores are borne as spherical cells on specialized swollen cells of
the multi-karyotic mycelium.

Nutritional and dietary importance

Apart from being delicious, this mushroom contains high quality
protein enriched in essential amino acids. Important vitamins and

minerals are also found in plenty amount and thus acting as a good supplement to normal cereal diet. Constituents of paddy straw mushroom are given in the table below:

Table 12.1
Showing different constituents such as fat, protein, minerals and vitamins in straw mushroom

S.N.	Contents	Quantity per 100 g fresh weight
1.	Moisture	90.40%
2.	Fat	0.25 g
3.	Protein	3.90 g
4.	Crude fibre	1.87 g
5.	Phosphorus	0.10 g
6.	Potassium	0.32 g
7.	Iron	1.70 mg
8.	Calcium	5.60 mg
9.	Thiamine	0.14 mg
10.	Riboflavin	0.61 mg
11.	Niacin	2.40 mg
12.	Ascorbic acid	18.00 mg

As stated earlier, straw mushroom contains essential amino acids found in plenty amount required for maintenance of health and normal well being. Different amino acids and their amount found in straw mushroom has been given as under:

Table 12.2
Showing different amino acids found in straw mushroom with their contents in milligrams

S.N.	Amino acids	Quantity in milligrams per 100 g protein.
1.	Leucine	3.5
2.	Isoleucine	5.5
3.	Valine	6.8
4.	Tryptophane	1.1
5.	Lysine	4.3
6.	Histidine	2.1
7.	Phenylalanine	4.9
8.	Threonine	4.2
9.	Arginine	4.1
10.	Methionine	0.9

Source – After Zakia Bano *et al.* (1971). *Jour. Food Sci. Tech.* **8**:180–82

CULTIVATION OF PADDY STRAW MUSHROOM

Traditional method of straw mushroom cultivation consists of different phases, namely, the spawn production, substrate preparation/wetting, bed preparation, spawning and spawn run, cropping and last the picking and marketing. The time of growing of this mushroom is June in northern India and April – May in eastern and peninsular India. In areas where minimum temperature during the growing period is lower than 30 C°, the cultivation of straw mushroom is not practicable. In case of indoor cultivation, this mushroom can easily be cultivated at any time during summer because both temperature and humidity can suitably be controlled.

1. Spawn production

Natural spawn and pure culture spawn may be used for straw mushroom cultivation. Pure culture spawn is superior to natural spawn as in case of *Agaricus bisporus*. The pure culture is obtained from the tissues of the cap of a healthy and firm fruit body. A small portion of tissue from the interior of the pileus or stipe is taken with the help of a sterilized needle and transferred to a solid nutrient medium like potato dextrose agar in test tube or petridish. Sub cultures are made from initial pure culture for preparation of spawn. The spawn is usually prepared on paddy straw or wheat/sorghum grains. Empty milk bottles (0.5 liter) or heat resistant poly propylene bags are filled with soaked and chopped paddy straw or cooked and firm grains of wheat or sorghum. When grains are used they are mixed with 1–2% calcium carbonafie to prevent clumping of grains. Spawn bottles are closed with cotton plugs and sterilized in autoclave at 1.1 kg / cm² (121 C°) for 30 minutes. After inoculation with pure culture aseptically, the bottles or bags are incubated at 32 ± 1C°. After about 2 weeks the spawn becomes ready for spawning. In straw mushroom cultivation, straw spawn is preferable to the grain spawn.

2. Substrate preparation/wetting

This mushroom grows best on paddy straw but several other straws can also be used for its cultivation. Some species like *Volvariella volvacea* can be grown on other kinds of straw like wheat and sorghum. Recently, composted cotton wastes and coconut wastes have given good results when used as substrate. Old contaminated and rotten straw may also be used for its cultivation. The straw is tied into bundles, measuring 1.2 m in length and 25 cm diameter in size. These bundles are steeped in water in a cemented tank for 24 to 48 hours. The bundles are taken out and put on a cemented floor for few hours for draining out the excess water.

3. Bed preparation, spawning and spawn run

Although there are many methods of straw mushroom cultivation such as Hong-Kong method, Malaysia method, Thailand method and modern cotton waste method. These methods are popular in different countries. In our country, traditional method is usually brought into practice. Beds are prepared by the methods described as under:

- The mushroom beds are usually prepared on a raised bamboo platform inside a thatched hut.
- Four pre-wetted bundles are placed side by side on this platform, facing all the loose ends on one side.
- Now another four bundles are placed with their both ends on the opposite sides.
- The loose ends of all the eight bundles meet and overlap each other in the middle.
- Spawn is applied on this first layer about 15 centimeters away from the outer edge. On the top of this spawned layer, a little quantity of red gram powder at the rate of about 200 g per bed should be applied along with the spawn.
- Now on the top of the spawned first layer of 8 bundles again a second layer of 8 bundles is placed in the same way.
- A third layer of 8 bundles is again laid on the top of the second layer.
- The final layer of 8 bundles is also placed on the third layer and all these 32 bundles make a single bed. The third and fourth series of bundles is placed with their butt ends at right angles to lower the spawn layer, which is also similarly spawned as above.
- Now the beds are firmly pressed to make it compact for efficient spawn run. Compact bed does not permit rapid water loss. Beds are covered with polythene sheets or gunny sheets in dry weather in such a way that it may not tough the straw. This produces the suitable humidity and temperature for spawn run.

- The individual beds are watered daily once or twice depending upon the climatic conditions with a rose-can. The weight of the straw/bed is about 25–32 kg and a minimum of 28–22 liters of water per bed should be sprayed to maintain the desirable moisture content.

4. Crop production

About 10 to 15 days may be required for complete spawn run under optimum conditions (temperature between 32–35 C° and relative humidity between 85–90%). After completion of spawn run polythene should be removed. Beds are exposed to fresh air and the mushrooms start appearing within a few days. The pinheads usually appear in about 10–12 days.

5. Picking and storage

Straw mushroom should be picked at button stage early in the morning. The fruiting bodies are carefully separated from the adhering straw. Mushroom production continues for a period of 2–4 weeks. Each bed of 30 kg dry straw can produce 4 to 6 kg of fresh mushrooms. When the mushroom production stops, the straw can be composted to form manure. This mushroom is very good to taste and valued for its excellent aroma.

OTHER METHODS OF STRAW MUSHROOM CULTIVATION

There are some other methods of straw mushroom cultivation such as Hong Kong method, Malaysia method, Thailand method, modern cotton waste method and improved case cultivation method.

1. Hong-Kong method

In this method, the cultivation of straw mushroom is conducted outdoors and the material used is paddy straw. This method is simple and useful for growers who can not afford the high cost of the modern technology.

1. In this method, the beds are made on a raised platform about 20–30 centimeters high from the soil on stone or wooden frame.
2. The ditches are dug around the platform, measuring 75 centimeters wide. Ditches filled with water are usually used as a source of water for the beds.

3. Beds are made in east-west direction to provide more uniform sunlight and temperature. The straw bundles are immersed in water in tank and thoroughly soaked. Soaked bundles are piled neatly on the base platform.

4. Layers are made in such a manner that first layer is laid and 4.5 kg rice bran for every 180 kg of dry rice straw is dusted and water is sprinkled over it.

5. This procedure is repeated for different layers by using rice bran in the similar fashion one over the other until the pile is about a meter high. Straw is tightly pressed during piling.

6. After about 3–4 days when the straw has become soft and turned brown in colour, it is considered to be ready for making the beds.

7. The straw bundles are united and laid length wise along the base/platform. Each layer alternates the position of panicles on the beds. Beds are made consisting of 5–6 layers and measure about 60–75 centimeters in height.

8. As the beds are ready, spawning is done simultaneously with the bed formation. Usually 1 to 1.5 kg grain spawn/100 kg dry straw is used. In case the straw spawn is used, the pieces of spawn are planted 10–15 centimeters apart and about 7 centimeters from the edges of the beds.

9. Now the beds are covered with straw mats to save them from direct sun light and in rainy season, water proof covering should be used.

10. Temperature of air between 28–30 C°, relative humidity of 85 –95 % and bed temperature between 34–37 C° have been found to be most suitable for high yield of the produce.

11. The average yield may be estimated to be 2–3 kg/bed of 30 kg dry straw.

2. Malaysia method

In this method straw is soaked first of all and is mixed with cattle manure before making the stack. Composting is done for about 10 days and turning is done after 2 to 3 days so as to maintain aerobic conditions. The beds are prepared from this composted straw in open sky and spawned thereafter. The spawned beds are protected with the straw mat.

3. Thailand method

In this method dry rice straw and cotton waste are used to prepare substrate by the procedure described as under:

1. Both the rice straw and the cotton waste are soaked in water. Inside a wooden mould, rice straw measuring 7.5 centimeters in thickness is paced properly.
2. Cotton waste used as food supplement is spread along the four sides of the mould leaving 10 centimeters from the edges. On the top of the supplement, grain spawn is spread, making it the first layer.
3. This procedure is repeated to make three layers. Again food supplement is spread and over the entire top surface of third layer spawning is done. It is now covered with soaked straw measuring about 2–3 centimeters in thickness. Now the wooden mould is taken off.
4. A number of beds or blocks are made in the same way and they should be set in a row. The distance between the rows should be about 15–20 centimeters. Such beds should be covered by polyethylene film. Mushroom buttons are observed with in 7–10 days of spawning.

4. Modern cotton waste method

This method was developed in Hong-Kong using cotton waste compost under controlled conditions. Temporary houses are built from iron frames covered with thick polyethylene film. Each house is provided with blowers for ventilation and is covered on the top with straw mats to protect it from the hot sun. Lighting arrangement is done inside the cropping room. Boiler is also installed outside the house for introducing steam through pipes when so needed. Procedures for making compost and spawning may be summarized as under:

1. For making compost, first grade cotton waste is taken and is supplemented with 4% wheat or rice bran. About 4 to 6% limestone is also added to it so as to maintain desirable pH level-6.5–7.0. Compost may also be made using cotton waste and chopped paddy straw in the ratio of 2:1 or 1:1.
2. The mixture so made is wetted thoroughly and a pile is made, measuring 150 centimeters × 150 centimeters × 150 centimeters.
3. The pile is given a turning on the second or third day. Now the compost will be ready within 3–4 days for filling in the beds on the fourth or fifth day.

4. The beds are filled with compost 10–15 centimeters deep and steam is introduced to attain a temperature of 60 C° quickly. This temperature is maintained for two hours.

5. After two hours, fresh air is blown in by a ventilation system and the temperature is maintained at 52 C° for about 8 hours.

6. Now the temperature is allowed to fall gradually in the compost so as to maintain it at 35 C° which is suitable for spawning.

7. The spawning is done at the rate of 2–4% of the wet substrate by weight.

8. By this method, a yield of about 25–35% of the weight of the substrate is usually expected after 25–30 days of spawning.

IMPROVED CAGE CULTIVATION

Recently, improved cage-cultivation is popular for cultivation of straw mushroom. For this, paddy straw bundles (60/cage), spawn bottles (2/cage), wooden cage (I no., measuring 1 meter x 50 centimeters x 25 centimeters), drum (1 no., 100 liters capacity), polythene sheet (4 meters), binding thread (3 meters), thermometer (1 no.) and hand chopper (1 no) are required. Besides these, rose can (I no.), Bavistin (1 packet), Malathion or any other suitable insecticide and formalin (1 bottle) are also needed. Method of the cultivation may be summarized as under:

1. Dry fresh and hand threshed paddy straw free from moulds and leafy portion is selected for the use of making bundles, measuring 25 centimeters in length and 10 centimeters in thickness. About 60 bundles are used for each cage (bed).

2. The bundles are soaked in boiling water for 20–30 minutes and there after should be allowed to cool and drain off excess water.

3. Now disinfect the cage and polythene sheets with 4% formalin or dettol solution.

4. Arrange ten straw bundles uniformly in the cage as the bottom layer. Now put some spawn grains over the bundles. Similarly put up the second layer of ten bundles over the first layer and spawn it as before. Repeat till six layers of bundles so as to fill the cage.

5. Spray solutions of 0.1% Malathion and 0.02% Bavistin all over the bed and cover the bed with polythene sheet and bind it with the binding thread.

6. Keep the spawned cage in a room or a shed for mycelial run. A warm place with temperature around 30C° is helpful for better mycelial growth.
7. Remove the polythene sheet after the mycelial run is completed. Maintain high humidity in the bed and the room till pinheads appear. Pin-heads usually appear within 10–15 days after spawning. Harvest the crop at the egg stage. Continued spraying of water for maintenance of proper temperature and humidity is essential. The next flush of mushroom usually appears within a week or so.
8. The straw mushroom should be consumed immediately after harvest. This mushroom may be preserved for 24 hours in refrigerator at 1–15 C° temperature. For preserving it for a week, immerse the mushroom in 10% brine followed by drying of surface moisture.
9. Mushroom should be washed properly before use to remove the salt. Straw mushroom can also be dried in the sun or by the heat provided under controlled conditions at temperature 50–55 C° in oven.
10. Dehydrated mushrooms are hygroscopic and should be packed in airtight containers or sealed in polythene bags. Dehydrated mushrooms can be powdered and used for making many preparations to be eaten.
11. Straw mushroom is not suitable for canning unless picked up very early in the button stage.

Chapter 13

Cultivation of Shiitake Mushroom

Introduction, distinguishing characteristics, taxonomic position, cultivation technology, the log preparation, spawn production, method of spawning, crop management, synthetic log cultivation, different formulations, synthetic substrate preparation method, bag filling technique, spawn and spawning, cropping and harvesting and characteristic feature of plastic bag methods.

Shiitake mushroom (*Lentinus edodes* (Berk.) Sing.), is known to be commonly cultivated in East Asia, particularly Japan and China. Besides China and Japan, this mushroom is also cultivated in Thailand, Taiwan, Korea and Malaysia. In Japan, it is well recognized as wood mushroom and is considered to be the next important cultivated mushroom after *Agaricus bisporus*. At present its annual production in the world is estimated to be about 8,26,200 tonnes. Japan is the highest producer of this mushroom in the world. More than 1,30,300 tonnes is harvested every year, about 45% of it is sold fresh and rest amount is dried. Besides being used as delicious dish, a refreshing drink has been prepared by adding some other ingradients to it. Concentrated extracts of this mushroom are sold as natural remedy for management of cholestrol in heart patients. It is liked by the consumers because of its unique taste and flavour. Presence of a chemical usually known to be useful in reducing plasma cholesterol level in blood has been observed to be found in this mushroom. Mainly cultivated in Japan, China, Taiwan, South Korea and United States of America, it grows in nature on the wood of broad leaf trees mainly oak and chestnut.

Recent taxonomic position
Kingdom – Mycota.
Phylum – Basidiomycota

Family – Lentnaceae
Genus – *Lentinus*
Species – *edodes*
(Ainsworth & Bisby's Dictionary of fungi 1995).

Distinguishing characteristics

1. Shiitake mushroom *(Lentinus edodes)* grows in nature on the dead wood of a number of hard wood trees mainly *Quercus* species (oak), *Castenopsis chinesis, Castenopsis tissa, Castenopsis fordli, Castenopsis lamontii, Elaeocarpus chinensis, Elaeocarpus japonicus, Elaeocarpus lancaefolius, Lithocaspus calophylla, Lithocarpus galber, Lithocarpus specicatus, Betula* species and *Carpinus* species.
2. This mushroom is cultivated round the year by adopting suitable strain of this mushroom which can fruit between the temperature range of 10 to 20 C°.
3. The mycelium of the *Lentinus edodes* is known to be saprophytic and wood rotting. Thus it grows well on dried wooden logs and absorbs nutrients from the cambium. The bark usually protects its mycelium from the competitor moulds.
4. Although it grows on logs of different ages, but the logs of 15 to 20 years old with 9 to 18 centimeters of diameter have been found to be the most suitable for its growth and cultivation.
5. The moisture content of logs should be around 45 to 50% If the moisture content is less than 20% there may be no growth at all. If the moisture contents are more than 60% with a pH level of 7.0 to 8.0, it may be contaminated with other moulds.
6. The Shiitake mushroom mycelium grows well between 5 to 30C° and the optimum temperature is 20–26 C° for its growth.
7. Various factors are known to affect the induction of fruiting. Some of the important factors are temperature fluctuation, high humidity, soaking concentration of carbon dioxide and physical socks.

CULTIVATION TECHNOLOGY

Lentinus edodes grows in nature on the dead wood of a number of hard wood trees including *Quercus* species (oak), *Castenopsis, chinesis, Castenopsis tissa, Castenopsis fordli, Castenopsis lamontii, Elaeocarpus chinensis, Elaeocarpus japonicus,*

Elaeocarpus lancaefolius, Lithocarpus calophylla Lithocarpus galber, Lithocarpus specicatus and *Betucla* species. This mushroom is known to be cultivated through out the year by adopting improved cultivation techniques. The techniques may be divided into four stages namely, the log preparation, the spawn preparation, the spawning of logs and the crop management.

THE LOG PREPARATION

Although *Lentinus edodes* grows on any size and age of logs, but the logs with 9–18 cm diameter and from 15–20 years old trees

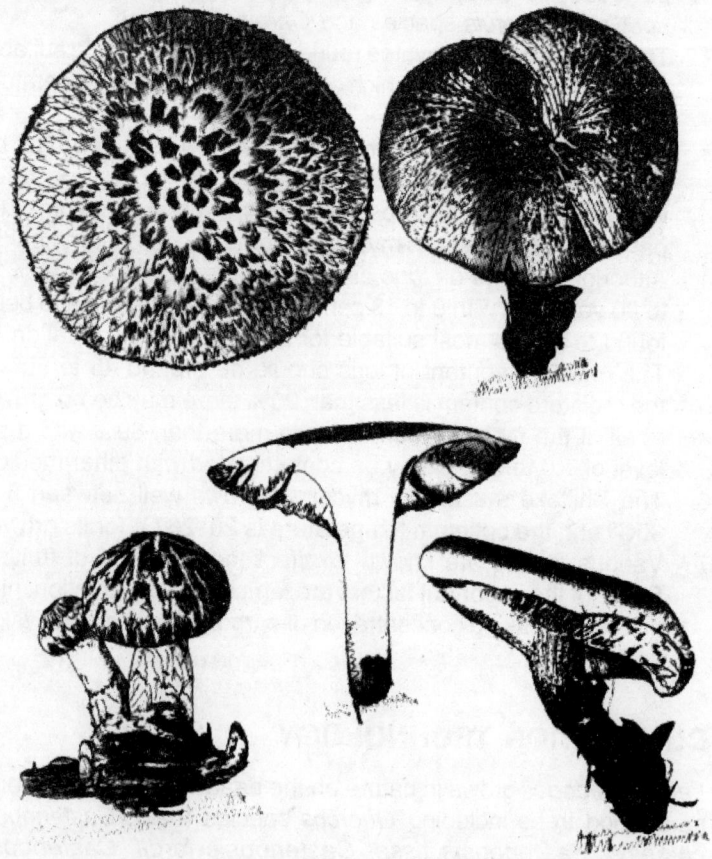

Fig. 13.1 Showing morphological characteristics of different Lentinus species.

Table 13.1
Showing different kinds of suitable trees used in different countries for wood log cultivation of shiitake.

Scientific name	Common name	Remarks
1. *Carpinus* laxiflora	Horn bean	Excellent quality
2. *Castanea crenata*	Japanese shii	Excellent quality
3. *Castanopsis cuspidate*	Shii	Excellent quality
4. *Quercus alba*	White oak	Excellent quality
5. *Osytrya virginianna*	Iron wood	Excellent quality
6. *Salix nigra*	Black willow	Excellent quality
7. *Betula lutea*	Sweet birch	Good quality
8. *Betula nigra*	Red birch	Good quality
9. *Acer nigrum*	Black mapple	Fair quality
10. *Malus sylvestris*	Mapple	Poor quality

are most suitable for its cultivation. The time of felling or cutting the trees is also equally important. The most suitable period for its cultivation is December and January to early March when the logs contain highest amount of carbohydrates and other organic substrates. Moreover, the outer protective layer of the bark is also tightly attached with the woody portion during this period. The logs should contain a moisture content of about 40 to 45% and pH should be between 4.5 and 5.5. The felled logs are usually left as such for 25–45 days that result in the lowering of the moisture contents to 40–45% being the optimum. Sometimes the logs are immediately inoculated when moisture content remains the optimum because further drying usually results in excessive moisture loss.

Logs of suitable species of oaks *(Quercus* species*)*, the shii-tree *(Pasania cuspidata)* and chestnuts (*Castanea* species) are cut into pieces, measuring 1 meter long with 10 centimeters of diameter. These logs are then inoculated using wood clips. Certain trees are used for wood log cultivation of shiitake in different countries.

Moisture content of the logs should be suitable for the mycelial growth. Moisture contents less than 20%, and more than 60% with pH of 7.0 to 8.0 are not suitable for mycelial growth.

PREPARATION OF SPAWN

There are two types of spawn namely, (1) saw dust spawn and (2) wood plug spawn. Saw dust spawn is prepared by using saw dust, wheat bran, rice bran, used tea leaves, calcium carbonate, sucrose, potassium nitrate and water etc. in recommended quantities and composition. Composition of commonly used saw dust spawn may be summarized as under. Any of the following formulae may be used depending upon the availability of the raw materials to be used in preparation of the spawn:

Formula-1

Saw dust	–	65%
Wheat bran	–	15%
Used tea leaves	–	20%
Water	–	65%

Formula-2

Saw dust	–	78%
Sucrose	–	1.0%
Wheat bran	–	20%
Calcium carbonate	–	1.0%
Water	–	65%

Formula-3

Saw dust	–	800	grams
Rice bran	–	200	grams
Sucrose	–	30	grams
Potassium nitrate	–	4	grams
Calcium carbonate	–	6	grams
Water	–	2	liters

After properly sieving, to remove bigger size of wood particles, the saw dust is thoroughly mixed with water. Normally one or two drops of water should ooze out when pressed between the fingers. It is now filled into either empty spawn bottles or in polypropylene bags. With the help of a rod, one incubation hole is made into the centre of the substrate. The spawn containers are plugged with non-absorbent cotton and covered with aluminum foil. It is then autoclaved at 1.1 Kg / cm^2 (121C°) for 2 hours. The actively growing mycelium of 10 days old culture should be inoculated aseptically and incubated for 30 days at 24 ± 2C°. During the incubation, contaminated bottles should be discarded.

Wood plug spawn is prepared by incubating mycelium on small wedge shaped or small cylindrical wood pieces. When the fungal mycelium impregnates the wood pieces, they are ready for inoculation.

METHOD OF SPAWNING THE LOG

For spawn inoculation, small holes measuring 1.0 × 1.0 centimeter in size and 1.5 to 2 cm deep should be made at a distance of 20–30 centimeters on long axis. Distance between each row should be kept about 6 centimeters. The holes between the two rows are made alternate in position. Now the saw dust spawn is filled in the holes or wood plug spawn is inserted by cutting out similar size pieces. The saw dust spawn should not be kept tightly pressed. The wholes inserted with wood plug spawn or filled with saw dust spawn are now sealed with paraffin wax. Spawning should usually be done in aseptic condition. The shiitake mycelium commonly grows between the temperature range of 5 to 30 C° but the most optimum temperature has been observed to be ranging between 20–26 C°. Low temperatures ranging between 14–20 C° are considered to be suitable for the spawning of logs. At low temperatures (14–20 C°), there is minimum growth of mould competitors.

CROP MANAGEMENT

Inoculated logs are kept in open at a place where the physical conditions are most favourable for the mycelium growth. The inoculated logs are kept in a flat pile with minimum exposure to light. The pile is covered with either straw or gunny bags to prevent excessive water loss of the logs. The vegetative growth of the mushroom in the logs will be completed within 8–12 months depending upon the culture strain and the type of wood used. Induction of fruit body usually requires temperature shock or temperature drop, high humidity and enough light which should be provided as desired. Following precautions are taken to induce fruiting:

1. The logs for fruiting are either sprayed with cold water or immersed in a tank of cold water.
2. If the logs are immersed in cold water, then during summer they should be kept for 24 hours in cold water (15–18C°) while during winter they should be kept for 2–3 days at 10–15C°.
3. The logs are then leaned against the supports and the cropping area is kept moist to maintain high relative humidity. The temperature should be maintained between 15–20 C° and the humidity around 80–90%.

4. Fruit bodies are harvested by first pressing and then twisting it gently.

5. Shiitake mushroom is harvested for three times and after a rest for 30 to 40 days they are again watered to get more mushrooms. It should be repeated for 3–4 times per year. These logs may produce crop for 5 to 6 years.

Synthetic log cultivation

Synthetic log cultivation method is popular in Taiwan, China, Singapore, New Zeeland, USA, Finland, Netherlands, Germany, Philippines, Sri Lanka and Thailand. The cultivation of shiitake mushroom is becoming very popular in these countries. The commercial cultivation is carried out by using saw dust spawn composed of oak (*Ouercus* species), maple (*Acer* species), birch (*Betula* species) or any other hard wood graded as excellent for log cultivation.

Various formulations have been recommended for growing shiitake. One can select the best after conducting the productivity tests. Some of the common suggested formulations are as under:

Common formulations

Formula-1

Saw dust		80%
Rice bran		20%
Water content	(adjusted)	65%

Formula-2

Rice straw	50%
Wheat straw	20%
Saw dust	20%
Cane sugar	1.3 %
Calcium carbonates	1.5 %
Citric acid	0.2%
Calcium sulphate	0.5%

Formula-3

Hard wood saw dust	89.8%
Rice bran	10 %
Calcium carbonates	0.2%
Water content (adjusted to)	60%

Formula-4

Corn cobs	40.0 kg
Saw dust	10.0 kg
Wheat bran	12.5 kg
Cane sugar	1.0 kg
Pectin	15.0 g
Urea	20.0 g

Formula-5

Saw dust	80%
(Mapple and birch in ratio of 60: 40)	
Millet	10%
Wheat bran	10%

Formula-6

Hard wood saw dust	32.8 to 34.2%
(100.0 kg)	
Rice bran	2.7 to 5.2%
(8.0–16.0 kg)	
Corn powder	1.4–2.6%
(4.0–8.0 kg)	
Calcium carbonates	0.2–0.3%
(0.6–1.0 Kg)	
Water content	59–62%

METHOD OF PREPARATION

Formulae given above have been suggested by different workers. These formulae are used commonly in different countries. To these formulae, the water should be adjusted to 60–65% as so desired. The pH should be stabilized at 5.5 to 6.0 by adding gypsum and the lime. Soluble ingredients such as citric acid and sugar etc. are usually first dissolved in water before mixing. Saw dust should be soaked at least for two days and rice straw for 3 hours before use. All the ingredients are thoroughly mixed.

Bags filling technique

After preparing the substrate, the bags should be filled at the rate of 1.5 to 4 kg per bag immediately after mixing and wetting the substrate, otherwise fermentation and contamination may cause deterioration and damage to the substrate. Polypropylene (heat resistant) bags are commonly used and the ends of the bags are sealed with heat there after. The bags are first loosely filled and later the substrate is pressed by putting gentle pressure, thus giving the bags cylindrical shape. Some growers make holes for inoculation before semi-sterilization while others make holes after the heat treatment. Generally holes are made of 15 millimeters in diameter and 20 mm deep. Such holes are punched on the opposite sides with an auger. After spawning, the holes are covered with 33 millimeters square adhesive medical tape. The time between mixing the supplements and sterilization should be less than six hours to avoid fermentation. Bags can also be plugged with non-absorbent cotton. It is now sterilized by heat treatment which can be carried out in an autoclave at 121°C. for 1 hour or on a brick and cement lined-tower at 90–95 C° for 5–7 hours. Both systems of heat treatment are used commercially.

Spawn and spawning

Some times holes are not made by some growers before sterilization. In such case the bags are cleaned and forceps sterilized with 70% alcohol are used to make holes. The substrate is now pressed back on the spot of inoculation side. The tape is applied over it after the spawn has been inserted. The saw dust amounting one cubic centimeter (1 cm^3) or a little less spawn amount per hole is spawned. In this way a bottle containing 750g spawn can inoculate 25–30 bags. Spawning can also be carried out by removing the cotton plugs. Spawn is introduced at the rate of about 2.5%. Spawn run may take 18–100 days. During this period, the bags are generally incubated in by providing specific light and dark cycles at 23–25 C°. When longer days or more than 40 days are required for spawn run, the surface of the colonized substrate may begin to turn brown. Some exudates may also be produced. Such changes should be considered to be normal.

The following changes can be recognized during the spawn run of shiitake mushroom:
1. Mycelial running may be observed followed by coat formation in the form of a thick mycelial sheet. It usually develops on the surface of the substrate about 2–4 week after inoculation.
2. Mycelial bumps which are clumps of mycelium are commonly formed on the surface of the most strains of the Shiitake mushroom. These bumps can turn into primordial. Practically,

at a later stage most of them may abort. Bump formation is promoted by fluctuation of temperature and high concentration of CO_2. Some aeration should be provided when the bumps have formed.

3. Pigmentation and coat hardening phase may also be observed in some of the cases. Now remove the plastic when bags have partially (half or one third) turned brown. The outside of the substrate may become hard and the inside should be soft and moist. At this stage the substrates may have moisture content of about 80%.

Fruiting and harvesting:

Various factors including temperature fluctuation, high humidity, soaking, removal of CO_2 and physical shocks are known to affect the induction of fruiting of the mushroom. A schedule of various parameters as given by Chalmers (1989) is given below:

S.N.	Stage/activity	Days	Temperature in C°	Light intensity (Lux)	Humidity %
1.	Incubation	30–120	20–30	None	65–70
2.	Induction	2–4	10–20	500–1000	85–95
3.	Fruiting	7–14	12–18	500–1000	60–80
4.	Rest	7–21	20–30	None	65–70
5.	Induction	2–4	10–20	500–1000	85–95

It has also been observed that the temperature range for fruiting is strain dependent and a dry period after harvesting usually prevent contamination. The artificial logs should be given water bath so as to restore high moisture content of the substrate. Generally, the logs do not require watering during incubation, therefore, maintenance of humidity as low as low 65–70% has been found suitable to prevent contamination. Removal of plastic too early or too late also affects the yield of this mushroom. Deformed fruit bodies during the first flush are signs of abnormal spawn run and high content of CO_2 during incubation.

Harvesting should be done by taking the stalks of the mushrooms and breaking them from the substrate. Do not tear them from the surface. Harvest the mushrooms at an early stage and do not water the scars left for 3–4 days. Yield may be obtained at the rate of about 15–30% of the wet weight of the substrate.

CHARACTERISTIC FEATURES OF PLASTIC BAG METHOD

Merits

1. The materials used to prepare synthetic logs are mainly saw dust and other agricultural by-products or residues such as biogases, sugar beet residue, cotton seed hulls, peanut hull and corn cobs.
2. This method is economical as it shortens the production period of mushroom and gives higher yield.
3. When using natural logs, the time required from spawning to first harvest is about 8–12 months and harvesting is completed in about 3 years.
4. About 100 kg of natural logs can produce about 10–15 kg of fresh mushroom.
5. In synthetic logs, mushroom can be harvested in about 80 days after spawning.
6. Completion of harvesting is generally within 8 months and biological efficiency of 80–145% is obtainable in this period.
7. Besides these, bag cultivation is relatively easy to manage.

Demerits

Quality of mushrooms produced on synthetic log is poorer than produced on natural logs.

FLOW CHART OF CULTIVATON

(Shiitake mushroom-*Lentinus edodes*)
Preparation of substrate
(Shaw dust, wheat strew, bran and other materials)

–

Sterilization of substrate

–

Spawning

–

Filling of substrate

–

Management during spawning

–

Management after spawn run

–

Fruiting

–

Harvesting

–

Yield (200–250g/kg substrate)

Chapter 14

Cultivation of Black Ear Mushroom

Introduction, distinguishing characteristics, taxonomic position, nutritional importance, different cultivated species, cultivation technology, log cultivation, bag culture cultivation and flow chart of cultivation.

Different species of *Auricularia* are known as black ear mushrooms. Genus *Auricularia* belongs to a group of fungi characterized by gelatinous fruit bodies. Like other mushrooms, it does not has gills or stalk and is disc like and ear shaped in morphology. All species of *Auricularia* known so far are edible. Among the commercially cultivated species, *Auricularia auricula*, *Auricularia fuscosuccinia* and *Auricularia polytricha* are economically important. *Auricularia auricula* is light coloured and small while the later two—*Auricularia fuscosuccinia* and *Auricularia polytricha* are dark coloured, large and hairy in morphology. Both of these do not turn slimy on cooking. Black ear mushrooms are believed to have medicinal importance and are used to cure sore throat, anaemia, and certain digestive disorders especially piles and chronic constipation. Among all the cultivated mushrooms, black ear mushroom has the oldest record to be cultivated by the Chinese. At present, its cultivation has become a major occupation in some of the Asian countries where cultivation farms have exclusively been set up for home consumption and export. Its production has steadily increased in recent years. According to Chang (1996), the total annual world production of this mushroom is estimated to be 420 x 1000 metric tones and it ranks fourth among the different cultivated species of mushroom in the world. Thailand is a major importer of this mushroom for local use and 80% of dried produce of Taiwan is exported to Hong Kong, Japan and U.S.A. In India, this mushroom is collected and consumed in the North Eastern hill regions where it grows naturally. Cultivation of this mushroom is considered to be recent in India.

Morphological characteristics

The genus *Auricularia* is known as ear fungus because of the resemblance of its basidiocarp to a human ear. The cut section of basidiocarp of *Auricularia* shows a hairy upper surface, a gelatinous layer and a broad hymenium on the lower side. The basidia are cylindrical and are divided by three transverse septa into four cells. Basidiospores are also called as ballistospores because they are discharged forcibly. Such spores on germination form a second ballistospores that form the primary mycelium. These may germinate directly or form secondary ballistospores by budding.

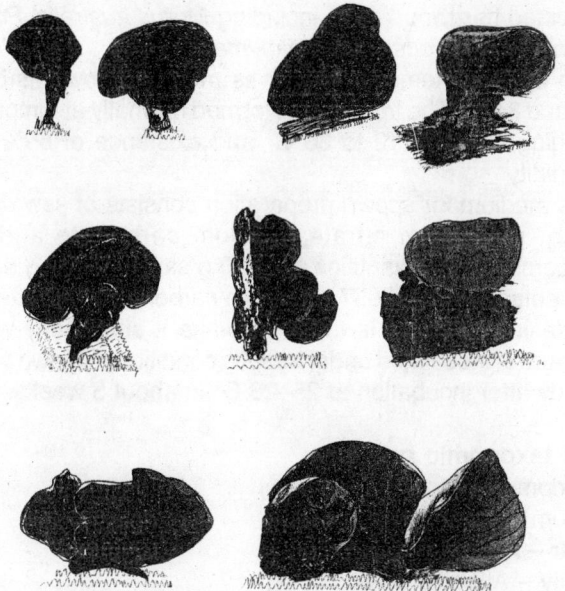

Fig. 14.1 Showing morphological characteristics of black ear mushroom (*Auricularia auricula*) as seen from different angles.

Life cycle

This fungus is heterothallic and is either of bipolar or tetra polar type and there are indications of multiple alleles. When two primary hyphae of compatible strains come together, they form anastomosis and plasmogamy takes place. It results in the formation of di karyotic mycelium which ultimately forms the fruiting bodies.

Distinguishing characteristics

1. This mushroom grows in hot and humid climate in countries suited to this mushroom like China, Taiwan, South Korea, Japan, Thailand and Philippines etc.
2. The mushrooms belonging to *Auricularia* species are simple to cook as they can be fried, stewed, boiled or steamed with meat, vegetable or fish. Its cartilaginous flesh has a pleasant texture.
3. It was being grown on wood logs years ago and is still being cultivated on wood logs where they are easily available.
4. The log cultivation is done similar to that of Shiitake *(Lentinus edodes)* cultivation. The logs are cut from the trunks of some selected hardwood trees including *Morus australis, Pongamia pinnata* and *Broussonetia papyrifera*.
5. The optimum temperature for its mycelial growth is between 20 and 34 C°. The fruit body is formed normally at temperatures ranging between 12 to 30 C° and existance of 85% relative humidity.
6. The medium for spawn preparation consists of saw dust, rice bran, potassium nitrate, calcium carbonate and water Recommended quantities are 100 g saw dust, 25 g rice bran, 5 g potassium nitrate, 7 g calcium carbonate and water. Water in desired quantity is taken to make it sufficiently wet. This mixture is inoculated under aseptic conditions. Spawn becomes ready after incubation at 25–28 C° in about 3 weeks.

Recent taxonomic position
Kingdom – Mycota,
Phylum – Basidiomycota
Order – Auriculariales
Family – Auricularaceae
Genus – *Auricularia*
— Ainsworth & Bisby's Dictionary of fungi (1995).

Nutritional importance
Auricularia contains more than ten species of wide distribution. *Auricularia polytricha* is edible and is cultured on poles of *Quercus* in China. It is canned or dried and offered for sale in western markets. It has been reported that in China a kit containing all the

necessary ingredients to cultivate this mushroom is made commercially available to the public. This mushroom is rich in nutritional constituents as shown in the table given below:

Table 14.1.
Showing nutritional composition of black ear mushroom in respect of their importance.

S.N.	Parts /constituents	Nutritional percentage
1.	Edible parts	100.00
2.	Water	9.19
3.	Protein	8.67
4.	Fat	1.64
5.	Carbohydrates	73.69
6.	Fiber	11.50
7.	Calories per 100 g	317.00
8.	Ash	4.50

Source : Based on reports from "*Essentials of nutrition* (1958), published by American Bureau for Medical Aid to China.

It is evident from the table given above, that this mushroom is rich in different nutritional constituents. This mushroom is also rich in different vitamins and minerals desirable for normal well being of the people as given below :

Table 14.2.
Showing minerals found in black ear mushroom.

S.N.	Mineral elements	Availability in percentage
1.	Potassium oxide	35.33
2.	Sodium oxide	5.98
3.	Calcium oxide	17.61
4.	FeO_3	2.36
5.	Aluminum oxide	4.70
6.	Magnesium oxide	0.5
7.	Manganese oxide	6.60
8.	Copper oxide	0.07
9.	Zinc oxide	0.09
10.	Potassium oxide	7.87
11.	Chlorine	2.29
12.	Other elements	Trace amounts

Source : Based on reports from "*Essentials of nutrition* (1958), published by American Bureau for Medical Aid to China.

Different cultivated species

There are more than ten species of *Auricularia* which are commonly known to occur in our country. Out of these, 7 are well known to be found and commonly cultivated in Taiwan. These are *Auricularia auricula* (Hook) Underw, *Auricularia polytricha* (Mont.) Sacc. *Auricularia delicata* (Fr.) Henn., *Auricularia mesenterica* Pers., *Auricularia cornea* (Ehrenb) (ex Fries) Ehrenb (ex Endl), *Auricularia peltata* Lloyd and *Auricularia fuscosuccinea* (Mont.) Farlow. Two important species of this mushroom – *Auricularia auricula* (Hook) Underw and *Auricularia polytricha* (Mont.) Sacc are the most popular edible species of this genus. In China, *Auricularia auricula* is called as Mu-Erb, meaning the ear of the trees and the other species *Auricularia polytricha* is called as the Jew's ear, being similar to human ear. Both the species are commonly cultivated there on logs of various woods.

CULTIVATION TECHNOLOGY

Log cultivation

1. Freshly felled logs are collected after autumn, because the moisture content of such logs varies from 50–80% in those days with enough sugar accumulation. Such logs are considered to be most suitable for cultivation.
2. Generally, logs measuring one-meter each of 3–6 centimeters in diameters are cut and preferred to facilitate handling.
3. To inoculate the logs, holes measuring 1.0 centimeter across and 1.0 to 1.8 centimeters deep are made. These holes are bored and filled with saw dust spawn and there after the holes are plugged with bark and sealed with molten wax. Prepared substrates made up of autoclaved saw dust rice bran mixture in polypropylene bags have also been used in Taiwan since the early seventies for its cultivation.
4. Inoculated logs are laid crosswise or stand upright in a growing yard where there is no direct sunlight and remains constant temperature and excellent air circulation.
5. Incubation of logs is done in shade at about 28 C° for about two months after which the logs are ready for cropping. After 30 days of watering, flushes appear and continue till natural temperatures prevail.

6. When the spawn run is complete which usually takes about 30–40 days, such logs are transferred to cropping yard that has a constant temperature of 23 to 28 C° with relative humidity about 80 percent.
7. The fruit bodies are cut at their base or simply twisted off by hand. No special care is needed after harvest and fruit bodies are formed repeatedly under favourable environmental conditions.
8. If the logs are protected properly, harvests can be taken from these logs every year in the natural growing seasons. It has been observed that one piece of sesbania log of 12–15 centimeters in diameter usually yields about 3–5 kg mushroom in 5–6 months. The total yield after several years of cropping may be expected to be 10–20 % of the original weight of the log.

Bag cultivation

Recently a new method of growing this mushroom in plastic bags has been developed in Taiwan. With the growing scarcity of wood, cultivation has shifted from log cultivation to bag culture. In bag culture, cultivation technique has been standardized for various substrates like saw dust, paddy straw, maize stems, corn cobs, cotton, seed hulls after supplementation and composting. Bag cultivation may be summarized as under:

1. At National research center for mushroom, Solan, (H.P.); wheat straw has given equally good results especially with fresh straw as compared to composted straw. Rice bran supplementation (4%) was found to enhance mycelial growth and yield of this mushroom. Autoclaved substrates have been observed to give contaminant free growth as compared to pasteurized ones.
2. The polypropylene bags are prepared which are heat resistant and each bag contains 0.5 to 2 kg substrate. It facilitates autoclaving.
3. For spawning the bags, saw dust is most commonly used. With the introduction of bag culture, grain spawn is also being used. Grain spawn has to be used fresh without storage for more than one month to avoid degeneration. However, saw dust span (supplemented with wheat bran etc.) was found to remain viable even after 3–4 months of storage. Spawning should be done @ 2% on wet weight basis of substrate.

4. For spawn run and cropping, the bags can be hung/placed in shelves in close proximity to each other (5–7 centimeters distance). Bags can be hung at irregular heights to accommodate more bags which will have the added advantage of reducing the risk of spoilage due to mites and ants etc.

5. A temperature range of 22–28 C° and relative humidity of 80 ± 10% should be maintained for spawn run and cropping.

6. On wheat straw, it takes 2–3 weeks for mycelial colonization after which the bags should be hung and slitted at regular intervals. Slitting of bags has been found more beneficial than complete removal of bags as the slitting prevents drying out of substrate.

7. Apart from temperature and humidity, light, aeration and watering are other pre-requisites for fruit body development and maturation. Watering is done with a fine sprayer once or twice a day depending upon the surrounding of the humidity.

8. Aeration and light for few hours (2–3 hours) are also required after the appearance of fruit body. It initiates development of normal mushrooms with higher yield.

9. When young, the mushroom has a conspicuously thick edge resembling a cup. At this stage, the mushroom should generally be picked for harvest.

10. Unlike other mushrooms, *Auricularia* is less perishable in nature in both fresh and dried forms. It stays in good condition on the substrate even up to 7–10 days after attaining maturity.

11. Yields as fresh mushroom on wheat straw (supplemented with rice bran) have been found to be variable ranging from 85g to 150g per 100g substrate. In China, 6–8 kg dry mushroom have been reported to be produced from 100 kg substrate composed of cotton seed hulls.

12. *Auricularia polytricha* mushroom harvested from wood logs has been observed to be tough in texture, less in colour attraction with larger production period in comparison to *Auricularia polytricha* mushroom harvested from substrate bags.

13. The fruit bodies of *Auricularia* mushroom can easily be sun-dried resulting in dry matter of 8–12%. This mushroom is known to retain its characteristic crispness on cooking.

FLOW CHART OF CULTIVATION

(Auricularia species*)*
Preparation of substrate

-

Spawning
(Filling 2kg substrate per bag)

-

Management during spawn run
(Temperature 22–28C° and relative humidity 70–85%)

-

Management after spawn run
(Temperature 22–25C° and relative humidity 70–85%)

-

Harvesting
Yield (500–800g per kg of substrate)

Chapter 15

Cultivation of Specialty Mushrooms

> *Cultivation of Calocybe indica, cultivation technology, substrate preparation and cultivation, spawn preparation, spawning and spawn run, casing soil and casing, cropping and harvesting; cultivation of flammulina velutipes, cultivation technology, substrate preparation, fruit bodies formation; cultivation of Tremella fuciformis; cultivation of Pholiota nameko, characteristics and cultivation technology; some other edible non-cultivated mushrooms.*

CULTIVATION OF *CALOCYBE INDICA* (MILKY MUSHROOM)

During the last decade, a number of wild edible fungi have been successfully brought under cultivation. The cultivation of such mushrooms still requires intensive research for improving the technology for quality and higher yield. Such mushrooms are *Calocybe indica*, *Flammulina velutipes*, *Pholiota nameko* and *Tremella fuciformis*. *Lentinus edodes* and *Auricularia* species have also been considered as specialty mushrooms whose cultivation techniques have been described earlier.

Calocybe is a large genus containing about 250 species. It belongs to family Tricholomataceae of order Agaricales. Characteristically, this mushroom produces whitish basidiocarp with fleshy stipe and broadly adnate to decurrent gills. It lacks ring or volva. Clamp connections are typically present. The basidiospores are smooth or ornamented. Some species of this mushroom like *Calocybe indica* is edible and grows well in nature on humus soil under the road side trees in forests. Many other species like *Calocybe dealbata* and *Calocybe aurantiaca* are poisonous. *Calocybe indica*, the edible mushroom is sold in different cities and village markets by collecting from the forests. In West Bengal, it is liked because of its attractive, robust and white basidiocarp. It has long shelf life and is eaten usually because of its unique taste.

Recent taxonomic position
  Kingdom – Mycota
  Phylum   – Basidiomycota
  Order – Agaricales
  Family – Tricholomataceae
  Genus – *Calocybe*
  — Ainsworth & Bisby's Dictionary of fungi, (1995).

Nutritional importance
  Young pinheads of *Calocybe indica* usually contain the lowest protein about 15% on dry weight basis, whereas, mature fruit body contains highest protein to the extent of about 17.2% on dry weight basis. It has been observed that this mushroom contains 12 amino acids namely alanine, aspartic acid, glutamine, glutamic acid, glycine, hydroxyproline, histidine, lysine, threonine, tyrosine, valine, arginine and proline. Out of all, glycine being a very useful amino acid is found in plenty amount (10.8g/100g protein).

CULTIVATION TECHNOLOGY

Substrate preparation
  The mycelium of *Calocybe indica* grows both on composted and fresh straw. For preparing compost following methods are followed:
1. Soil, sand and maize meal taken in ratio of 12:6:1 are mixed. Now water is sprinkled on it to moisten it properly.
2. It is then autoclaved for sterilization so as to avoid contamination.
3. Fresh paddy straw is chopped properly and is soaked in clean water for 18–24 hours. Subsequently, it is soaked in hot water at 65–80C° for 2–3 hours.
4. Soaked straw is now supplemented either with maize meal or wheat bran @ 5% of the wet weight of the straw. After supplementation, it is disinfected and filled in metal or wooden trays. Pasteurization of substrate gives good results.

Spawn preparation

Wheat grains free from diseases and insect pests should be boiled for 15–20 minutes so that they may become soft but should not split at all. After draining out of the excess water, boiled grains are spread over on a muslin cloth overnight. On next morning, gypsum (calcium sulphate) and chalk powder (calcium carbonate) are thoroughly mixed at the rate of 2% to 6% wet weight of grain. It is then filled in empty milk or glucose bottles. Such bottles are autoclaved at usual temperature for one hour on 2 consecutive days. After cooling of the bottles, they are inoculated with a little bit of mycelium taken aseptically from the 10–15 days old culture. Inoculated bottles are incubated at 26–28 C° for 3–4 days and light is provided for 6 to 7 hours daily. The grains are thoroughly shaken after 6th 9th and 12th days to avoid clumping of grains.

Spawning and spawn run

The compost or straw as described above is filled in trays and spawned by broadcasting. The spawned trays are kept in cropping rooms for 8–10 days for mycelial growth and spread. The trays are covered with sterilized moist newspaper sheet for 3–4 days and should also be kept moist by spraying water regularly. Benomyl @ 10 ppm (25ml/ tray) is sprayed on the newspaper sheet to avoid the moulds infestation. The paper sheet should be removed from the top surface when the mycelium completely impregnates the substrate.

Casing soil and casing

Casing soil is prepared by mixing dried loam soil or garden soil and sand in ratio of 1:1 and calcium carbonate @ 12% of soil and sand mixture. The pH of 6.5 to 7.5 is suitable for casing mixture. About 2 kilograms of pasteurized casing mixture is applied uniformly per tray. It should now be slightly pressed.

Cropping and Harvesting

After 2 to 3 weeks of casing, pinheads will start coming up. These will mature within a week. The trays are kept moist by covering with cellophane paper boxes. First flush of fruit bodies can be harvested within 3–4 week of casing. While harvesting, individual fruit bodies are picked up without disturbing adjoining young pinheads. From one tray of 4kg wet paddy straw, approximately 500–600g fresh mushrooms can be harvested.

FLOW CHART OF CULTIVATION

(Generalized method of *Calocybe indica* cultivation)
Substrate preparation

−

Sterilization of substrate

−

Filling the substrate in trays/bags

−

Spawning and spawn run
(Maintain temperature between 22–30 C° and R.H. 70–85%)

−

Management after spawn run

−

Casing and case run
(3–4 cm thick case layer. Maintain pH of 6.5 to 7.5
and temperature 25–35C°)

−

Cropping and Harvesting
(fruiting temperature 26–30C°)
(After 10–12 days of casing)

−

Cropping period Feb. to April
Yield
(500–700 g/ tray of substrate)

CULTIVATION OF *FLAMMULINA VELUTIPES*

Flammulina velutipes forms small fruit bodies and is liked by all due to its delicious taste. This mushroom usually appears in winter season in Japan; therefore, it is called as winter mushroom. Being an important wood destroying fungus, it grows commonly on trunks of broad leaved trees. Both log and sawdust cultivation methods are popular. Sawdust cultivation is preferred because quality mushrooms are produced through this method.

Recent taxonomic position
 Kingdom – Mycota
 Phylum – Basidiomycota.
 Order – Agaricales
 Family – Tricholomataceae.
 Genu – *Flammulina*
 — Ainsworth & Bisby's Dictonary of fungi (1995)

CULTIVATION TECHNOLOGY

The whole cultivation process from spawning to cropping usually takes about 3 months. The sawdust cultivation method may be summarized as under:

Substrate preparation
 Substrate is composed of sawdust preferably taken from broad leaf trees and rice bran in the ratio of 4:1. Water content is adjusted to 58–60%. It is now filled in propylene bottle of 800 to 1000 ml capacity. About 540g of substrate is filled in a bottle. These bottles are capped to prevent contamination and drying out. These bottles filled with substrate should be autoclaved for an hour at 121 C°

Spawn and spawning
 Sterilized bottles are inoculated with sawdust spawn. For mycelial growth, temperatures ranging between 22 C° to 26 C° have been found suitable. The spawn run becomes complete with in 20 to 25 days. The upper layer which consists of sawdust spawn is then removed. These bottles are now placed in darkness at temperature between 10 C° and 12 C° and relative humidity between 80 to 85%.

Fruit body's formation
 After 10 to 15 days, fruit body formation is initiated. The temperature in this phase is lowered to 5 C°–8 C°. When the stipes have reached to the length of 2 centimeters, the neck of the bottle is wrapped with waxed-paper in a plastic- film to hold the mushroom upright. It is removed when the stipes are 12–14 centimeters long. After being cut off they are packed in bundles.

Yield
About 100 to 150 g mushroom per bottle may be obtained in the first flush followed by considerable reduction in second phase.

CULTIVATION OF *TREMELLA* SPECIES

This mushroom is popular as white jelly fungus and is also recognized as silver ear. This mushroom is known to have medicinal importance, therefore, Chinese not only use it as a medicine but they consume it as a delicious dish as well. This mushroom is mostly found in subtropical regions of the world usually growing on hardwoods.

Recent taxonomic position
Kingdom – Mycota
Phylum   – Basidiomycota.
Order – Tremellales
Family – Tremellaceae
Genus – *Tremella* (=*Tremellodendrdron*)
— Ainsworth & Bisby's Dictonary of fungi (1995)

Characteristics
The fruit body of this mushroom consists of a number of rather large blade likes lobes. It is found in clusters, measuring 10 centimeters or more in width. They are characteristically translucent to opaque, white, gelatinous and agar like in the beginning which changes to soft and mucilaginous later on.

CULTIVATION TECHNOLOGY

Method of cultivation of this mushroom is usually similar to that of *Lentinus edodes* and *Auricularia auricula* as described earlier. A brief description of the cultivation method may be summarized as under:

Spawn and spawning
1.   The spawn for the cultivation of this mushroom should be made in the manner similar to *Auricularia auricula*.

2. To prepare spawn, saw dust and 20% rice bran mixture is used. After inoculation, it is maintained at 23 C° to 26 C°. The spawn becomes ready in about 2 weeks.

3. The inoculation of logs is done in the same way as described for *Lentinus edodes* and *Auricularia auricula*. The tree selected for cultivation should be cut in late autumn or early spring when water content remains as desired.

4. After inoculation, the logs are placed upright and incubated for 35 to 45 days.

5. During the period of spawn run, environmental conditions should not be too moist because it increases the growth of weed moulds.

Cropping and yield

6. The fruiting phase requires 85% to 95% relative humidity and temperature range of 20 C° to 27 C°. It is a little higher than the temperature required for vegetative growth.

7. Timely watering should be done to accelerate the cropping and maintenance of proper temperature.

8. Fruiting bodies having diameter of 10–15 centimeters, should be harvested in the course of 7 months during which fruit bodies are continuously formed.

CULTIVATION OF *PHOLIOTA NAMEKO*

This mushroom is known to be the most popular cultivated mushroom in Japan. It occurs in nature at the high altitude regions of Japan and Taiwan.

Characteristics

The common name "nameko" means viscid mushroom as called usually in Japan. The mushroom grows on the woods of *Fagus* species and *Quercus mongolica*. The pileus of the mushroom is yellow brown, glabrous usually covered with glutinous mucilage.

Taxonomic position
   Kingdom – Mycota
   Phylum – Basidiomycota
   Order – Agaricales

Family – Strophariaceae
Genus – *Pholiota*
— Ainsworth & Bisby's Dictonary of fungi (1995)

CULTIVATION TECHNOLOGY

The mushroom is cultivated on logs or on the mixture of saw dust supplernented with wheat bran. Temperature between 8 C° to 15 C° is suitable for cultivation because temperature above 15 C° affects the fruit body in such a way that the formation of pileus of the mushroom remains small. Temperature below 8 C° also affects the normal formation of the fruiting body resulting in formation of fruit bodies to grow longer. This mushroom requires more moisture for fruiting than the moisture required by other mushrooms under cultivation.

Chapter 16

Diseases of Mushrooms

Introduction, diseases of button mushroom, competitor moulds, fungal diseases of button mushroom—dry bubble, false truffle, cobweb disease or mildew, weed fungi and competitor moulds; physiological diseases—rose comb disease, stroma and sectors or sectoring, flock hard cap, open veil, hollow core, brown pitch, purple stem, scales or crocodiles and long stemmed mushrooms; bacterial disease of button mushroom-bacterial blotch or brown blotch, ginger blotch, mummy disease, drippy gall and pit disease.

Like all other crops, mushrooms are also affected adversely by a large number of biotic and non-biotic disease causing agents. Among the biotic agents, fungi, bacteria, viruses, nematodes and insect-pests are of paramount importance, as they cause considerable damage to mushrooms either directly or indirectly. Abiotic agents include high or low temperature, air pollutants, extreme light and excess moisture which initiate different kinds of abnormalities in mushrooms at different stages of development.

DISEASES OF BUTTON MUSHROOMS

Disease may be defined as "a physiological or structural abnormality incited by a biotic or abiotic pathogen that is harmful to the plant or to any of its part or products that reduce the economic value". Although a number of harmful fungi, bacteria and viruses encounter to cause diseases in button mushroom but the most common and economically important diseases known to be of great economic importance may be summarized according to their occurrence at different stages of cultivation.

1. **Compost moulds:** Competitor moulds and pathogenic fungi occurring mainly in compost are olive green moulds (*Chaetomium olivaceum*), ink caps (*Coprinus* species), green moulds (*Aspergillus* species, *Penicillium* species and

Trichoderma species) , black moulds (*Mucor* species and *Rhizopus* species) and some others which include species of *Sporotrichum, Sepedonium Fusarium* and *Cephalosporium*.

2. **Compost and casing soil moulds:** Fungi occurring in compost and in casing soil mostly include white plaster moulds (*Scopulariopsis fimicola*), Brown plaster mould (*Papulospora byssina*), lipstick mould (*Sporendonema purpurescens*), false truffle (*Diehliomyces microsporus*) and green molds (*Aspergillus* species, *Penicillium* species and *Trichoderma* species).

3. **Casing soil and growing mushroom moulds:** Such moulds include cinnamon mould (*Peziza ostracoderma*), wet bubble (*Mycogone perniciosa*), dry bubble (*Verticillium fungicola*), cobweb (*Cladobotryum dendroides*) pink mould (*Trichothecium roseum*) and green moulds (*Aspergillus* species, *Penicillium* species and *Trichoderma* species).

4. **Fungi attacking fruit bodies:** Such fungi include species of *Fusarium* causing fusarium rot of mushroom fruit bodies.

In intensive and continual cropping, the growing conditions sometimes trend to be unfavorable and temperature above 20C° coupled with excess moisture in the beds usually encourage the development of many diseases and competitor moulds. These diseases may be incited by both pathogenic and non pathogenic agents. Pathogenic diseases are incited by fungi, bacteria, viruses and nematodes

FUNGAL DISEASES OF BUTTON MUSHROOMS

Dry Bubble
Symptoms
The disease is characterized by the deformation of the young mushrooms and the formation of muddy brown and sunken spots on the cap of the mushroom. A grayish white mouldy growth may be seen on the pileus resulting in a dryness and leathery appearance of the mushroom. Some mushrooms attacked during the early stage never develop beyond a small dry bubble like form.

The causal agent
This disease is caused by different species of *Verticillium* chiefly *Verticillium malthousei, Verticillium psalliotae* and *Verticillium fungicola*.

Etiology

The fungus is known to be found in soil. It produces one celled, thin walled, oblong to cylindrical hyaline conidia, measuring 3.5 – 15.9 m× 1.5 – 5min size. Conidiophores are slender and tall. Conidia accumulate in clusters and are surrounded by sticky mucilage.

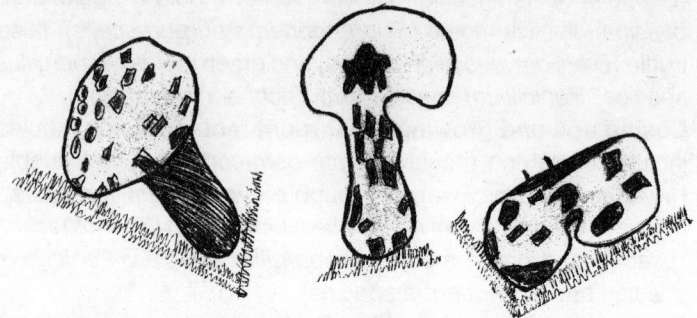

Fig. 16.1 Showing mushrooms infected from *Verticillium* species.

Disease cycle

The debris and dust on the floors of growing houses are the important source of infection. The spread of the fungus takes place by means of water splashes on the neighboring healthy mushrooms and by flies to mushroom of long distances. *Verticillium* the species are carried onto the mushroom farm by infected casing soil and spread is also carried out by infected equipments and flies.

Management

1. Maintain proper temperature, ventilation and humidity as this disease is favoured by temperature above 23 C°, poor ventilation and high humidity.
2. The diseased mushrooms should be picked carefully and destroyed so as to prevent the diseases to spread.
3. Perfect sanitary conditions should be maintained in growing houses and when the disease appears, the temperature should be lowered to below 28 C°.

False Truffle
Symptoms

The disease is characterized by the appearance of cottony-weft of mycelium on the bed surface. These wefts soon become denser and develop into small, reddish brown and wrinkled stromatic bodies resembling a truffle. The infected beds usually have a peculiar disagreeable odour. The yield of the mushroom crop is reduced significantly.

The causal agent

This disease is caused by the fungal species *Diehliomyces microsporus*. Sometimes, it is considered as competitor and not the pathogenic fungus to the mushroom. It was first reported by Lambert (1930) from Ohio, USA.

Etiology

Ascocarps are formed from the dense tangled hyphal knots. These are fleshy, first white then brownish and finally reddish brown with 3–8 ascospores. Chlamydospores may also be formed in the hyphal web of ascocarp.

Disease cycle

The spores of the causal fungus is usually introduced in the mushroom houses through casing soil.

Management

Soil used should be well sterilized. After casing, excessive moisture in bed, temperature above 20 C°, poor ventilation and high humidity should be avoided. Proper temperature, moisture, ventilation and humidity should be maintained in cropping houses.

Cobweb Disease or Mildew
Symptoms

A white silky growth usually grows over the surface of the casing soil. It sometimes climbs up and covers some mushroom in its pith. The older mycelium of the pathogen changes from silky to granular white. The infected mushrooms become discoloured and soft. Later on, such diseased mushrooms are engulfed in a cottony ball of mycelium. The disease is serious where year round cropping is practiced.

The causal agent

This damaging disease is caused by *Dactylium dendroides*. It is the imperfect stage of *Hypomyces rosellus*. Sterile hyphae form a turf and are branched, septate and hyaline Conidia are 2-3 septate.

Disease cycle

Infected casing soil is the most important source of this disease. High relative humidity and temperature encourage the disease.

The pathogen is soil inhabiting and mode of spread is by means of conidia through movement, tools and workers.

Management

Proper sterilization of casing soil is significantly important. As soon as the disease spots are located, complete soil related with infected spots should be removed and destroyed. Other hygienic conditions should be maintained to prevent the spread of the disease.

Wet bubble Symptoms

The disease was first described from Paris in 1888 and now occurs in France, England and USA. When the infection, takes place before the differentiation of the stipe and pileus, there are thickening of stipes and deformation of gills. White mouldy growth on the mushrooms may be commonly observed, resulting in putrifaction with a golden brown liquid exudate. It gives foul odour. Young pin heads if infected may exhibit cytological changes as a result of infection. The disease is also known as white mould, bubble, La mole and mycogone disease.

Causal agent

Mycogen perniciosa. The perfect stage of this fungus is *Hypomyces perniciosa.*

Etiology

Mycelium of the pathogen is white, compact and felt-like. Hyphae are branched, interwoven, septate, hyaline and measure 3–5 nm broad. Conidiophores short, slender, branched, hyaline and measure 200 × 3.5 nm in size. Conidiophores bear conidia that are thin walled, single celled and measure 5–10 × 4–5 nm in size. Large two celled chlamydospores are also observed.

Disease cycle

The disease is known to spread through casing soil, spent compost and many other agencies. The infection of the pathogen may be air borne, water borne and also through flies and mites. Chlamydospores found in casing soil serve as primary source of inoculum. It may survive upto 3 years in the soil.

Management

(1) Benomyl spray at the rate of 0.5 – 4g per square meter immediately after casing has been reported to be very effective for protecting the crop.

(2) Aerated steam at 54.4C° for 15 minutes can eliminate the pathogen from casing soil.

(3) Use of plastic pots to cover mushroom showing wet bubble symptoms during the cropping season should be done to prevent spread of disease.

Weed Fungi and Competitor Moulds

Moulds acting both as competitors and pathogenic fungi are undesirable for proper growth and development of mushroom. They adversely affect the quality and yield to such a great extent that sometimes complete failure of the crop may be observed. *Competitor moulds, also known as weed moulds or indicator moulds are those fungi which adversely affect the growth of the mushroom mycelium during the spawn rum (colonization) on the substrate/compost/casing soil.* They compete with the mushroom for nutrition, oxygen, water and space. As a result of such competition, the mushroom growth is checked and in some cases there is no growth at all. A partial list of important competitor moulds along with the symptoms and methods of management have been given as under.

Table 16.1

Showing symptoms and management of different diseases produced by the competitor moulds.

Name of the diseases	Causal fungi	Symptoms	Management
1. Brown plaster	*Populospora bysinna.*	1. White patches on the casing. 2. Compost usually turning to rust colour.	1. Regulate moisture content of compost. 2. Treat patches with formalin (2%) and 3. Spray-Bavistin (0.05%).
2. White-plaster moulds	*Scopulariosis fimicola.*	1. Dense white patches of mycelium on casing soil. 2. Flour like appearance.	Adjust compost pH to 8 and spray Bavistin (0.05%).
3. Inky-cap moulds	*Coprinus altramentarius, C. lagopus, C. comatus* and *C. fimetarius.*	1. Rapid appearance of long slender stalks and thin caps. 2. Stalks and thin caps disintegrate into black slimy mass of spores.	Adjust compost pH to 8 and spray Bavistin (0.05%)

264

4. Olive-green moulds	*Chaetomium olivaceum* and *C. globosum.*	1. Greyish white appearance of mycelium on the compost. 2. It changes later into olive green.	1. Proper pasteurization during peak heating. 2. Spray Bavistin (0.05%).
5. Yellow-moulds	*Myceliphthora lutea* (mat-disease*)*, *Chrysosporium merdarium* and *Sepedonium chrysospermum.*	Brown yellow patches with white fluffy edge generally on bottom beds.	1. Maintain hygienic conditions. 2. Pasteurization should be done properly. 3. Correct moisture content.
6. Lipstick-moulds	*Sporendonema purpurascens.*	1. White crystal like colonies. 2. White grey mouldy fluff with little white balls on straw. 3. Colour changes to cherry red on spore formation.	1. Maintain hygienic conditions. 2. Do proper pasteurization. 3. Correct moisture content.
7. False-truffle	*Diehlimyces microsporus.*	1. White fluffy mycelium later turning to creamy yellow in colour. 2. Thick solid wrinkled mass resembling brain like structures.	1. Lower the temperature. 2. Maintain good hygienic conditions. 3. Destroy infected beds.
8. Green-moulds	*Aspergillus* species *Penicillium* species and *Tricherma* species.	1. Small blue green cushions on spawned and cased tray. 2. Caps turn brown.	1. Good pasteurization of compost. 2. Remove dead mushrooms. 3. Spray Bavistin (0.05%).
9 Black and grey whisker moulds	*Doratomyces stemonitis.*	Mycelium dark and forms black or grey bristles.	1. Proper fermentation. 2. Peak heating and 3.Maintain hygienic conditions.
10. Cinnamon moulds	*Peziza ostracoderma.*	1. Round white mycelium patches are formed on casing layer. 2. Turning yellow brown with thick fluffy white edge. 3. Brown fruit bodies.	1. Maintain relative humidity after casing to 95%. 2. Use recommended quantity of formalin.
11. White mould	*Cephalothecium roseum.*	White mouldy growth turns pink in due course in compost or casing soil.	Spray Bavistin (0.05%) at 7–10 days intervals.

Source - Adapted from training manual of NRCM, Solan (H.P.)

Weed mushrooms

Weed mushrooms usually appear when the compost is under preparation. These may come up as the spots and may escape through composting. The most common weed mushroom - *Coprinus cinercus* has a long and scaly buttons. It is not a serious menace as it does not harm the crop if proper care is taken to avoid it. Besides these competitor moulds, pathogenic fungi and weed mushrooms, there are other agents also that cause diseases of different descreptions. Some important abnormalities may be summarized as under:

Physiological diseases

In addition to biotic agents which adversely affect the mushrooms, there are a large number of abiotic agents which create unfavorable environment for the proper growth of mushrooms, resulting in the quantitative as well as qualitative loss. These abiotic agents include low or high moisture in the substrate, unusual pH, low or high temperature, low or high CO_2 concentration in the room, wind velocity, fumes and unsuitable relative humidity. Many of these agents make the substrate non-selective for mushroom mycelium and encourage other moulds and pests while some interfere with the normal mushroom production. As compared to white button mushroom, there are few physiological disorders recorded in oyster mushrooms. Reduced light in the cropping room results in longer and thicker stipes and pileus. Insufficient ventilation (1–2% carbon dioxide) and low light exposure induce bunched growth regeneration. Management of environment is of great significance in mushroom cultivation and any deviation from the optimum requirements may lead to various kinds of abnormalities.

Since a major proportion of button mushroom is being produced under natural climatic conditions in India, the following abiotic disorders are quite frequently observed.

Rose Comb Disease

Symptoms

The disease is characterized by the malformed mushroom along with distortion of pileus and formation of lamellae on the upper surface of the pileus. Such mushrooms are referred as "Morchelloid mushrooms". Large lumps and swelling may be visible on the

Fig. 16.2 Showing morphological abnormality in mushroom with characteristic rose comb.

mushroom cap. The gills often grow on the top of the cap tissue. These abnormal gills make the swellings and look spongy in appearance. The mushrooms can even burst or split and then turn brown.

The causal agent

The damage is caused by the smoke from burning oil or coal. When mushroom primordial come in contact with smoke from fire, the stipes become bulky and the growth of the pileus is retarded. The abnormality is also caused by gases or vapors coming from solvents, paint or oil products and polluted casing soil.

Management

Avoid smoke resulted from burning oil and coal.

Stoma and Sectoring Diseases
Symptoms

Stroma is noticeable aggregation of mushroom mycelium developed over the surface of spawned compost or on the casing soil. Discrete aerial patches of white mycelium form a dense tissue layer on the substrate surface. Stroma can be easily peeled from the surface layer of the compost or casing. Stroma formed on the compost surface may be small and localized. Later on, the small patches can coalesce with each other covering larger areas of the surface. Mushroom can develop on stroma but ramains somewhat unusual in appearance. A sector is that portion of spawn which is distinctive when compared with normal appearance of spawn. It may be extra white, extra dense or extra fluffy and is always different from the normal spawn. Sectors appear on or in the compost and on the casing. These usually trend to disappear as the crop grows. A few sectors will not affect yield adversely but the presence of excessive stroma may reduce yield.

The causal agents

Stroma or sectors are related to the genetic character of the spawn but are sometimes induced if spawn is mishandled or exposed to harmful petroleum based fumes or chemicals or certain detergents during preparation, storage and transit. Excessive carbon dioxide and prolonged spawn run period also results in stroma formation.

Management

Large patches of stroma should be removed from the compost or casing surfaces. Next growth of the spawn may be expected to be normal.

Flock, Hard Cap and Open Veil
Symptoms

The cap opens pre-maturely and the gills of the affected mushrooms are rudimentary and poorly developed having little

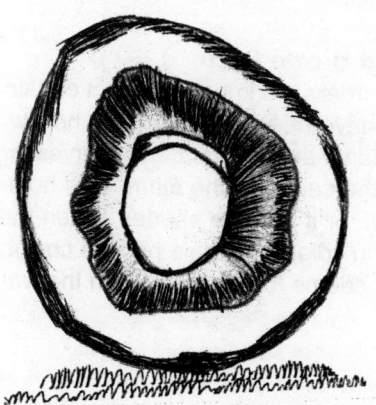

Fig. 16.3 Showing abnormality in mushroom—characteristic open veil.

pigmentation. The flocked mushrooms generally appear in first flush and may disappear in subsequent flushes but in some cases it continues increasing in subsequent flushes. Hard cap means the loss of harvestable mushrooms. Hard cap is a variation of flock syndrome. In hard cap, caps and gills tend to be disproportionately small in relation to stem diameter. Hard cap mushrooms are restricted to a limited area on the casing but at times 30% areas may produce hard caps.

The cause of the disease

The mechanism that causes the mushrooms to be flocked is genetic and certain strains have greater tendency to develop this abnormality. Environmental conditions including diesel exhaust, oil-based point fumes and certain anticorrosive chemicals in steam boilers or certain diseases like dieback, brown plaster mould and false truffle induce flock symptoms. Open veil is the premature opening of veil with abnormal gills development. Open veil sometimes occurs when a period of water stress of 1 to 3 days is followed by a generous watering. It also occurs when fumes of certain organic chemicals drift into or are released in a growing room.

Management

Overall, if open veil appears, it is safe to conclude that the mushroom had been under stress during its development. This abnormality is of common occurrence in Himanchal Pradesh and Haryana especially during the termination of the crop or under high temperature conditions.

Hollow Core and Brown Pitch

These two disorders are known to affect certain strains. Usually off-white strains have been found to have hollow core. When the bottoms of the stems are trimmed after harvesting, a circular gap may be seen in the centre of the stem. This hole may extend the length of the stipe or it may be shorter. When the hollow cut end portion is brown in colour, the sale price is considerably reduced. This abnormality seems to be related with the watering and water stress.

Purple Stem

The disease is also called as black leg disease. Cut stems of the mushrooms develop a deep purple colour within few hours of harvest or after being in cold storage overnight. At times, colour is closer to black than purple and it occurs in all strains including smooth white, off-white, cream and brown strains. Generally, mushrooms from 3rd break to the end of the crop are most susceptible. Polyphenol oxidase which is an enzyme is known to influence such pigment formation. Conditions that predispose mushrooms to this phenomenon are unknown but the frequency and amount of water applied before harvest seems to affect its occurrence.

Scales or Crocodiles

Scales arise through the surface tissue failing to grow while the cap develops further. The main reason for scales formation is improper climatic control. Strong vapors of formaldehyde or pest-control products in excess can also cause the outer layer of the skin of half-grown mushrooms to tear off. As the mushroom continues to grow, the skin bursts and so-called 'crocodile skin' is formed. The off white and cream mushroom strains are more sensitive to such scales formation than white mushrooms.

Long Stemmed Mushrooms

The presence of long strems in combination with a number of other symptoms can be the indication of virus diseases. Practically, it is not the virus disease and is often the result of too high CO_2 concentration. With the improvement of aeration such conditions can be avoided.

BACTERIAL DISEASES OF MUSHROOMS

Bacteria are among those micro-organisms which are having the size in the range of microns and can not be seen by naked eyes. First time in 1876, Koch proved that bacteria can cause diseases as observed by him through a series of experiments. T.J. Burrill in 1878, first time proved the association of a bacterium with a plant disease. Bacteria have been defined "*as being extremely microscopic, unicellular organisms usually rigid in structure without chlorophyll but rarely containing other photosynthetic pigments. They multiply mostly by fission although a few may reproduce sexually. They are characterized by not having a readily demonstrable nucleus*". There are four important diseases in winter button mushroom which are induced by bacteria. Only one disease is known to occur in summer button mushroom which is suspected to be of bacterial in nature and etiology.

Bacterial diseases of Button Mushroom
There are five important bacterial diseases of button mushroom. These are as under:
1. Bacterial blotch or brown blotch (*Pseudomonas tolaasii*).
2. Ginger blotch (*Pseudomonas gingeri*).
3. Mummy disease (*Pseudomonas* species)
4. Drippy gall (*Pseudomonas agarici* or *Pseudomonas cichorii*).
5. Pit disease.

1. Bacterial Blotch
Bacterial blotch in mushroom was described for the first time by Tolaas from America in 1915. Paine (1919) in England named the bacterium after Tolaas together with other *Pseudomonas*. This disease has also been reported from India in 1976. An extra cellular toxin "tolaasin" was found responsible for this disease. The toxin is an ion channel farming lipo peptide having bio-surfactant property. It involves five protein encoded by five loci. This disease was studied well by Fletcher *et al.* (1986).

Symptoms
1. When mushrooms remain moist for longer time, yellowish-brown patches or blotches occur initially which in serious cases usually turn dark brown in colour.
2. Gradually, these patches spread over the whole surface of the mushroom cap.
3. Brown pits can also sometimes be observed in such mushrooms.
4. Mushrooms with bacterial blotch seem sticky.
5. In serious attacks, the pin heads can turn completely brown and they do not develop further.

The causal pathogen
The disease is caused by *Pseudomonas tolaasii*. It has been observed that persistent moisture on sporophore for more than three hours after watering usually encourage the symptoms development. High relative humidity with low evaporation rate also favours the development of the symptoms.

Table 16.2
Showing different bacterial diseases of mushrooms with their causal pathogens and distribution.

Mushroom host	Name of the disease	Causal pathogen	Distribution
1. *Agaricus bisporus*	Bacterial blotch	*Pseudomonas fluorescens, Pseudomonas tolaasii*	World wide
2. *Agaricus bisporus*	Mummy	*Pseudomonas species*	U.K. and U.S.A.
3. *Agaricus bisporus*	Ginger blotch	*Pseudomonas_ gingeri*	Netherlands and U.K.
4. *Agaricus bisporus*	Drippy gall	*Pseudomonas agaricii* and *Pseudomonas_ cichorii.*	Netherlands and U.K.
5. *Agaricus bitorquis*	Soft rot	*Pseudomonas gladioli* pv *agaricola*	U.K.
6. *Pleurotus* species	Brown blotch	*Pseudomonas_ gingeri*	Japan, Australia, Netherlands, Belgium, Italy and Europe.
7. *Pleurotus* species	Yellowing	*Pseudomonas alcaligen* and *Pseudomonas agarici*	India and U.S.A.
8. *Pleurotus* species	First shaped fruit bodies	*Pseudomonas floorescens*	Belgium, Italy and India
9. *Volvariella* species	Bacterial rot	*Pseudomonas species*	India and Indonesia
10. *Lentinus edodes*	Immature browning	*Pseudomonas floorescens*	Japan
	Malformation	RLO	Japan
11. *Flammulina Velutipes*	Brown soft rot	*Erwinia species*	Japan and India

The disease cycle

The pathogen usually seems to be endemic at many mushroom farms. It survives probably between crops on surfaces, in debris, in tools and on various materials of the farms.

Management

1. Store all casing materials in an area free from contamination before and after mixing it. Also avoid surface condensation on developing mushroom.
2. When the disease has established, removal of all affected mushrooms is desirable. Also ensure preventive measures to check disease spread. Pasteurization of casing soils by steam/air mixture and short wave length radiation have been reported to be effective. However, over heating should be avoided.
3. Spray suitable bactericide such as streptomycin for the control of the disease. Application by terramycin 9 mg per square foot, streptomycin (200 ppm), oxytetracycline (300 ppm) have been found effetive in managing the disease.
4. Spraying of Zinc salt has been found to be effective in controlling the disease.
5. Adjust the conditions within the cropping house so that whenever possible, evaporation may take place from the surface of the developing mushrooms.
6. Biological control should be explored with antagonists like *Pseudomonas fluorescens* and bacteriophages.
7. Management of *Aphelenchoides composticola* (nematode) infection is also important as it helps in spreading the disease.
8. In some countries, a software system has been developed to manage the disease.

2. Ginger Blotch

This disease is closely related with bacterial blotch caused by *Pseudomonas tolaasii*. This disease is most commonly observed in England and Netherlands (Fletcher *et al.*, 1986).

Symptoms

The ginger colour of blotches which do not change with the advancement of age, distinguishes this disease from bacterial brown blotch. The blotches are not deeper than 1–2 millimeters. Unlike *Pseudamonas tolaasii*, *Pseudomonas gingeri* does not give a positive reaction in the white line test.

The causal pathogen

The disease is caused by the bacterium—*Pseudomonas gingeri*. The ecology and epidemiology of the disease is similar to that of bacterial brown blotch.

Disease cycle

The contaminated casing material is probably the most important primary source of the disease.

Management

Control measures are similar to those recommended for bacterial blotch.

3. Mummy Disease

This disease was first reported by Tucker and Routein in 1942. It is known to be very popular in U.K. as reported by Wuest and Zarkower, 1991. Royse (1980) using what he called the 'mummy bacterium' demonstrated the intracellular growth of the bacterium in artificially infected mushroom by electron microscopy. It has been found very difficult to induce artificial infection producing same symptoms with bacterium isolated from mummy-diseased tissues.

Fig. 16.4 Showing mushrooms with characteristics mummy disease.

Symptoms

1. During spawn run no symptoms of infection are noticeable. But after casing, the spread of spawn and development of pin heads are observed in patches.
2. The pin heads which have not emerged may remain stuck in the casing soil.
3. The fruit bodies can turn grayish in colour and open prematurely.
4. In second flush, the stipe becomes crooked and caps tilt.
5. The stem is often thickened at the base and the base is usually surrounded by a fluffy edge of mycelium.
6. The mushrooms become tough and spongy or leathery dry

(mummy) and they change in colour from grayish white to brown.

7. At pickings, a cracking sound is heard.
8. When the stem is cut through, cut surface seems reddish brown.
9. Under some situations, very fast spread of the disease has been reported.

The causal pathogen

The disease is caused by *Pseudomonas aeruginosa*.

Disease cycle

The spread of the disease is through infected mushroom mycelium and not through spores. The disease has been reported by placing of compost or casing material from diseased beds to healthy compost at the time of spawn running.

Control

Observe and select affected boxes or areas of beds by digging 20 centimeters wide channel and treat them with 0.5% formalin. Strict hygienic measures should be followed.

4. Drippy Gall Disease

The disease is observed to be most severe in autumn and winter months. Fletcher *et al* (1986). Studied the discase in detail. It is known to occur in U.K. and Netherland in severe form.

Symptoms

Gills are attacked by the bacterium before the veil of the mushroom is open. Affected gills are often under developed. Underdeveloped affected gills exhibit small, brown and decaying areas with creamy white bacterial ooze on them. Hence the name drippy gall has been given.

The causal pathogen

This disease is reported to be caused by *Pseudomonas agaricii* and *Pseudomonas cichorii*.

Disease cycle

Probably flies, pickers and water splashes are helpful for spreading the disease within the crop. As the gills are attacked before veil breaks, it seems that the bacteria are systemic.

Management

Spray suitable insecticide to control the flies and follow strict hygienic precautions to avoid infection and spread of the disease.

Fig. 16.5 Showing diseased mushroom-bacterial pit.

5. Pit Disease

This disease is fairly common but rarely causes considerable crop losses. The cause of the disease is not yet established but is suspected to be a bacterium. Mites and nematodes have also been implicated.

Symptoms

Small dark (often black) and slimy pits appear on the cap surface. The depth of pit may be few millimeters deep and their numbers may range from 1 to 10 per cap. Pits are generally seen in 3rd or 4th flush.

Management

Same control measures as recommended for bacterial blotch should be used to reduce the incidence and spread of the disease.

BACTERIAL DISEASES OF OYSTER MUSHROOM

Several bacterial diseases have been reported on *Pleurotus ostreatus, Pleurotus sajor-caju* and *Pleurotus eryngii.* Such bacterial diseases are known to be caused by *Pseudomonas tolaasii, Pseudomonas agarici, Pseudomonas fluorescens* including some unidentified bacteria and some other species of *Pseudomonas.* Different symptoms induced by the bacterial pathogens are brown blotch, black spotting, yellowing and mottling of fruit bodies. However, very little work has been done on bacterial diseases of oyster mushroom in our country. Some very common diseases reported in India are as under:

Four bacterial pathogens, namely, *Pseudomonus alcaligens, P. tolaasii, P. agrici* and *P. fluorescens* have been reported to parasitize *Pleurotus* fruiting bodies. Among these, *P. agarici* and *P. alcaligens* have been reported from India.

1. Bacterial Rot Disease

This disease was first reported from West Bengal on *Pleurotus sajor-caju* in India.

Symptoms

It induces appearance of water-soaked areas and yellow brown discoloration on young sporophores. Rotting of grown up fruit bodies, starts from the centre towards periphery. The gills on the lower surface usually turn yellow and caps get crinkled and rolled upward.

The causal pathogen

The bacterium - *Pseudomonas alcaligens* causes this disease. It produces whitish effused growth on PDA medium.

Management

Follow strict hygienic precautions and spray suitable bactericide well in time for the management of the disease.

2. Brown Spot Disease

A common substrate competitor bacterium - *Pseudomonas stutzeri* has been reported from Karnataka on paddy straw substrate used for cultivating *Pleurotus sajor-caju.* The bacterium, being a common soil saprophyte, induces brown spots in the substrate. It causes a reduction in the yield of *Pleurotus sajor-caju.* Streptocycline dip beyond 100 ppm and formalin dip beyond 25 ppm controlled the competitor bacterium as reported.

3. Yellow Blotch disease

This disease has recently been reported on *Pleurotus sajor-caju*. The incidence of the disease has been reported from 42 to 89% during 1989–93. In and around Solan, it causes complete crop failure in some cases.

Symptoms

The disease appears on pileus as blotches of varying sizes which are sometimes depressed and yellow, hazel-brown or orange in colour. When disease appears during primordial formation, entire flush may be affected. The infected fruit bodies rot and emit foul smell under high temperature and humid conditions. The slimy appearance on infected fruit bodies is the characteristic symptom of the disease.

The causal pathogen

The pathogen has been identified as *Pseudomonas agarici*.

Epidemiology

The disease incidence is high under warm and humid conditions. The pathogen usually spread through water splashes, workers, tools and mushroom flies. When the humidity is above 90%, the fruit bodies gave slimy appearance that may result in rotting of fruit bodies with foul smell.

Management

Oxytetracycline, streptocycline and sodium hypochlorite (400 ppm each) have been reported to be effective for the management of the disease.

VIRUS DISEASES OF CULTIVATED MUSHROOMS

A virus disease in cultivated mushroom (*Agaricus bisporus*) later having various names including 'La France disease' and 'die-back disease', was first reported in 1948 in the United States of America. In 1957, devastating crop losses occurred in Britain due to a similar disease. It was demonstrated by the experiments that three types of virus particles were associated with the disease under investigation. The disease was named as 'Die-back disease' to distinguish it from any other possible disorder. Disorders of this type were not reported in the Netherlands until 1994. After few years, a heavy outbreak occurred causing significant losses in yield;

278

Fig. 16.3 (a) Showing cultivated mushroom infected by watery stipe
disease known to be causes by virus.

therefore, serious attempts were made to investigate these diseases
incited by viruses. *Viruses are obligatory parasitic pathogens with
dimension of less than 200 millimicrons. Being ultramicroscopic,
they are infective entities that multiply only intracellularly in the
form of nucleic acid and are potentially pathogenic. Viruses act as
living organism in the host plant tissue and behave as non living
molecule/chemical outside the host plant.*

In Australia, mushroom diseases of viral nature, probably dated
back to the early days of mushroom growing were reported. From
India, spherical virus particles associated with *Agaricus bisporus*,
measuring 25 nm and 35 nm in diameter have also been reported
years back.

VIRUSES AND VIRUS LIKE PARTICLES (VLP)

Virus and VLPs have been commonly observed in *Agaricus
bisporus*. There are few reports of virus particles found associated

Table 16.3
Showing viruses and virus like particles found associated with different diseases and mushroom hosts.

Name of the disease	Shape of the viruses	Size of the virus particles	Distribution
Host - *Agaricus bisporus*			
1. La France	Spherical	25 nm in diameter	Australia
2. Watery stipe	Spherical	29 nm in diameter	England
3. X-disease	Spherical	35 nm in diameter	Holland
4. Die -back	Spherical	40 –50 nm in diameter	France, U.S.A. and India.
	Bacilliform	18×50 nm	U.K.
	Club shaped	60–70 nm in diameter	France
		or 120–170 nm in length	West Germany
		with a spherical body of 40–50 nm and a cylindrical tail of 20–30 nm in diameter.	South Africa
	Rods of varying length	19×9 –90 nm	Poland
		19–35 nm	German Democratic republic.
		20–130 nm	China
Host -*Pleurotus* species			
Pleurotus colombinus	Spherical	26 ± 2 nm in diameter	France
Pleurotus ostreatus	Spherical	24 nm in diameter	China
Pleurotus pulmonarius	Spherical	24 nm in diameter	China
Pleurotus sapidus	Flexuous rods	40×600 nm in length	China
Pleurotus florida	Flexuous rods	40×600 nm in length	China
Host-*Volvariella volvacea*	Spherical	35 nm	China
Host - *Lentinus edodes*	Spherical	20 nm 23 nm 36 nm 45 nm 30 nm	Japan
	Flexuous rods	17×200×1200 nm 15×700–900 nm 18×1500 nm 15×16×300 nm	China

Source : Adapted from training manual of NRCM, Solan (H.P.)

with *Pleurotus* species and *Lentinus edodes*. Different shapes and sizes of the viruses and VLPs have been reported from different parts of the world. A partial lists of such viruses and virus like particles have been summarized in the table 16.3.

DETECTION AND MANAGEMENT OF VIRUSES

Viruses produce different kinds of symptoms on different parts of the mushroom, resulting in deterioration of the mushroom quality and yield of the produce. The wide variations in the symptomatology of diseases caused by viruses usually reflect variations in the economic impact of mushrooms. General symptoms produced by the viruses may be summarized as under:

Symptoms
   The general symptoms produced by the viruses on different parts of the mushrooms have been given below:
1. Mushrooms appear only in dense clusters. Mycelium does not develop properly or develops hardly in the casing layer and sometimes disappears after normal spread.
2. Mycelium isolated from diseased sporophores in agar media show a slow and degenerated growth.
3. Delayed appearance of the pinheads during the first flush or formation of fruiting primordial below the surface of casing layer may be an important indication of the disease incited by viruses.
4. Symptoms on sporophores are highly variable. These variations may show following abnormalities as listed below:
   - Off-white colour of the caps and early maturity.
   - Slow development of pin heads and dwarfing.
   - Elongated and slightly bent stipes are formed. These stipes are thin.
   - Mushrooms are loosely attached to the substrate and at the slightest touch they are pushed over.
   - Watery stipes and streaking in the stipes are observed. Stipes are spongy and they quickly turn brown on wetting. Thickened and barrel shaped stipes may be formed. Pileus may remain small and under developed.
   - Brown and slimy caps may occur owing to a secondary bacterial rot.

- Abnormal or absent veils with hard gills may be observed.
- A specific and musty smell in diseased mushrooms may be found.

Epidemiology of Virus Diseases

Various factors like time of infection, cultural conditions and strain of the spawn used, greatly affect the incidence and loss in yield. The viruses usually infect the mushroom spores and the mycelium. The spread of viruses through infected spores or mycelium can spread the diseases in a number of ways such as via air flow through ventilation, through flies, through dirty containers, by means of transport which have not been disinfected and also by persons with dirty clothing and footwear etc. Disease spread may also be due to poor disinfection of wooden furniture, floor, walls and/or side planks after harvesting.

Infected spores of mushrooms on germination, produce infected mycelium which by means of anastomosis transmits the virus to healthy spawn/mycelium. Viruses are also known to be transmitted through mites and fungi.

Difficulties in detection of viruses

Diagnosis of virus infection in mushrooms is difficult because of the following reasons.

1. Symptoms induced by viruses are similar to the symptoms produced by the different biotic and abiotic agents. Such as elongation of stipe incited by virus infection may be similar to the symptoms incited by concentration of high carbon dioxide. Water-logging of the stipe tissue is usually incited by virus infection, however, it may also be induced by higher moisture conditions. Loss in yield and bare patches may be induced by a number of factors.
2. The second difficulty in detection of virus is due to its low concentration in host mushroom.

Detection methods

1. Electron microscopy through ultra-thin sectioning, dip method as well as through purified preparations.
2. Serologically specific election microscopy (SSEM).
3. Poly-acryl amide gel electrophoresis of viral ds RNA (PAGE).
4. Enzyme linked immuno-sorbent assay (ELISA).

Management of suspected virus related problems

Virus related problems should be managed in following methods. In case the disease is not present in the mushroom house, following precautions should be taken.

When the disease is not present

1. Steam the compost for 12 hours at a temperature of 70 C°. At emptying, take away the compost quickly.
2. Spray the wood with 2% sodium penta-chloro-phenate to which 0.5–1.0% sodium carbonate has been added. After drying, spray and wash with water.
3. Disinfect doors, little holes in the floor, shutters, racks, floors and walls with formaldehyde solution. Also clean the manure yard and adjacent patches of ground with formaldehyde.
4. Before filling, fit spore filters. During growing time these spore filters should be replaced once or twice according to the amount of dust in the air. Use a fan for extracting air.
5. Immediately after spawning, use a suitable pesticide against flies then cover the compost with paper. Keep the paper moist. Wet the paper twice a week with 2% solution of the 40% commercial formaldehyde. Never use sodium penta-chloro-phenate here. Moisten the paper before removing it carefully. The entire farm and its surroundings should be kept very clean and maintained. In the working corridor, formaldehyde should be sprayed. Machines, refrigerators and other utilities should he disinfected with formaldehyde solution. Cuttings etc. should be removed and destroyed immediately.
6. Diseases can be controlled best by immediately steaming out the concerned room and materials as soon as the first contamination is detected.

When the disease is already present

1. Steam the compost for 12 hours at a temperature of 70 C°. At emptying, take away the compost quickly.
2. Immerse the wood in a 4% sodium penta-chloro-phenate solution to which 0.5%–1% sodium carbonate has been added.
3. Disinfect doors, little holes in the floor, shutters, racks, floors and walls with formaldehyde solution. Also clean the manure yard and adjacent patches of ground with formaldehyde.

4. Spore filters should be replaced once or twice according to the amount of dust in the air. Use a fan for extracting air.

5. Pick the mushrooms when still closed. First pick from the healthy parts then from the diseased patches. Have a short picking period only (not more than 4 weeks). Often wash hands with antiseptic soap.

6. Keep each room as a separate entity with separate clothes, shoes, steps, buckets, picking knives, picking racks and fans etc. Kill off diseased patches with salt and cover with plastic. Make the limits of the different patches.

7. Admit no visitors in the diseased rooms and keep the door towards the working corridors closed.

8. Maintain insect-pests and mites free mushroom house by spraying suitable insecticide at suitable time. Do not change over to brown strains of spawn too quickly.

Chapter 17

Insect-pests and Nematodes

> *Common insect-pests of mushroom, flies as insect - pests, management and control of flies; springtails as insect-pests and their management; beetles as insect-pests and their management; mushroom mites and their management; nematodes as pests and their management.*

Like the field crops, mushrooms are also attacked by several pests. Insect-pests, mites and nematodes usually cause damage to the mushrooms right from spawning to harvesting of the crop. Sciarid flies, phorid flies, cecid flies, springtails and mites are the important arthropod pests of cultivated mushrooms in India. Mushrooms, being the indoor crop, provide a very suitable habitat for the insect-pests. More over, maintenance of optimum temperature and humidity in the cropping room provides ideal condition for the development and survival of the pests. Therefore, measures should be taken to prevent the entry of insect pests into the cropping room. However, chemical method of control, should be taken as the last step rather than the first.

COMMON INSECT PESTS OF MUSHROOMS

Flies as Insect - Pests
1. Sciarid flies (Diptera: Sciaridae)
Morphology

Sciarid flies are also called as mushroom flies. Mushroom sciarids are small flies, measuring 3–4 mm in length. They are black gnat like flies with long thin antennae which are held characteristically erect.

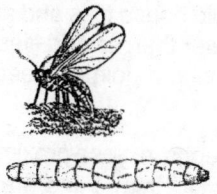

Fig. 17.1 Showiing morphology of mushroom fly and its larva.

Characteristics

Females usually trend to rest on the surface of the walls and trays while males often remain on the surface of the casing. A single female lays about 110 eggs in clusters or single or in chains. Different species of sciarid flies are known to be found through out the year in and around the mushroom farms. Most important species which cause much harm to mushroom crops are *Lycoriella solani, Lycoriella mali, Lycoriella auripila, Bradysia paupera* and *Bradysia tritici.*

Economic importance

The damaging stage of the pest is larva which is white and legless maggot, ranging from 1 mm to 8 mm in length. The larva bears shiny black head. Larvae cause damage by making tunnels in the stipes. They cause most serious injury to pin heads and buttons of the mushrooms. Mycelial attachment can he damaged, causing the pinheads to become brown and leathery. Pinheads may become hollow or may even be consumed entirely. Adults act as vectors of *Verticillium fungicola.*

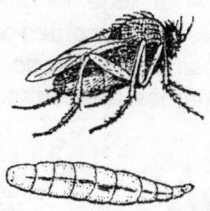

Fig. 17.2 Showing morphology of compost fly (*Megaselia* species) and its larva.

2. Phorid flies (Diptera: Phoridae)
Morphology

Phorid flies have small hump on the back having inconspicuous antennae. They resemble house flies and are brown black in colour. Generally, they are stouter than sciarid flies. The larvae are creamy white legless maggots with a pointed head, which is not black.

Characteristics

Female lays upto 50 eggs in close proximity to the growing hyphal tips of the mushroom mycelium. Flies are attracted to mushroom houses due to the odors resulted from fermentation of the compost during the cool down period of peak heat. After the laying of eggs, new generation of adults emerge from the compost within 2–3 weeks. By this time, crop has been cased and it is the casing layer in which the subsequent generations of these flies develop.

Economic importance

Larvae feed on mushroom tissue and moves upward to the cap forming tunnels. Larvae hatching from the eggs laid on mushroom gills directly bore into the mushroom cap. Larvae hatching from the eggs and laid in spawned compost or casing material make tunnels through the button of mushroom stalks. The colour of the infested mushroom becomes yellow brown when attacked during the pin head stage. Maximum infestation of 11–74% occurs during March– April. The various species of phorid flies are *Megaselia halterata*, *Megaselia nigra* and *Megaselia agarica*.

3 Cecid fly (Diptera: Cecidomyiidae)
Morphology

Cecids are rarely identified from the fly stage because they are so minute to be seen. Larvae are legless maggots either white or orange. They have no discernible heads but there are two eyes-spots at the head ends which together give the appearance of "X. Six species of cecids have been recorded on mushroom throughout the world. Only three namely, *Heteropeza pygmaea*, *Mycophila speyeri* and *Mycophila barnesi* are common in occurrence.

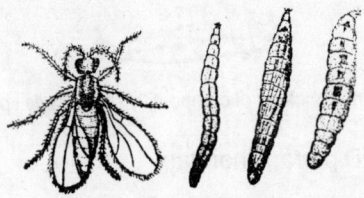

Fig. 17.3 Showing morphological appearance of cecid fly and its larvae.

Characteristics

Larvae, being sticky is usually carried out by trays, tools, shoes and clothes of workers. Reproduction in cecids is through pseudo genesis. Each cecid larva becomes mother larva in due course. It can give birth to 12–20 daughter larvae within a week of its own birth without being any adult cecid present.

Economic importance

Occurrence of a cecid fly species-*Heteropenzina cathistes* has been reported on oyster mushroom from Jind and Chandigarh. Any serious damage by these flies to this mushroom has not been observed so far in India. Initial infestation probably arises from the infested casing soil. Larvae feed on the mycelium. The white or orange larvae are first noticed. During watering, they move on to the mushroom where they feed on the outside of stipes or at the junction of stipe and gills. Bacteria present on the skin of the larvae usually results in brownish stripes on gills. Gill tissues break down to produce tiny pustules with black fluid. They usually cause spoilage of mushrooms upto 50%.

MANAGEMENT AND CONTROL OF FLIES

The flies should be controlled so as to get better crop of mushroom. Both prophylactic and curative measures should be taken at proper time as described below :

Prophylatic Measures
1. *Maintenance of hygiene and sanitation*

Hygiene is very important at every step of mushroom cultivation. The first step in the compost preparation is to clean the composting yard properly and thereafter, the composting yard should be sprayed with 2% formalin about 24 hours earlier of compost preparation. Hygiene and sanitation will check the prevalence of insect pests in the composting yard. Pasteurization of compost kills insect pests at its all stages.

2. *Treatment of compost and casing material*

About 20 ml of Lindane 20 EC after diluting it in water should be mixed into the compost at the time of last turning. If the mushroom flies are present in the mushroom house before casing, then mix thoroughly 15 ml of Lindane 2O EC after dilution in 3–4 liters of water in 100 kg of ready to use casing material before use. Incorporation of any other suitable insecticide in compost and in casing soil may also serve the purpose of controlling the larvae of flies.

3. Screening of doors and other inlets of mushroom house

Mushroom flies are attracted to spawn and mushroom compost due to their odour. During cropping period, the flies enter the mushroom house and breed in the spawned compost and mushroom beds. Since the body size of mushroom flies is too small, they can pass through an ordinary wire screen. Therefore, it becomes imperative to prevent the entry of the flies into the cropping rooms by screening of doors and ventilators with nylon or wire nets of 14–16 mesh/cm. It is effective in checking the entry of the flies into the mushroom house.

4. Poison baiting

If flies are present during the cropping period, various other methods can be employed for the control of adult pests. Poison baiting with baygon diluted in water at the ratio of 1:10 should be used with the addition of little sugar into it. It is also an effective method for controlling adult flies.

5. Light traps

Polythene sheets coated with sticky material and attached with flurescent strip light may be used continuously in each cropping room. It also helps in controlling the adult flies to a great extent.

Curative Measures

Following curative measures should be taken into account for the management of flies:

1. Spraying of non persistent and safe chemicals

Presence of mushroom flies in the mushroom house helps in further built up of the fly population resulting in high infestation of mushrooms. Under such circumstances, the flies should be killed by using non-persistent and comparatively safe chemicals. This can be done by the methods as given below:

- After 7th day of spawning, Malathion (0.01%) should be sprayed on beds.
- Flies can also be controlled by spraying 30 ml of Nuvan 76 EC in fine droplets. After spraying, the mushroom house should be closed for 2 hours. Direct spraying on beds should be

avoided. An interval of 48 hours between spraying and picking of mushrooms must be observed.

- Judicious and need based application of only safer insecticide should be done. However, care should be taken that same insecticide should not be used again and again. Continuous application of same insecticide helps in building of resistance in insects. Therefore, rotation of insecticides should be done at each application.

2. Disposal of spent compost

The spent compost and casing material contains the immature stages of pest, nematodes and mites. Damping of spent compost and casing material in moist and shady places become ideal substratum for fly breeding. Putting spent compost and casing material in manure pit and covering it with 10 centimetres layer of manure helps in checking the fly breeding.

3. Other precautions to be taken

Sticky traps should be used to monitor the number of flies in the spawn running room. Besides, effective screening of doors and ventilators should be arranged. During cropping, pyrethrums may be used to kill the flies. At the end of cropping, suitable cook out temperature should be maintained and all the spent compost should be removed from the farm. In addition to these, strict hygienic conditions should be maintained at the farm and casing ingredients must always be stored and mixed in a clean area.

SPRINGTAILS AS INSECT-PESTS

Springtails mostly cause more serious damage to oyster mushroom because of its preferred host. Seven species of springtails namely, *Lepidocyrtus cyaneus*, *Lepidocyrtus lanuginosus*, *Xenylla mucronata*, *Achorutes armatus*, *Proisotoma minuta*, *Proisotoma simplex* and *Seira iricolor* have been recorded in different parts of the country including H.P., Delhi, Rajasthan and Punjab. They move by jumping and rarely by walking.

Morphology

Springtails are wingless pests and have ground colour with light violet coloured band along the sides of the body. Dark and round scales are observed to be characteristically present all over the body of springtails. Body length including appendage measures about 2.85 millimeters.

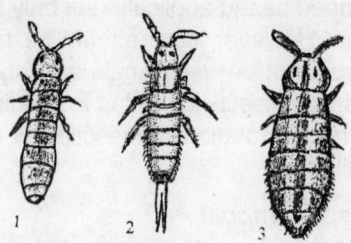

Fig. 17.4 Showing three species of mushroom springtails
(1) *Isotoma* species (2) *Lepidocyrtus cyaneus* and (3) *Achorutes armatus.*

Economic importance

Both the adults and nymphs of springtails, usually feed on mycelium by scraping it from the spawn grains and cutting the mycelial strands there after. They produce shallow pits on the sporophores. Springtails are usually found at the base of the stem, resulting in arrested growth of young primordial showing withered look and small pits.

Management

Springtails are managed by the measures given below:
- Clean properly the surroundings and inside of the mushroom house.
- Proper disposal of spent compost and casing material should be done immediately.
- Raising of the crop above the floor level should be preferred.
- Efficient pasteurization of the compost and timely spraying of the infested place with any suitable insecticide must be done.
- In case the compost is infested by springtails, mixing of 15 ml of diazinon 20 EC after dilution in water should be mixed in 100 kg compost at the time of filling.

BEETLES AS INSECT-PESTS

Three species of beetles have been reported to cause damage to oyster mushrooms. The most common beetles reported are staphylinid beetles from Kerala, cucujoid beetle from Chandigarh and *Alphitobius laevigatus* beetle from Solan.

Morphology
Damaging stage of the beetle is grub which is whitish and long in appearance with tubular terminal segments.

Characteristics
The adults are attracted to the small newly developed mushrooms. They lay eggs in the over-matured pileus and discarded mushroom debris. Grubs feed on the soft gills and crawl over the beds. The life cycle is completed within 3 weeks.

Economic importance
Grubs feed on the softer tissues of the stipes, gills and pileus. At initial stage, grubs make small irregular holes in the hymenium and stipes. In severe cases, adults bore windows in the pileus. Eaten margins of gills and edges of the fruit bodies give a fringed look to the damaged mushroom.

Management
Removal of wastes and debris of the mushrooms from the mushroom house and surrounding areas should be done. It prevents the adults from laying of eggs and thus checking further built up of the population. Over-matured mushroom should be harvested immediately. Bleaching powder usually repels the adults. Its application should be done in mushroom houses and premises to repel the adults.

MUSHROOM MITES AS PESTS

There are more than 54 species of mites which have been reported on mushrooms from various parts of the world. Among these, 16 species have been identified to be economically important in our country. Cultivated mushrooms are generally infested by several groups of mites. The recent advances in mushroom culture, has led the availability of mushrooms throughout the year. Such conditions have resulted in typical ecological atmosphere which is highly conducive for enormous population built up of mites. Maintenance of optimum temperature and humidity inside the mushroom house are favourable for the development of most of the mites.

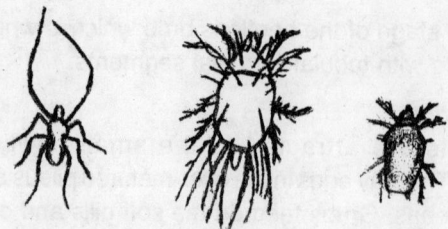

Fig. 17.5 Showing three species of long tailed mites—(1) *Linopodes antennaepes* (2) *Tyroglyphus longior* and (3) *Pigmephorus*.

Morphology

Tyrophagus species of mites are 0.3–0.5 millimeters in length. They are translucent white in colour, having long hair on the body. The symptoms of damage caused by the mites vary with the species.

Characteristics

Mites such as *Tyrophagus* species are capable of their introduction into the compost and cropping rooms through the flies especially the sciarids on whose bodies these mites cling or attach themselves. The migratory stage of mites is produced when the mites become overcrowded. Mites belonging to different groups are known to cause damage in following ways:

1. Mites belonging to Anoetidae usually feed on the tissues already in the state of decay.
2. Mites belonging to Tarsonemidae are also serious pests of mushrooms. They damage stem and caps forming tiny pits on the lower parts of the stipe.
3. Mites belonging to Pyemotidae feed on the mycelial body beneath the casing layer. Their presence on mushroom caps usually devaluate the mushrooms. This mite has also been reported to cause allergic reactions.
4. Mites belonging to Eupididae, cause damage primarily on the root system, resulting in a constriction at the base of the stipe. In severe attack, the mushroom is held to the surface of the bed by only a few withered filaments.

Economic importance

Tyrophagus species of mites belonging to *Tyroglyphidae*, have been reported to damage the mushrooms in Himachal Pradesh and its adjoining states and West Bengal. The initial infestation of mites into mushroom houses comes through raw materials used for the preparation of mushroom beds. *Tyroglyphus dimidiatus* is a major pest of mushroom throughout the world. It is usually found in large numbers in hay, straw, grains and similar materials used for preparing mushroom beds. These mites usually feed on the mycelium and damage sporophores by causing shrunk caps and brown rusted spots on the buttons. They sometimes hollow out tiny buttons while in larger mushrooms they form cavities of various sizes on stalks and caps.

Some of the mites are beneficial to us because they predate on the harmful mites, nematodes and immature stages of different insect pests. Therefore, while initiating the control measures, such beneficial prey mites should be identified and appropriate measures should be taken to save them.

Management
Preventive measures
1. The mites can be controlled by proper pasteurization of compost and casing soil. An efficient cook out (71 C° for 2 hours) and safe disposal of spent compost are essential for controlling mites. Cleaning of the mushroom house and disposal of all organic debris is also important for avoiding saprophytic mites.
2. Disinfest the mushroom house by spraying floor, wall and premises with the solution of suitable disinfectant. Disinfect empty rooms also.
3. Make sure that all the spent compost is removed from the farm.
4. Burning of sulphur in the empty mushroom houses at the rate of 2–3 lbs per 100 cubic feet helps in controlling the mites.
5. Control of mushroom flies by spraying suitable insecticide time to time is essential.
6. Observe strict hygienic conditions throughout the mushroom house and make sure that composting and peak heating are efficient.

Curative measures
If mites are present in the compost, spray the compost with diazinon emulsion at the time of filling. About 1.5–2.0 milliliters of diazinon 20 EC should be used in 10 liters of water for spraying.

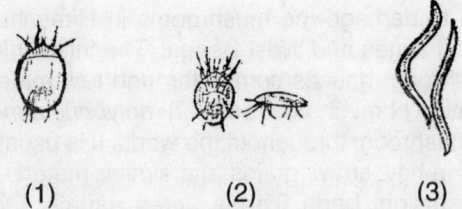

Fig. 17.6 Showing dormant stage of mite-(1) Rhizoglyphus and (2) Histiostoma. (3) shows a common species of the nematode.

Fig. 17.7 Showing differenet species of mites-(1) Rhozoglyphus, (2) Histiostoma and (3) Tarsonemus.

NEMATODES AS PESTS IN MUSHROOMS

A number of nematodes are also encountered in mushroom beds along with insect pests and mites as described earlier. The nematodes are small and microscopic. They belong to the animal kingdom, measuring about 0.2 to 10 millimeters in length. They easily swim in the surface film of water in compost and casing. The mycelium of the fungi including mushroom is the favourable source of food for many species of nematodes. These nematodes may sometimes cause complete failure of the crop.

Morphology

Nematodes are slender, cylindrical, filiform and tapering at each ends. The body of the nematode remains covered with an impermeable cuticle which may be smooth or marked by different types of sculpturing. Beneath the cuticle layer is a sub-cuticle layer followed by the muscular layer. They undergo four mounts from egg to adult and at each stage they cast off the cuticle, getting larger each time. At the anterior end , there is a mouth where a number of papillae or setae are present which act as sensory organs. At the posterior end, there is an anus. After copulation, the body of a female becomes filled with elliptical and hyaline egg in a jelly-like sac. These nematodes are free living and may be present in large numbers.

Mycelio–phagous nematodes have a needle like structure (stylet) in their mouth part with the help of which they puncture the hyphal cell and suck the contents resulting in the destruction of the mycelium. These nematodes have rapid rate of multiplication (50–100 folds a week) hence their infestation with few nematodes may result in the complete failure of crop in later stages. These nematodes multiply at faster rate during spawn run period at temperature ranging from 22 to 28 C°.

Economic importance

Nematodes being one of the most dangerous pests, once enter the crop bed, can not be eradicated without complete destroying the crop. Their presence in the beds usually mean very poor yield or total crop failure. In all twenty one nematode species representing two orders namely, *Aphelenchida* and *Tylenchida* have been found associated with the mushroom cultivation throughout the world. Among these, twenty species belong to four genera- *Aphelenchoides*, *Aphelenchus*, *Paraphelenchus* and *Seinura*. *Ditylenchus* species has been reported to be myceliophagous nematode belonging to Tylenchida. *Aphelenchoides composticola*, *Aphelenchoides sacchari*, *Aphelenchoides saprop ilus* and *Aphelenchoides agrici* have been found to be highly pathogenic.

Saprophytic nematodes have also been recorded from the severely damaged mushroom beds. However, the exact role played by them in interference of mushroom cultivation is not well understood. Pathogenicity of these nematodes have not yet been proved so far. Mouth parts of these nematodes are such that they are unable to puncture the hyphal cell. However, these nematodes are known to create unhygienic conditions in the compost or sometimes these may produce and carry harmful or pathogenic bacteria on their body parts.

Mode of infestation

Nematode contamination in a mushroom farm may occur at any time from composting to cropping. Improperly pasteurized compost and casing soil are known to be the main sources of infestation. Spent compost, unclean wooden trays, dirty spray water and contaminated implements are also the main sources of nematode contamination. Sometimes mushroom flies also carry nematodes in their body parts.

Symptoms

Since the growers remain not in favour to disturb the beds after casing; therefore, the early symptoms resulted from the attack of nematodes are overlooked. Different symptoms appear in nematode infested beds in succession. The mycelial growth is sparse and patchy in appearance. The surface of the compost sinks and mycelium turns stingy. Whiteness of spawn run slowly changes to brown. Pin heads also change to brownish in appearance. Flushes are poor, delayed and alternately high and poor yields are received in successive flushes. Sometimes complete crop failure may be observed.

Management

Prophylatic measures

There is no curative method to control nematodes once these nematodes gain entry into the mushroom beds. Hence, integrated pest management strategies as given below are advised to be followed for management of mushroom nematodes.

1. Maintain strict hygiene and sanitation in mushroom house. Disinfect the composting yard with 4% formalin about 24 hours earlier to compost preparation.
2. Materials used in preparation of compost are the main sources of nematode infestation. The composting ingredients should always be stored in a clean area. Safe disposal of spent compost is also desirable.
3. Disinfection of instruments, walls, floors and galleries with 4% formalin is important. All the rooms should be fly proof. Besides it, proper pasteurization of compost and casing material must be done. Furadan 3G at the rate of 1/2 g per kg of straw and recommended amount of neem cake should be mixed during the final compost turning.
4. The spray water should be clean and treated with bleaching powder (50 ppm). Only recommended insecticides should be used and sprayed in appropriate strength.
5. Growing of *Pleruotus sajor-caju* in rotation with white button mushroom has been found to reduce the population of nematodes.
6. Grow moderately resistant variety/strain K-32 of *Agaricus*

bitorquis where nematode infestation is considerably insignificant.

Curative measures

7. Suitable nematicide like thionazin at the rate of 80 ppm has been recommended for the control of myceliophagous nematodes. However, this nematicide is not yet available in India.

Chapter 18

Post-harvest Handling and Processing

Introduction, short term storage, long term storage, different methods of storage, canning of mushrooms, freeze-drying method; pickling of mushrooms, drying of mushrooms, vacuum cooling method; marketing, difficulties in marketing , suggestions to improve marketing, future prospects in mushroom marketing and packaging of mushrooms.

Mushroom after harvesting, is usually consumed, sold or preserved for consumption or marketing in future. Mushrooms have very short shelf life, therefore, efforts should be made to consume or sell them in fresh state as soon as be possible. The produce should not be exposed to the temperature of more than 10 C° for longer time. Keeping in view the trend of market, produce should be preserved for using and consuming it in various ways. Various methods of preservation of rnushroom have been evolved.

Short term storage
Storage for few days

Fresh mushrooms are usually packed in poly packs of less than 100 gauge thickness. Generally, packs measuring 200 g and 400 g should be made for retail sale. Poly packs should be properly sealed by sealing instrument. In few regions of Northern India, some growers wash the mushrooms in low concentration of potassium meta-bi-sulphite (0.25%) because few buyers insist on such washing of mushrooms before packing them in packs. Although, this practice should not be recommended and if so desired, the concentration of potassium metabisulphite should be reduced to 0.05%. Poly packs so made, should be stored at low temperature (below 5 C°) till they are consumed or sold. These poly packs should not be stored even at this temperature for rnore than 3 days. Higher storage temperature usually results in blackening, cap opening, weight loss and microbial spoilage of mushrooms.

Storage for a month

Steeping preservation is a method useful for short period preservation usually for a month or so. The practice is useful in canneries to accumulate the desired quantity needed for operational efficiency. Cleaning of mushroom is done through washing it in water or in chemical of suitable concentration. Usually low concentration of potassium metabisulphite (0.05%) solution should be used. After such treatment, mushrooms are filled in large plastic containers and brine (10–12%) is added into the cans completely steeping the produce. Some preservatives are also added in the brine by few processors.

Long term storage

In event of the difficulties in the sale of fresh mushroom, long-term preservation methods have been evolved in order to meet the demand of preserved mushrooms. Canning is the most popular method of preserving the mushrooms. Canned produce may be traded in the international market. Asian countries like China, Taiwan and Korea usually export their produce to the American and European countries in the form of canned mushrooms. Besides canning, freeze drying and pickling are also practiced in different countries including India for long term storage of mushrooms. Thus, there are following 5 methods of mushroom preservation. These methods are canning, freeze drying, pickling, drying and vacuum cooling.

Canning of Mushrooms

Canning is the most popular method of preservation of white button mushrooms. Mushrooms are graded according to their size and stems are cut to less than 1 centimeter in size. These are canned as whole mushroom or in the form of sliced mushroom parts. Mushrooms are washed several times and are blanched for 45 minutes in a solution made of 1% brine + 0.1% citric acid. After cooling the blanched mushrooms in running water, these are filled in cans. Cans are then filled with hot brine (1.5 or 2% with citric acid or ascorbic acid as per the customer's requirement) and then passed through steam jacket exhaust box.

Normally cans at the exit of exhaust box have the desired temperature of 85 C° in the centre and there after these are sealed properly. Sealed cans are then sterilized either on 'steriflame' or in autoclaves at proper temperature and pressure for recommended time. Crates of hot cans are then immersed in running water cooling tanks. These are then taken out, wiped dry, labeled and stored in a cool and dry place.

Canning units of various sizes ranging from 200 cans to 3 tons/ shift are commercially available. Such firms usually provide complete services including installation, demonstration and maintenance.

Freeze-Drying Method

This is another method of preservation of mushrooms. It is a costly and energy-intensive process in which special machines called as freeze-dryers or lyophilizers are used. First of all, mushrooms are cleaned, washed well and there after mushroom is sublimed by slowly raising the temperature under a very low vacuum for 10–12 hours. Freeze-dried mushrooms usually appear very similar to that of fresh mushrooms. These are packed in sturdy containers under inert gas atmosphere. Though the process has failed to maintain its economic viability but recently there is renewed interest in the process.

Pickling of Mushrooms

Mushroom pickling is another method of mushroom preservation. This method is gaining popularity as it is the simplest and cheapest method of preservation. This method can easily be practiced by small growers also. Generally, the mushrooms are blanched or fried before normal pickling procedures. Now the mushrooms are used in making the pickles as per normal pickling procedures. Vinegar and other preservatives are generally essential in making the mushroom pickles. Mushrooms preserved as pickles can be stored up to 6–12 months.

Drying of Mushrooms

Drying is the most common method for preservation of the oyster, shiitake and paddy straw mushrooms. These mushrooms are traded mostly in dried form. Drying procedure varies with the scale of operation, financial inputs and customer's requirement. Oyster mushrooms can easily be sun-dried. The sun-dried product should be oven dried at 55 C°–60 C° for 6 hours before packing in sealed containers. Mechanical driers (electric as well as steam operated) are available in the market for drying fruits and vegetables and the same driers could be used for drying mushrooms as well.

Vacuum Cooling Method
Principles

Vacuum cooling or evaporative cooling is based on the principle that as liquids evaporate, they absorb heat from their surroundings and evaporation can be increased by vacuum.

Method of vacuum cooling

In order to ensure high quality mushrooms in the market place with enhanced shelf-life, vacuum cooling method is considered to be a safe and suitable method of preservation. In this method, mushrooms must be cooled as quickly as possible after picking and washing. There after, it is kept cool throughout. Rapid cooling can conserve the quality of mushrooms better than just leaving them in cold storage. Large stacks of fresh mushrooms can be loaded directly into a cold storage, with little consideration for the time it takes to cool the mushroom at par to the temperature of the store.

Factors affecting vacuum cooling

Following factors are responsible in cooling and maintenance of quality:

1. To maintain proper quality, water in mushrooms should be conserved.

2. The rate at which the product is cooled is very important in mushrooms. Therefore, packs of mushrooms should be placed in very cool atmosphere.

3. Packaging and over wrapping usually retard the heat exchange. In the absence of ventilation for heat removal, the mushrooms in the centre of the stack may get heated.

4. After releasing the vacuum, the mushrooms are kept in conventional stores till its marketing. But there is loss of fresh weight during vacuum cooling.

5. Cooling with positive ventilation is another modification where cold air is directed over or through boxed produce. For this,

perforated boxes containing the produce are placed. The air is drawn to promote rapid heat exchange.

6. In conventional cooling systems, drying of mushrooms is done and the air is generally dehumidified during refrigeration. One method of humidifying air is to pass it through ice-cold water which cools and saturates it with water vapor. Ice is made by conventional refrigeration. Since the produce is cooled by water saturated air, there is little loss of moisture. Ice bank cooling with forced ventilation is now becoming common.

PACKAGING OF MUSHROOMS

Packaging plays an important role in marketing and exports of fruits and vegetables including mushrooms. Improper packaging often results in rejections and under-valuation of the produce affecting price realization. Therefore, following precautions should be taken in packaging of the produce.

1. With a view to compete in the highly sophisticated and discriminating markets especially abroad, the packages should be attractive and distinctive.
2. Packaging of mushrooms in India is primitive as they are unlabeled and simple in appearance. Polyethylene or polypropylene pouches are preferred for retail sale. Bulk packaging is not in existence.
3. In developed countries, packaging is given due importance. Modified atmosphere packaging (MAP) and controlled atmosphere packaging (CAP) are in vogue there.
4. Retail packs are mostly made of polystyrene or card board punnets over wrapped with differentially permeable films which create a modified atmosphere of CO_2 and O_2 within the punnets extending shelf-life. Such packaging increases the consumer's confidence in the product.
5. Bulk packaging for super market includes polystyrene containers and easy-to-carry card board boxes of different sizes.
6. Besides the packaging for fresh mushrooms, attention should be paid to the packaging of processed mushrooms. Dried oyster mushrooms are being packed in poorly printed poly pouches which besides giving shabby appearance result in breaking up of the dried fruit bodies.

7. Laminates can also be used for packing mushroom pickles. But future is going to be ruled by 'environment-friendly' recyclable and biodegradable packaging materials.
8. A combination of rigid and flexible packging is expected to find significant place in future.

MARKETING OF THE PRODUCE

Difficulties in marketing

There are many difficulties in marketing of white button mushrooms. Some of the difficulties may be summarized as under:

1. It is well known that production of white button mushrooms, has gone up in recent years but marketing problems exist to great extent. There have frequent reports of marketing problem in north Indian states during the winter months forcing the distress sale of the mushrooms.
2. Now a days, the marketing of fresh mushrooms determines the future of mushroom industry in India. Therefore, it should be borne in mind that efforts for increasing the production of mushroom, without proper marketing facility, will not be profitable.
3. Despite the changing trends, there is not good market for the processed mushroom till now. Fresh vegetables and fruits are still preferred in our country.
4. Fresh mushrooms have very short shelf-life. They can not be transported to long distances without refrigerated transport facility. Therefore, they are sold in highly localized markets in and around production areas.
5. The cultivation of white button mushrooms under controlled condition is restricted to few commercial units where mushrooms are produced throughout the year. However, much of the production is being done under natural conditions during the winters. Mostly the problems of marketing are usually experienced for 2 to 3 months during December, January and February in winter season when more than 75% of the annual production comes in market for sale.
6. Because of the limited duration and limited marketing area, farmers face the consequences of over-saturated market. Thus they are forced to sell their produce at less remunerative prices.

Important tips to solve the marketing problems

Some of the suggestions to solve the marketing problems of mushrooms especially of white button mushrooms are given below:

1. Expand the market area and strengthen the demand by popularization of mushrooms as nutritive food, having significant medicinal value on mass media through Doordarshan, posters and by other means of publicity.
2. Demonstration of recipes should be done and free recipe booklet must be given to those who are interested.
3. Free samples of mushrooms and its products should also be distributed in new areas.
4. Cooperative societies should be formed for promoting and management of sales of mushrooms.
5. Facilities of cold storage, refrigerated transport and processing should be created. Besides this, distributors should be appointed for big cities. Train the retailers about handling and storage, explaining about food value and recipes of mushroom so that they may be helpful to popularize the mushroom among public.
6. Supermarkets, chain vegetable stores, mother dairy retail counters should be approached for establishing retail counters.
7. Good and eye appealing packing measuring 200 g, 400 g or 500 g should be made for retail sale.
8. Minimize the cost of production and bring down the sale price to boost up the demand.
9. Different state governments should fix minimum support price for their respective states as in Himanchal Pradesh. Public sector marketing, processing and export organizations should also come forward and assist in marketing, processing and export of the mushroom.
10. For maintaining fixed price, assured supply of mushrooms throughout the year at a reasonable constant price is the key for good marketing. Therefore, efforts should be made to cultivate mushrooms during off season under controlled condition in order to maintain proper supply of mushroom throughout the year.
11. In a limited area, like a village or a cooperative, the mushroom crops should be time-scheduled so as to get a reasonably

uniform production daily to meet the requirements of the consumers.

Need for Organizing Mushroom Marketing

Marketing of mushrooms in India is not yet organized. The producers sell the produce directly to retailers or even to consumers. Such kind of marketing has its own limitations. Per capita consumption of the mushroom in India is hardly 5 g as against over a kg in many foreign countries. Besides these, mushroom is a novel food item for such a vegetarian country like India. Although, some of us are aware of its flavour, texture and nutritive value but many are not aware of 'what is mushroom and whether it is vegetarian or non-vegetarian diet'? Thus, it is clear that no serious efforts to promote the product, to strengthen and expand the market in order to increase its consumption, have so far been made in our country.

Future Prospects of Marketing

1. Marketing problem is usually experienced only in case of fresh white button mushrooms. In the coming years there is going to be good demand for processed and fast foods. In such case, mushrooms may be canned to meet the demand in off-season and in the non-producing areas.

2. Regarding the problems of sale/export of canned mushrooms, serious thought has to be given to minimize the cost of production and processing in order to compete in the international market.

3. There is not much problem in the sale of fresh *Pleurotus* mushroom due to very low production but there have been problems in selling dried 'Dhingri'.

4. Generally, the export orders are too big to be met by a single grower. Therefore, growers should form a cooperative society where they may pool their product and trade.

5. Export corporations in central as well as state sectors should provide help to the growers in arranging export to other countries.

Chapter 19

Transfer of Mushroom Technology

Introduction, need for transfer of technology, need to modify existing transfer of technology, challenges faced in transfer of mushroom technology, principles for transfer of technology, sources of information for various inputs and guidance; training for mushroom cultivation, important mushroom journals, finance facility offered; sources of spawn and international sources of spawn.

Mushroom is highly profitable, eco-friendly, less labour intensive and cost effective nutritious food that remains safe from natural calamities. The climate of our country is much conducive for the cultivation of a variety of mushrooms. However, the yields of the cultivated mushrooms are lesser than the expectations as compared to other horticultural crops in our country. India and Taiwan entered in the field of mushroom cultivation earlier than the China, Korea and Indonesia, but these countries are much ahead in mushroom production from India.

NEED FOR TRANSFER OF TECHNOLOGY

Despite of many efforts made by various research and development organizations, mushroom cultivation in our country is still restricted to only few states like Himachal Pradesh, Punjab, Haryana, J&K, some parts of U.P. and Delhi Union Territory. Out of many factors responsible for slow progress in mushroom cultivation and consumption in our country, the transfer of technology system is also one of the most important factors that is responsible for such slow progress. Therefore, transfer of mushroom technology should be given due importance because of the following reasons –
1.   The transfer of technology plays a vital role in the diffusion of

research findings. Research related with the substrate selection, choice of casing material, genetic improvement, temperature requirement and different other methods of manipulations that are useful for the profitability and high yield may have no use until and unless these techniques are transferred to its ultimate mushroom growers.

2. In general, every scientist engaged in the field of mushroom research, is very particular in making as many research as possible for the higher productivity of quality mushrooms. However, such findings cannot be translated in to practice as long as these are not popularized among the actual cultivators. Therefore, faster transfer of mushroom technology requires strategies keeping in mind the importance and applicability of past transfer of technology programmes.

3. In the past, the strategy adopted was based on the principles of all round development of the rural community through the *Community development programmes* along with the parallel programme of *National extension service*.

4. Before green revolution in our country, the agricultural production was critical and insufficient to feed the population. In view of enhancing the yield, overall development with emphasis on area specific development was adapted. To achieve this objective, programmes like IADP (*Intensive agriculture district programme*), IAAP (*Intensive agriculture area programme*), HYVP (*High yielding varieties programme*) and many other such programmes were started one by one. Consequently, the *great revolution* was brought out. All these development programmes created regional imbalance and widened the gap between rich and poor.

5. Keeping in view, various programmes like SFDA (*Small farmers development agency*), MFALDA (*Marginal farmers & agricultural labourers development agency*), DPAP (*Drought prone area programme*) and IRDP (*Integrated rural development programme*) were launched. These programmes adopted different strategies which were different from that of earlier agricultural development programmes. However, in such programmes participatory approach of farmers was lacking.

6. In addition to these multidimensional development programmes, ICAR launched *Front line transfer of technology programmes* that included *National demonstration, Operational research*

308

project and *Lab to land programme so as* to demonstrate the valuable proven technologies at farmer's field. It was done to redress the operational constraints faced by farmers and to establish linkage between scientists and farmers. These programmes also could not make much headway and the adoption of technologies as not achieved up to the desired level because the existing technologies were not based on farmers' need and resources.

Need to modify existing transfer of technology

It was widely accepted by the extension workers, social scientists and policy makers to modify the existing transfer of technology approaches, keeping in view the following conditions–

l.   That the development programmes should be problem oriented through active involvement of farmers.
2.   World Bank funded Project- IVLP (*Institute village linkage programme*) was launched with core objective of technology assessment and refinement.
3.   In nineties, ICAR launched World Bank funded *National agricultural technology project* (NATP) at national level, in which innovation in technology dissemination was a transfer of technology component. Under this component, single window access to information and integrated technology management through ATIC (*Agricultural technology information centre*) and ATMA (*Agricultural technology management agency*) was given emphasis.
4.   *Agricultural technology management agency* was based on bottom up planning procedure with intensive use of information technology. The extension approaches/strategies adopted in these programmes were based on the principles that consisted of community approach, area approach, group approach, employment approach and participatory approach.

During such a long period, great emphasis was given on development and standardization of mushroom technologies. Transfer of mushroom cultivation technology was initiated mainiy in the form of organizing training programmes for mushroom lovers, entrepreneurs and farmers. With the growing interest of business minded people, mushroom cultivation was preferred by most of the people because of its utility and profitability. Other methods of transfer of technology were also taken into consideration that included organization and active participation of farmers in national and state level exhibitions.

Demonstrations on mushroom production at the farmers mushroom growing centres were also organized with a view to transfer the technology. Publication of extension literature and holding mushroom meal celebrations were also arranged to popularize the mushroom cultivation technology. The Government institutions and non government organizations engaged in development work also gave top priority to mushroom cultivation as cottage industry in villages.

In the beginning of this millennium, mushroom cultivation emerged as income and employment generation activity. As a result, demand for training in mushroom cultivation has increased significantly. Various Central and State sponsored schemes and programmes are assisting in training in various ways.

Today, the mushroom cultivation is a major component of activity in the Government run programmes like *Institute village linkage programme* (IVLP), *Agricultural technology management agency* (ATMA) and *District rural development agency* (DRDA). Under the umbrella of these agencies, office bearers are being trained in mushroom cultivation.

During the last few years, NRCM (*National research centre for mushroom*), Solan (H.P.) alone has organized many training programmes on mushroom cultivation. In these training programmes, many farmers, unemployed youths and farm women were trained. Trained and experienced private mushroom growers/consultants/agencies all over the country are also providing technical help to those interested in mushroom cultivation. However, they guide and train people in mushroom cultivation on payment of handsome amount but indirectly they are also transferring of technology thereby creating awareness about mushroom cultivation.

Challenges faced in transfer of mushroom technology

Mushroom is a non-traditional vegetable crop. Despite of various nutritive and medicinal qualities, mushroom is not much acceptable among the rural people because of the reasons given below —
1. *Negative attitude and superstitions*–Some rural people have developed bad feeling and superstition towards mushrooms which formed negative attitude amongst them. Change in

attitude of rural people about mushroom is thus a challenge to extension worker.

2. *Reluctant on cropping systems* – Majority of the farmers in India are strongly adhered to their existing farming system and are reluctant for such a change due to low risk taking ability.

3. *Complexity* – Complexity in the mushroom cultivation technology process is another obstacle in transfer of mushroom technology.

4. *Innocent about agro based enterprises* – In, the present global competitive environment, agriculture has become more specialized and commercialized. Progressive farmers now adopt different agro-based enterprises including mushroom cultivation to maximize their profit. However, most of the farmers do not take it seriously.

5. *Spawn unavailability* – Spawn is an unique type of critical input in mushroom cultivation which is not available at common seed stores or agencies. Due to not availability of spawn in open market, farmers do not adopt mushroom cultivation willingly.

6. *Lack of organized market* – Marketing of the product is not well organized. The producers have surplus quantity of quality mushrooms. Hence, there is need to develop well organized market.

7. *Preservation and processing* – Preservation of mushroom for longer period is difficult in rural areas. Due to these reasons, farmers do not adopt mushroom cultivation.

PRINCIPLES FOR TRANFER OF MUSHROOM TECHNOLOGIES

In order to popularize the technologies with maximum adoptability among farmers and mushroom growers, following strategies are needed to be kept in mind —

There should be need based transfer of mushroom technologies

Developed mushroom technologies should be based on the needs of the farmers. Need based technology generation process require bottom up approach with active involvement of farmer at various stages. In order to develop such need based technologies following strategies should be adopted as suggested by NRCM (ICAR), Chambaghat, Solan (H.P.) —

- Studies on resources available, agro-ecology and socio-economic aspects in the area should be done through participatory rural appraisal techniques.
- Evaluation of the existing mushroom production technologies should be done so as to generate the new one through experimentation.
- Most suitable mushroom cultivation technologies should be approved at farmers field with the active participation of farmers through demonstration trials.
- Rectification in mushroom production technologies should be done in consultation with the participating farmers and mushroom growers.
- Recommendation of refined mushroom production technologies should be done for the adaptation by the mushroom growers.

There must be integration among mushroom cultivation and related enterprises

There should be integration among mushroom cultivation and related enterprises. Mushroom cultivation should be inter dependent with agricultural, horticultural, animal husbandry and allied enterprises. Such integration has already been tried that showed promising results. The mushroom cultivation could be taken up in integration with cereals, vegetables and fruit crops by making best use of their residues - wheat straw, paddy straw, sugarcane, pea nut shells, maize stalk, dehaulled corn cobs and tree leaves etc. These are the base materials for substrate. The other ingredients needed for mushroom substrate can be obtained from livestock and poultry enterprises. The casing soil essentially required for fruiting of button mushroom could be collected from biogas. This relationship indicates that mushroom cultivation could play a vital role in integrated farming systems as under –

- The mushroom cultivation had placed itself at third place just after crop and animal husbandry as far as monetary gain is concerned.
- A single strategy cannot be suitable for a country with vast diversity. Different types of strategies would be needed for different kinds of mushroom growers.
- Agricultural and horticultural crops waste, animal waste and

industry waste available in huge amounts, can be utilized for mushroom cultivation.

- Spent compost and substrate that are the waste products obtained from mushroom cultivation could be utilized in agricultural & horticultural crops and animal husbandry for various purposes.

- Adding spent compost to unfertile soil or soil lacking in organic matter improves the fertility of the soil. The use of spent compost as an exclusive soil nutrients resulted in good yields and quality of the produce in many crops.

- The chemical analysis of spent compost shows that it is rich in nitrogen, phosphorus and potash which are essential nutrients for plant growth. Thus, spent compost can be used as organic fertilizer.

- Spent compost can be used as manure for vegetable production.

- Spent compost as animal feed has also been tested in the laboratories. It needs to be popularized among live stocks owners. Spent compost resulted from oyster mushroom substrate can be added to animal feed for calves and sheep.

- Biogas is a main source of energy for light and fuel in rural areas and is successfully being used as an alternative to electricity. Spent compost can be used for biogas production in place of cow dung as the availability of cow dung is low in rural family. Besides, the biogas solid known as *cabutz* may be used as casing material for mushroom production.

- Besides above uses of spent compost, it can also be utilized for making *vermi-compost* or *vermin-culture* which is very useful organic manure for agricultural crops. The chemical analysis of vermin-compost prepared of mushroom spent compost (wheat straw) revealed high nitrogen content up to 1.85%, phosphorus content up to 0.3% and potash content up to 0.2%.

- The results indicated that such *vermi-compost* will be highly useful manure for vegetables and rose cultivation.

Developed technologies should be suitable to small farmers

As mentioned earlier, different types of farmers require different kinds of strategy because of the heterogencity amongst the farmers in respect to the socio-economic status, education and farm size etc. Thus a strategy designed for the commercial production system cannot be appropriate for small production system. Small production system is usually operated by resource poor farmers who cannot understand technologies of complex nature. In order to motivate resource poor farmers for adopting non-traditional crop is a challenging task as they resist against such change due to low risk bearing capacity. Under such conditions, extension workers have to move step by step starting from awareness about the technology to its adoption. The following strategies may be most suitable for effective transfer of mushroom cultivation technologies amongst the resource poor farmers.

- First of all create awareness about mushroom cultivation amongst the farming community by organizing exhibitions, mushroom fete, workshops, seminars, distributing photographic leaflets, pamphlets, bulletins and through broadcasting talk on AIR.

- This amount of exposure will be sufficient for developing interest about mushroom cultivation among farmers. Through such exposures, they may take keen interest to seek more information about how to cultivate mushrooms.

- Selected and interested farmers from the locality should be asked to visit nearby mushroom research station or mushroom growing unit. They should be made familiar with the activities related to mushroom cultivation.

- Now few enthusiastic farmers should be trained in mushroom cultivation through training arranged at the research stations or mushroom growing centers.

- After providing training to the enthusiastic farmers, demonstration trials should be conducted at farmer's farms with the help of nearby mushroom research station.

- At this stage farmers should be allowed to do all operations by their own hand under supervision of mushroom experts.

- When the crop is ready to harvest, it should be exposed to the other farmers that will help in convincing them.

- Calculation on the monetary gain should also be made out and the profit gaining story should be told to other farmers also. If possible, story of success made by the farmer should be published and distributed among the farmers. Once the farmers are convinced, the work of transfer of technology usually becomes easy.

Modern information technology should be preferred

In the past, the diffusion of technology was through print media, radio and television that were very slow means of transfer of technology. These sources of information were time consuming also. Now the agriculture in general and mushroom cultivation in particular has become globally competitive. Therefore, needs of modern information technologies have increased many folds. Thus, the enhanced information needs can now be met out only through the use of modern *Information and communication technology* (ICT). The urban population is making good use of ICT for information access fo. various purposes.

Future status of transfer of mushroom technology

The Ministry of information technology is planning to convert over six lakhs P.C.O.'s into public *Tele-info-centres* which will offer a variety of services including internet, browsing, fax, e-mail and many other services. The Maharashtra state Government is said to have plans to link 40,000 villages with *Agronet* which is a specially developed software package for farmers. It aims at to provide the latest information on agriculture. Such facilities should be provided by different state Governments.

Likewise there are so many ICT enabled projects and programmes including Gyandoot, SARI (*Sustainable access in rural India*, Tarahaat of Development Alternatives, e-Choupal, Gramin Information Centre Scheme of Maharashatra. Chamber of commerce, Industries and Agriculture provide information on various aspects of agriculture and rural development. Such programmes can also be developed for information on mushroom cultivation.

Single window experts system for transfer of technology

During the last decade, information needs of mushroom growers cultivation technology and marketing have increased tremendously. Mushroom growers' information needs on technological aspect could be satisfied through single window experts system. Different agricultural universities are providing such facilities through *Krishak help line* and also through *Agricultural technology information centers* (ATIC). Similarly information on marketing should be made available through networking of *Mandies* of the regions.

National infotech centers and mobile hand set services
In near future, mobile hand sets are expected to be provided to the farmers so that they may receive agricultural technological information including mushrcom technology through the experts. Besides, interested farmers may also receive information through the government sponsored web site – *Agmark net. nic. in.*

SOURCES OF DIFFERENT INFORMATION

Mushroom is a non-traditional vegetable crop. The inputs and facilities required for mushroom cultivation are not easily available as compared to other agricultural and horticultural crops. The unavailability of inputs and lack of proper guidance are two important factors responsible for non-adoption of mushroom cultivation. Reliable source of information for proper guidance may be summarized as under :

TRAINING FOR MUSHROOM CULTIVATION

Training is an important component in mushroom cultivation without which one cannot be perfect in mushroom growing. National Research Centre for Mushroom (NRCM) Solan (H.P.) conducts training programme on various aspects related with mushrooms cultivation.

Entrepreneurs training course
This course is meant to serve the personnel of existing mushroom farms as well as the entrepreneurs who are likely to establish mushroom farms in future.

Subject matter specialists training course
This course is designed for extension specialists, horticulture officers, bank Officials and other functionaries of the development departments and universities etc. Such training programme is usually sponsored by Directorate of extension, Ministry of agriculture, Government of India.

Introductory training course for farmers & unemployed youths of India

This course has been designed that aimed to serve the rural farmers and unemployed youths who wish to grow mushroom at low to medium input level with a limited investment.

International training course

This course is open to trainees of other countries particularly from under-developed/developing countries. The medium of instruction for such course is English.

Sponsored training course

The centre organizes off-and-on-campus sponsored training courses on request in order to serve the weaker section of the society including poor small and marginal farmers and farm women from different areas of the country, Persons participating in such training, remain not in position to attend regular training programme at their own cost. Some development and financial institutions usually sponsor them.

Individualized training

Short term training courses are also organized by NRCM for individuals who want to be trained in some specific area of their interest such as spawn production, composting, specialty mushroom cultivation or in post harvest management.

All India Coordinated Mushroom Improvement Projects of N.R.C.M. in different states provide training in their respective states. A partial list of such centers may be summarized as under:

1. Department of Plant Pathology, G.B. Pant University of Agriculture and Technology, Pantnagar (Uttaranchal).
2. Department of Plant Pathology, N.D. University of Agriculture and Technology, Faizabad (UP).
3. Department of Plant Pathology, Tamil Nadu Agricultural University, Coimbatore (TN).
4. Department of Microbiology, Punjab Agricultural University, Ludhiana (Pb.).
5. Department of Plant Pathology, Indira Gandhi Krishi Vishwavidyalaya, Raipur (MP).
6. Department of Plant Pathology, Rajasthan Agricultural University, Udaipur (Raj.).

7. Department of Plant Pathology, Mahatma Phule Krishi Vidhyapeeth, Pune (MS).

OTHER SOURCES OF TRAINING

Besides these training centers organized under NRCM and its All India Coordinated Mushroom Improvement Projects network, there are many other institutions including State agricultural universities, State departments, Funded Projects & N.G.O's which provide training on various aspects of mushroom cultivation. Some of the important centers are listed below:

1. Department of Plant Pathology, Orissa Agricultural University, Bhubaneshwar (Orissa).
2. Department of Plant Pathology, Vidhan Chandra Krishi Vishwavidyalaya, Kalyani, West Bengal.
3. Department of Mycology and Plant Pathology, IARI, Pusa, New Delhi.
4. Department of Plant Pathology, IIHR, Bangalore (Karnataka).
5. H.P. Krishi Vishwavidyala, Palampur (HP).
6. HAIC Agro R&D Unit, Murthal, Sonepat (Haryana).
7. Department of Horticulture, Meghalaya, Shillong,
8. Directorate of Horticulture, Arunachal Pradesh, Naharlagun, Itanagar.
9. Indo-Dutch Mushroom Project, Jeolikot, Nainital (Uttaranchal state).
10. Manipur Tribal Development Corporation, Lamphelpat, Imphal.
11. Mushroom research laboratory, C.S.A. University of Agriculture and Technology, Kanpur (UP).

TRAINING THROUGH CORRESPONDENCE

Besides residential training courses, training through correspondence in mushroom cultivation is offered by many institutions. Indira Gandhi National Open University (IGNOU) has also started a correspondence course on mushroom cultivation in collaboration with National Research Centre for Mushroom (NRCM) in the year 2000. IGNOU offers three to six moths training course on mushroom cultivation using printed reading material and educational television channel-*Gyan Darshan*. Correspondence training courses are conducted at various institutes where mushroom development facility exists. Apart from IGNOU, National Open School is already providing training through correspondence courses.

INTERNATIONAL SOURCES OF TRAININGS

The entrepreneurs who want to establish export oriented mushroom units, need exposure to an international institute. For such types of information seekers, there are foreign institutes which provide training on mushroom cultivation. A partial list of such centers are as under :

1. Horticulture Research International, Wellesbourne, Warwick United Kingdom, CV35 9EF.
2. Fungi Perfecti, PO Box 7634-AMI, Olympia, WA 98507, USA. Website- *www.fungi.com*
3. C Point, PO Box 6035, 5960AA Horst, The Netherlands. Website- *www.cpoint.nl*
3. GAMU Ltd, Gesellschaft Fur angewandte Mykologie U. Umweltsludien GmbH, Dr. Jan I Lelley, D-47800 Krefeld, Hutbenallee 235, Germany.
4. McGreay Group (Head Office), 53-58 Armagh Road, Moy Dunganvon Co., Tyrone, Northern Ireland, UK, BT171 7HZ.
5. Korona National Mushroom Union, H-3396 Kerecsend, pf. 8, Hungary.
6. Traymaster Ltd, New Road, Catfield, Gt Yarmouth Norfolk, United Kingdom, NR29 5BQ. Website- *www.traymaster.co.uk*

IMPORTANT MUSHROOM JOURNALS

Indian Mushroom Growers Association
Mushroom Research Laboratory, Chambaghat,
Solan-173213 (H.P.)
The Mushroom Journal
Mushroom Growers Association, Agriculture House,
Knights Bridge, London SWIX 7NJ England.
Mushroom Journal for the Tropics
Department of Botany, Chinese University of Hong Kong,
New Territories, Hong Kong.

Mushroom News
American Mushroom Institute,
Baltimore Pike Kennett Square,
PA 19348, USA.

Mushroom Science
Mushroom Growers Association, Agriculture House,
Knights Bridge, London SWIX 7 NJ UK.

Mushroom Research
Mushroom Society of India, NRCM, Chambaghat,
Solan-173213 (H.P.)

FINANCE FACILITIES OFFERED

After receiving training for mushroom cultivation from any of the training centers mentioned above, nationalized banks like State Bank of India, State Bank of Patiala, Punjab National Bank and many other banks may be approached to get their project financed for establishing big units. Besides, Ministry of food processing industries, *Panchsheel Bhavan*, New Delhi, *National horticulture board*, Gurgaon (Haryana) and *Khadi village industry commission*, Mumbai may also provide finance for cultivation and processing unit of mushroom.

SOURCES OF SPAWN

Spawn of mushroom is another important input in mushroom cultivation. In India, NRCM and many other institutions and State Agricultural Universities provide spawn to entrepreneurs and farmers. The AICMIP centers and some many other training centers mentioned above also provide spawn of mushroom. A partial list of some important spawn producing and supplying units may be summarized as under :

1. Dr. Y.S. Parmar, University of Horticulture and Forestry, Nauni (HP).
2. Division of Plant Pathology, IARI, New Delhi-110012.
3. Department of Plant Pathology, Haryana Agricultural University, Hisar (Haryana).
4. Directorate of Horticulture, Mushroom Spawn Laboratory. Kohima.

6. Govt. Spawn Production Laboratory, Horticulture Complex, Chhouni Kalan, Hoshiarpur (Pb.).
7. Vigyan Samiti, Udaipur (Rajasthan).
8. Regional Research Laboratory, CSIR, Srinagar (J&K) and Department of Agriculture, Lalmandi, Srinagar (J&K).
9. Department of Plant Pathology, J.N. Krishi Vishwa Vidyalaya, Jabalpur (MP).
10. Department of Plant Pathology, Assam Agricultural University, Jorhat (Assam).
11. Department of Plant Pathology, C.S.Azad University of Agriculture and Technology, Kanpur (U.P.).

Besides these, different private persons and agencies are engaged in mushroom spawn production especially at places like Solan (HP), Kurukshetra (Haryana), Delhi, Patna (Bihar) and Mumbai (MS) etc.

INTERNATIONAL SOURCES OF SPAWN

Most of the export oriented mushroom units usually prefer to procure spawn from out side the country in order to get better strains for higher yields. For the convenience of such units few important foreign spawn suppliers may be listed below :—

1. Amycel/Spawn Mate
   Corporate Office 260 Westgate Drive, Watsonville CA 95076 USA.
2. Amycel (UK) Limited
   PO Box 211, Stretton House, Derby Road, Burton-on-Trent Staffordshire, United Kingdom DE 13 OZZ
   Email: amycel@orangenet. co.uk
3. Amycel s.a.r.l.(France)
   13 boulevard de Industrie 41100 Vendome, FRANCE
   E-mail: AmycelHHAY@aol.com
4. Amycel BV (NL)
   PO Box 3703 Ittervoort 6014 ZG
   The Netherlands.
   E-mail: amycel@worldonline.nl
5. Euromycel S.A.
   Zone Industrielle de St-Benoit la-Foret 37500
   Saint & Noit la-Foret, FRANCE
   E-mail: euromycel@wanadoo.fr

6. Field & Forest Products Inc.
   N3296, Kozuzek Road ,Peshtigo WI 54157-9610, USA
   E-mail: ffp@mari.net
7. Fullhouse
   Spawn & Supplement
   Mushroom Growing Products, USA
   Eastern U.S.
8. Gurelan S. Coop.
   Spawnmaker, Poligono de Areta.
   31620 Huarte-Pamplona,
   SPAIN,
   E-mail: gurelan@encomix.es
9. International Spawn Laboratory,
   Beechmount Industrial Estate, Navan Co. Meath,
   IRELAND
10. IPP Limited 'Le Lion'
    PO Box 4, Wilmslow, Cheshire, UK SK9 6YB

Source – Adapted from manual of NRCM, Solan (H.P.)

Practicals in Mushroom Cultivation

Experiment No. 1

Object

Study of the morphology and different parts of a typical mushroom.

Material required

A full developed mushroom preferably a white button mushroom, needle, glass slide, white blotting paper, pencil, rubber, paper and light microscope.

Observation

The fruiting body of a typical mushroom consists of following parts:

1. *Stipe or stem:* it is situated in centre of the pileus and is solid when young becoming hollow later on. It measures 30-120 mm × 10–15mm in size.

2. *Pileus (Cap):* It is white, creamy or brown in colour and almost smooth in texture. It is ordinarily easily separable from the stipe and is situated just above it.

3. *Lamellae or gills:* These are situated on the under side of the pileus. The gills bear spores on their surface.

4. *Annulus on ring:* Annulus is present in the sample of white button mushroom.

   (*Gills or lamellae in the young stage remain enclosed by a membrane that extends from the margin of the pileus to the stipe. This membrane is known as partial veil and is usually tears around the margin of the pileus. It remains attached to the stipe forming a ring like structure called as annulus*).

5. *Volva or universal veil:* Initially the entire fruit body of some mushroom species is found covered by the cup like structure which is called as volva or universal veil.

6. **Spores:** These are formed within the gills in a typical mushroom. Spores are microscopic and are different coloured and shaped.

Experiment No. 2

Object
Method of pure tissue culture preparation for spawn production.

Material required
A large sized healthy mushroom with intact membrane selected from cropping bed/ tray, knife, 0.1% mercuric chloride solution, sterilized inoculating needle and autoclaved nutrient agar medium.

Procedure
1. Take a large sized healthy mushroom with intact membrane selected from cropping bed/tray.
2. Cut lower portion of the mushroom stem with the help of a sharp knife.
3. Dip it in 0.1% mercuric chloride solution for 1 minute and thereafter wash it properly with tap water.
4. Cut a small portion of stem and remove a very small sized piece of the tissue with the help of sterilized inoculating needle.
5. Inoculate the autoclaved nutrient agar with the piece of tissue.
6. Incubate it at 25±2C° for 10–15 days.

Observation
The surface of medium becomes covered with mycelial growth. Now the pure culture is ready for inoculation of spawn grains.

Experiment No. 3

Object
Collection of spores for pure culture through spore print method.

Material required
Desired mushroom species, knife, a half black and half white paper, a glass bowl and light microscope.

Principles – The spore print is a simple method used for selection, identification and collection of pure spore culture. This method is most frequently used in gilled fungi. When the cap of mushroom is held stationary on a paper in a cooled chamber for a long period, the impression of pattern of gills is printed and the spores get accumulated onto the paper. The invisible spores appear coloured. Single spore from the spores collected in this way may be used for pure spore culture.

Procedure for spore print
1. A fresh mushroom of desired species is taken and with the help of a sharp knife cap is cut from stipe properly.
2. Now place the gill side down of the cap on a half black and half white paper in such a way that half of the gill should be towards black side and half towards white side.
3. Place a drop of water on the cap of mushroom and cover it by a glass bowl.
4. Leave this set up for about 8 hours or overnight undisturbed.
5. Next day gently remove the glass bowl and cup from the paper.

Results
On the paper prints of the gills and spore deposits may be observed. Gill pattern and spore colour should be studied.

Observation
Compare the colour of the spore observed on the paper with the colour of mushroom genus as given below in the table.

Table showing colour of spores of different mushrooms as observed by spore print

Mushroom type/Genus	Spore colour
1. Gilled mushroom	
Amanita	White to pale
Chlorophyllum	Green
Clitocybe	Fleshy colour
Hebeloma	Rusty to yellow brown
Hygropharus	Cream
inocybe	Brown or Cinnamon
Lepiota	Green
Naematoloma	Purple brown
Paneolus	Black
Pleurotus	Lavender colour
Russula	White, cream or yellow
Schizophyllum	Pink, salmon or flesh
2. Tubed mushrooms	
Boletus	Yellow to olive brown
Cyrodon	Yellow to yellow brown
Suillus	Yellow brown to cinnamon
3. Puffball mushroom	
Scleroderma	Purple black

Experiment No. 4

Object

Method of preparation of master mushroom/spawn for commercial mushroom production.

Material required

Wheat grain, calcium carbonate, gypsum, half litre milk bottle and cotton plugs.

Procedure

(After preparing pure culture, one of the mushroom mycelium is multiplied on a suitable medium which is used for further multiplication for preparation of con,mercial spawn. It is called as master spawn of mushroom).

1. Take desired amount of wheat grains which are fresh, unbroken and free from insects and diseases.
2. Wash the grains properly and boil such grains for 15–20 minutes in such a way that they remain fresh, soft and unbroken.
3. Allow the boiled grain to stand for about 60 minutes so that it may cool properly.
4. Now mix calcium carbonate @ 0.5% and gypsum @ 2% of the dry weight of the grains.
5. Fill the grains in half litre capacity of well washed and autoclaved milk bottles (commonly used by milk powder manufacturing company) upto 60% of its capacity. Inoculate it with a bit of pure culture of the mushroom under aseptic condition.
6. Plug the grain filled bottles properly with plugs prepared by non-absorbent cotton.
7. Incubate theses at room temperature for 15 days and in the mean time keep it mixing smoothly.

Results

After 10–15 days, spawn will be ready for spawning and further multiplication.

Experiments on mushroom cultivation

In recent years, cultivation of edible mushroom is gaining momentum through out the world. In these experiments, cultivation of *Pleurotus* species and *Volvariella volvacea* has been described.

PRINCIPLES OF DHINGRE MUSHROOM CULTIVATION

Different species of *Pleurotus* such as *P. ostreatus, P. sajor-caju, P. sapidus, P. cornucopieae, P. florida* and *P. flabellatus, etc.* are seen growing on dead and decaying organic materials in summer and rainy season in different parts of the country. However, some of these species can be artificially grown on waste cellulose materials, easily available as waste products generated from houses and through agricultural products and by-products. Such products and by-products include sunflower stalks, ropes, cotton wastes, paddy straw, wheat straw, sugarcane wastes and leaves, rice husk, banana leaves, saw dust and papers etc. These materials can be used as substrate for the cultivation of *Pleurotus* species.

Experiment No. 5

Object
Method of cultivation of edible Dhingri mushroom (*Pleurotus* species) near the laboratory or in green house on house hold wastes.

Materials required
Pure culture of *Pleurotus* species, wheat grains (100 g), waste paper (2–4 kg), black gram flour (10 g), polythene bags (1 kg capacity), Flask (500 ml capacity), Sprit lamp, Cork borer (5 mm diameter), incubator, inoculating needle, Petri plates and autoclaved nutrient aga medium.

Spawn production
1. Obtain pure culture of *Pleurotus* species or isolate spores from the healthy mushroom and prepare its pure young culture on nutrient agar medium.
2. Now take 100 g of wheat grains and soak it in water overnight in 500 ml flask. Next day, decant excess water by inverting it in such a way that grains should not come out from the flask.
3. Plug the flask with cotton plug and autoclave it at 121 C° for 30 minutes.
4. Now cut agar blocks with sterile cork borer from active mycelium of pure culture and transfer 8 or 10 blocks into the flask containing sterilized grains. It should be mixed properly with the grains.

5. Incubate the flask at 25 ±1 C° for 10–15 days with regular agitation so as to mix the inoculum with grains for proper mycelial growth and infestation. Mycelial growth and infestation on the grains inoculated with the inoculum act as spawn.

Spawning

1. Take 4 kg of waste paper and cut it into small pieces. Boil 5–6 liters of water in a large sized container.
2. Filled the waste paper into it and mixed properly so as to pasteurize the paper in boiled water.
3. After 30–35 minutes, the waste paper is decanted and squeezed. Now the waste paper should be placed in sterilized polythene paper bags.
4. Now sprinkle small amount of black gram flour @ 10g/kg and spawn @ 50 g/kg onto the centre of substrate.
5. Now transfer moistened paper in sterilized polythene bags and pack tightly. Make a hole in the center so as to facilitate proper aeration.

Spawn running

After spawning, the spawned bag is kept at 25 ± C° for about 15 days for spawn running.

Observation

In the mean time, white mycelia grow profusely on the waste paper substrate and form mycelial mat. Under such circumstances, cut polythene bags from four sides so as to expose the mycelial mat. When required, sprinkle sterilized water in order to maintain 70–80% relative humidity. Incubate it further at 25±1 C°.

Result

Gills of different sizes of *Pleurotus* appear in several flushes. Cut it with knife at each flush and use as desired.

Experiment No. 6

Object

To find out the cost of cultivation of Dhingre oyster mushroom.

Principles

Cultivation of oyster mushroom is simple as compared to white button mushroom cultivation. A small mushroom production unit may require a space, measuring 20 feet × 15 feet × 10 feet in which 300 to 325 bags, each filled with 6.0 Kg of wet cut pieces of wheat straw may be accomodated. For this purpose, 4 to 6 quintals of dry straw may be needed.

Procedure

Cost of cultivation may be calculated on the basis of expenditure and income received by the mushroom production unit.

1. Capital used
- Cost of sprayer
- Cost of tank to wet the straw
- Cost of strawcutting machine
- Others expences

Total... Rs. =

2. Reccurring expenxes
- Cost of paddy/wheat straw
- Cost of preparation of bags
- Cost of spawn
- Fungicides, Insecticides and other Chemicals used
- Labour
- Other expences

3. Depreciation and interest on capital
- Depreciation on at the rate of 10%.
- Interest on capital at the rate of 10%

Total... Rs.=

4. Total expenditure
- Total of items 2 + 3

5. Income received
- Total production of mushrooms in Kgs.   =
- Mushrooms sold @ Rs. – per Kg.   =
- Total Net income (= Gross income – Total expenditure)
          =

Results
- Cost of production per kilogram of mushroom   =
- Income and cost ratio   =

PRINCIPLES OF PADDY STRAW MUSHROOM CULTIVATION

Paddy straw mushroom (*Voivariella volvacea*) is also called as tropical mushroom or Chinese mushroom. This mushroom is cultivated mostly in different parts of China, Malaysia, Indonesia, Philippines and India. Many species are known and the most important edible species is *Voivariella volvacea*. It is grown chiefly using paddy straw as substrate in different parts of our country. It has whitish to dull brown fruiting bodies growing singly or in groups. In India its cultivation was first started in Coimbatore and now its cultivation is being popularized by Agricultural Research Institute, Coimbatore (T.N.); Indian Agricultural Research Institute, New Delhi; Regional Research Institute, Jammu (J.K.); National Botanical Research Institute, Lucknow; G.B. Pant University of Agriculture and Technology, Pantnagar (Utranchal State); C.S. Azad University of Agriculture and Technology, Kanpur (U.P.) and by different other Agricultural Universities situated in Punjab, Haryana, J.K. and Karnataka.

Harvested fresh paddy straw mushroom should be consumed or preserved by drying the gills of mushroom at 50–60 C° or exposing it in the sun to remove the moisture content. It should be packed in polythene bags.

Experiment No. 7

Object

Cultivation of paddy straw mushroom (*Volvariella volvacea*) near the laboratory in open place/green house.

Materials required

Spawn of paddy straw mushroom, paddy straw, small water tank, bamboo cuttings, bricks, gram, polythene sheets and thermo meter.

Paddy straw bed preparation and spawning

1. Collect fresh paddy straw of not more than 1 year old being free from insects and diseases.
2. Prepare several bundles of paddy straw by putting butt and end one side. Pour water in small tank and put all the bundles into it so as to immerse all the bundles in water.

3. Take out the bundles after soaking overnight and drain off the excess water thereafter.

4. Prepare 1m ×1m bamboo frame and place it on the bricks. Make square shaped straw beds measuring 1m × 1m × 1m by placing the soaked straw bundles in such a way that their butt ends may be on one side and look square shaped. It is the first layer.

5. Over the first layer, place the second layer of straw bundles in such a way that their butt ends may be on one side but should be opposite to that of the first layer.

6. Inoculate the beds by placing spawn so as to make 8–10 cm thick layer. Again prepare the third layer by placing moist paddy straw bundles keeping the butt in opposite direction and spread spawn as done earlier in previous step.

7. Repeat the above step of making further layers of paddy straw and spawning it so as to achieve a cube shaped structure of beds.

8. Finally spread all the spawn over the bed and cover the inoculated layers with loose straw and press the bed down properly.

9. Cover the bed with transparent polythene sheet to maintain moisture and save the bed from rats, rodents and birds.

Spawn running

After spawning, maintain temperature of bed between 30 C° 35 C° and moisture between 60–68% by sprinkling boiled then cooled down water when ever required. After about 10 days of spawning, remove polythene sheet so as to grow small buttons of this mushroom. In the mean time, the mushroom attains maturity.

Results

There are 5 different stages of mushroom formation. First of all, pin head stage, then button stage, thereafter egg stage are formed. Egg elongates in due course giving rise to full grown stage. Full grown stage may be considered as maturation when the volva of the *Volvariella volvacea* is about to rupture. Harvest the fruiting bodies at this stage by twisting it gently or by cutting with knife.

FLOW CHART OF
PADDY STRAW MUSHROOM CULTIVATION
(GENERALIZED METHOD)

-

Preparation of substrate
(Requirement : 3–4 kg paddy straw, 100 g spawn, 200g gram powder)

-

Preparation of bed
(Spawning 100g spawn)

-

Crop management
(Maintain temperature for spawn run 30–35C° and moisture 60–80%)

-

Mushroom formation
(1. Pin head stage, 2. Button stage, 3. Egg stage, 4. Egg elongation stage, 5. Full grown stage).

-

Harvesting
(4–5 kg mushroom /kg of dry weight of substratum)

COST OF CULTIVATION OF PADDY STRAW MUSHROOM

Paddy straw mushroom can be grown outside the mushroom house. There is no need to expend money on mushroom house construction. It may be easily grown in hut, polythene houses and in bricks made rooms. Cost of cultivation may be calculated in following manner:

- Cost of paddy straw
- Cost of spawn
- Fungicides/ insecticides
- Cost of labours used
- Cost of electricity and water
- House rent
- Other expences
- Approximate weight (on 15% dry weight basis) of produce =
- Total income (mushroom sold the rate at the market place calculated per kilogram) =

- Net income = Gross income – Total expenditure =
- Cost of mushroom production per kilogram =

$$\frac{\text{Net income}}{\text{Total yield in kilograms}}$$

- Profit and cost ratio = $\dfrac{\text{Gross income in rupees}}{\text{Gross expenditure in rupees}}$

COST OF CULTIVATION OF WHITE BUTTON MUSHROOM

Cost of cultivation of white button mushroom may be calculated as under:

1. Capital
- Cost of bulk chamber construction
- Cost of moter and blower
- Construction of cropping rooms (preferably two)
  A. Big room (34 feet × 18 feet × 9.5 feet) (capacity 750 bags)
  B. Small room (25 feet × 15 feet × 9.5 feet) (capacity for 45 bags)
- Cost of iron racks (3 tiers)
- Boiler and pipe fitting
- Others (computer etc.)

2. Recurring expenditure
- Paddy or wheat straw
- Chicken manure
- Brewer's grain
- Urea
- Gypsum
- Spawn
- Polythene bags
- A permanent labour
- Temporary labours
- Casing soil and its sterilization expenses
- Fuel, water and electricity
- Other common expenses

3. *Interest on capital*
   A – Interest on total capital (15%).
   B – Depreciation on building and equipment etc.
   Total expenses = 1 + 2 + 3

4. *Details of income*
   Mushroom production in kilograms =
   Money received from sale of mushroom =
   Net income = Total gross income – Expenditure (2 + 3)
   Profit and cost ratio = Total income/Expenditure (2 + 3)

FREQUENTLY ASKED QUESTIONS AND THEIR ANSWERS

Q.1–What do you mean by mushrooms?
A. Mushrooms are spore bearing fruiting bodies of edible fungi that are available as food material in the market place.

Q.2–What short of mushroom should be consumed?
A. Mushroom produced by any mushroom growing unit/farm should only be consumed. Mushrooms collected from other places like hills, pastures, gardens and such other places should not be consumed at all. .

Q.3–Why?
A. Because mushroom collected from such places other than produced from the mushroom farms may be poisonous. Such mushrooms if eaten may cause death of the person consuming it.

Q.4–What are the different parts of a typical mushroom?
A. Different parts of a typical mushroom are the stipe, the pileus, the annulus, the gills or lamella and the volva.

Q.5–Whether all these parts are found in all kinds of mushrooms?
A. No. All parts are not found in all kinds of mushrooms.

Q.6–What are the characteristic features of white button mushrooms?
A. The stipe of the mushroom is found in the center. It is white, annulated solid when young and becoming hollow bellow the annulus. At the base it is thicker slightly tapering upwards. The pileus is easily separable from the stipe. It looks white, cream or brown in colour. Lamellae are free, crowded and pink in colour at first later becoming dark brown in colour.

Q.7–Why do you call it button mushroom?

A. Because it looks like a button when it is quite young.

Q. 8–What is the colony character of this mushroom?

A. On the agar medium, the colony of *Agaricus bisporus* appears to be circular. Apical growth of hyphae produce repeated branching.

Q.9–Is there any other species of *Agaricus* button mushroom which is cultivated in our country?

A. Yes. *Agaricus bitorquis*. It requires higher temperature than *Agaricus bisporus*.

Q.10–In what respect *Agaricus bitorquis* differs from *Agaricus bisporus*?

A. Temperature requirement for *Agaricus bitorquis* is about 5 C° higher than that of *Agaricus bisporus*.

Q.11–What are popular mushrooms which are cultivated in our country?

A. Three kinds of mushrooms are most commonly cultivated in our country. These are white button mushroom, paddy straw mushroom and oyster mushroom.

Q.12–Name some other edible species of paddy straw mushrooms?

A. *Volvariella volvacea* is the most commonly cultivated straw mushroom. However, other edible species are also known which include *Volvariella esculenta* and *Volvariella dyspepsia*.

Q.13–What are the characteristic features of paddy straw mushroom?

A. Paddy straw mushroom also called as straw mushroom or Chinese mushroom differs from *Agaricus* species as in this mushroom ring around the stipe is absent. The colour of the colony is initially grayish white which turns pale with the advancement of age. This mushroom is easily perishable and should be consumed immediately.

Q.14–What are environmental requirements for paddy straw mushroom?

A. The optimum temperature range for mycelial growth is 30–35 C°, moisture content of the substrate should be between 70–80% and relative humidity should be 75–85% for cultivation.

Q.15–What are different methods of paddy straw mushroom cultivation?

A. There are many methods of cultivation which include Traditional method, Hong Kong method, Malaysia method, Thailand method, and Modern cotton waste method. Traditional method is most popular method in our country.

Q.16–What are different cultivated species of Dhingri mushroom?

A. *Pleurotus ostreatus, Pleurotus florida, Pleurotus eryngii, Pleurotus cystidisus, Pleurotus sajor-caju* and *Pleurotus sapidus* are most popular species.

Q.17–What are the environmental requirements for *Pleurotus* mushroom?

A. Temperature requirement of *Pleurotus sajor-caju* for mycelial growth is 25 C°, temperature requirement for fruit body initiation is 15–25 C° and during spawn run humidity should be 84–85%.

Q.18–What are the important characteristics of oyster mushroom?

A. Oyster mushrooms (*Pleurotus* species) are characterized by the rapidity of mycelial growth and high saprophytic colonization activity on cellulosed substrates.

Q.19–How many species of *Pleurotus* have been named as cultivated species?

A. As many as 8 species of *Pleurotus* are well known to be cultivated. These species are *Pleurotus ostreatus, Pleurotus florida, Pleurotus eryngii, Pleurotus cystidiosus, Pleurotus flabellatus, Pleurotus cornucopiae, Pleurotus sapidus* and *Pleurotus sajor-caju.*

Q.20–What are the morphological characteristics of *Pleurotus sajor-caju.*?

A. This mushroom is soft and white in hot weather and grayish in cold weather. Stipe is very short and pileus is depressed.

Q.21–How much yield do you expect from oyster mushroom?

A. It is possible to get 700 g to 1 kg of fresh mushroom per kg of dry weight of the substrate.

Q.22–Do you know the name of some other edible species of mushroom which are being cultivated?

A. Yes, I know. *Flammulina velutipes, Pholiota nameko, Calocybe indica, Auricularia auricula, Lentinus edodes* and *Tremella fuciformis* are most common edible and cultivated mushrooms.

Q.23–Can you name some non cultivated edible mushrooms?

A. Yes, I can. *Morchella* species, *Phellorinia inquinans* and *Podaxis pistillaris* are not cultivated edible species.

Fill up the blanks by adding suitable word/words.

24. Mushrooms are non-chlorophyllus fruiting bodies of _____ which are fleshy and edible.

25. Most common edible button mushroom usually grown in India is _____.

26. Ring like structure seen on the stipe of a typical mushroom is called as _____.

27. Volva remains _____ in Agaricus *bisporus*.

28. Edible mushrooms are rich in _____.

29. In most of the mushrooms, percentage of carbohydrate is _____.

30. Button mushrooms require _____ compounds for their growth.

31. Compost made for button mushroom must have _____ percent moisture.

32. Pure culture spawn may be prepared on wheat grains which are suitable as _____ for spore germination and spawn multiplication.

33. Fruiting body of button mushroom is _____ shaped.

34. *Agaricus bisporus* produces _____ basidiospores are its basidia.

35. *Volvariella* species are called as _____ mushroom.

36. Optimum temperature for crop production of *Volvariella* species should be _____ C°.

37. Most commonly cultivated species of oyster mushroom is _____.

38. Optimum temperature for oyster mushroom cultivation is _____ C°.

39. Most important common species of shiitake mushroom is _____.

40. Commonly cultivated mushroom species of wood ear fungus are _____ and _____.

41. *Chaetomium olivaceum* is a harmful fungus related with _____

42. Inky cap is a disease incited by the fungus _____.

43. Bacterial blotch of *Agaricus bisporus* is caused by the species of _____.

44. Important insects of mushrooms are flies, termites and _____.

45. Springtails are harmful _____ commonly found in

shelves, bags and trays below the compost and casing soil.

46. Mushroom should be kept below the temperature of 5 C° and moisture content should be below _____.

Whether following statements are true or false? Correct those which are false.

47. Mushrooms collected from pastures, orchards and forests are not suitable to be consumed. (True/ False).

48. Common edible mushrooms are rich in protein and lack chlorophyll. (True/ False).

49. Most common species of straw mushroom is *Pleurotus ostreatus*. (True/False)

50. Basidiospores are not found in gills. (True/False)

51. Uni-factorial type of sexuality exists in *Auricularia auricula*. (True/False)

52. *Lentinus edodes* is known as Shiitake mushroom. (True/ False)

53. *Agaricus bitorquis* produces two basidiospores on each basidium. (True/False).

54. In all the edible species of mushrooms, death cups remain absent. (True/ False).

55. In commonly used edible mushrooms, sodium salt and fat are found in very little amount. (True/False)

56. Casing soil preserves the moisture of the substrate for longer time and protects it in different ways. (True/ False)

Answers — 24. Fungi, 25. *Agaricus bisporus,* 26. Annulus, 27. Absent, 28. Protein, 29. 4.5%, 30. Carbon, 31. 68 to 70%, 32. Substrate, 33. *Umbrella,* 34. Two, 35. Paddy straw or straw, 36. 25–37C°, 37. *Pleurotus ostreatus.* 38. 20–32 C°, 39. *Lentinus edodes* 40. *Auricularia auricula, Auricularia polyricha* 41. Compost, 42. *Coprinus* species, 43. *Pseudomonas.* 44. *Springtails,* 45. Insects, 46. 4–6, 47. True, 48. True, 49. False, 50. True, 51. True, 52. True, 53. False, 54. True, 55. True and 56. True.

Glossary

Å (Angstrom) – a unit of length, equal to 1/10 millimicrons (mm) or 1 /10,000 micron (m).

A cellular – lacking cellular organization.

Acerate – needle shaped.

Achlorophyllous – without chlorophyll, non-chlorophyllous.

Achromatic lens – an objective lens in which a chromatic aberration has been connected for two colours.

Acid equivalent – It is the active ingredient of a commercial material responsible for required chemical reaction.

Acid fast – the property of certain bacteria that retain their initial stain and do not decolorize after washing.

AIDS – Acquired Immune Deficiency Syndrome.

Acuate – pointed.

Aculeate – bearing a sting or homologous organs.

Acute toxicity – rapid poisoning produced by a single exposure or a few repeated exposures to excessive amount of toxic materials.

Adeniform – glans like.

Adnate – attached squarely to the stipe.

Adnexed – attached slightly to the stipe.

ADP – adenosine diphosphate.

Agar – a gelatin like material obtained from sea weed and used to prepare culture media.

Agar gel column – are used in analytical processes where it is necessary to-hymeniurn separate chemicals with different sized molecules.

Agaricoid – bearing gills.

Ambient temperature – The natural i.e. outside temperature at the time.

Amorphous – shapeless.

Amino acids – a class of organic compounds containing an $(-NH_2)$ and a carboxyl (COOH) group.

Ammonification – the release of ammonia from nitrogenous organic matter by microbial action.

Anaerobic – a microorganism that lives on a process that occurs in the absence of molecular oxygen.

Annulus – the interval between adjacent annulations on the cuticle.

Annulus – the ring around the stem of a mushroom.

Antagonistic effect – antagonistic effect and the process as antagonism.

Antenna – whip like sensory appendage to the head of an insect.

Antibiotic – chemical compound/metabolites of an organism that inhibits or kills other microorganisms.

Antidote – a treatment given to counter act the effect of a poison.

Antigen – a substance, usually a protein which\when injected into the body of warm blooded animal induces antibodies production.

Apathogenic – causing no disease.

Aphis (aphids) – one of the member of species of plant lice which are extremely prolific causing mush damage by sucking the sap of leaves.

Apiculus – a particular point at the end of spore where it is attached to the sterigmata.

Appendiculate – remnants of veil attached with cap margin.

Applanate – shape of a pileus almost flat.

Apterous – wingless.

Arachunoid – cobweb – like.

Aseptic techniques – precautionary measures taken in microbiological work and clinical practice to prevent contamination.

Asporogenous – non–spore forming.

Abortive – Imperfectly formed.

Acute – sharp edge, tapering to be pointed.

Adnate – gills joined to the stem along entire width.

Agaric – Any fungus with gills.

Anastomosis – branching so as to form a network.

Applanate – flat in appearance.

Appressed – flat, not raised.

Azonate – without zones.

a.i. – active ingredient .

Basidiospore – a sexually produced spore borne on basidium.

Basidiocarp – fruiting body of a basidiomycetous fungus.

Button – a button mushroom which has reached the development stage where the cap and stalk are fully differentiated and partly expanded but the tissue covering the gills is not broken.

Bulbous – with a bulb like swelling at the base.

Canning – method of preservation of foodstuffs including mushrooms. In it suitably prepared foodstuffs (mushrooms) are paced in metal containers that are heated, exhausted and thermetically sealed.

Cap – a part of fruit body which bears spores bearing structures on its under surface.

Carbaryl – a good contact insecticide.

Carbendazim (Bavistin) – broad spectrum fungicide systemically active against ascomyceteous fungi, fungi imperfecti and some of the basidiomycetous fungi.

Cabofuran (furadan) – broad spectrum systemic insecticide, acaricide and nematicide.

Carrier – a material serving as diluent and vehicle for the active ingredient *i.e.* fungicide.

Casing – a mixture of peat and lime stone which is placed as layer on the top of the mushroom compost for colonization and fruit formation especially in button mushroom.

Catalyst – a substance that accelerate a chemical reaction.

Chloropicrin – soil fumigant.

Clamp connection – a bridge-like hyphal connection characteristic of the secondary mycelia of many Basidiomycetous fungi.

Circumscissile – splitting transversely at the middle.

Coenocytic – having a multinucleate mycelium without cross walls.

Context – the substance of the pileus.

Cover crop – a rapidly growing usually annual crop planted together with a more slowly growing usually biennial or perennial crop which is harvested usually one year after the cover crop has been harvested.

Crustose – like a crust.

Culture – a general term used for the growth of a microorganism *in vitro* or *in vivo*.

Cup fungi – Ascomycetous fungi with cup shaped ascocarps.

Cupulate – cup shaped.

C.O. – causal organism.

Caespitose – in tufts, in dense bunches.

Cartilaginous – cartilage like in texture.

Concentric – Successive circles of increasing size around a common centre.

Context – portion of the fruit body above the pores or gills.

Convolute – curved irregular furrows.

Conk – term used in forestry for sporophores of Family Polyporaceae.

Crenulate – with tiny scallops.

Culturing – artificial propagation of organisms on nutrient media or living plants.

Daedaloid – pores that are very irregular in shape.

Decurrent – gills that run down the stem.

Decurved – curved downwards.

Denticulate – having small teeth.

Dentate – edge irregular, suggesting teeth like structure.

Detoxification – the inactivation or destruction of a toxin.

Difolaton – fungicide closely related to Captan, marked as 80% WP or emulsified concentrate.

Dimethoate (Rogar) – systemic insecticide used against sap feeding insects.

Dimidiate – semicircular or nearly so.

Disk – the central part of the surface of the pileus.

Disease – harmful deviation from the normal conditions of any plant, animal or man.

Disinfect – to free diseased plant parts from infection.

Disinfectant – an agent that kills organisms present on the surface.

Distant – said to lamellae when they are far apart.

Dissemination – transfer of inoculum from its source to healthy plants.

Dust – a pesticide formulation in dry and finely powdered form used for dusting without further dilution.

Dwarfing – decrease in overall size.

Dyer's rule – an empirical law based on the observation that the head capsule and certain other parts of caterpillars grow in geometric progression, increasing in size by constant ratio at each molt.

Dysentery – an infectious disease characterized by inflammation and ulceration of the lower part of the bowels.

Dichotomous – forked into two branches.

Economic threshold (ET) – The pathogen density at which control measures may be determined to prevent a population build up to the economic injury level.

Economic injury level – the amount of infestation at which control must be applied to prevent the infestation rising to the level causing economic loss.

Eccentric – not centrally attached.

Echinulate – minutely spiny.

Equal – said to the stipe when of uniform thickness.

Ecosystem – the complex of plants, animals and environmental factors in an ecological niche.

ELISA – enzyme – linked immuno-sorbent assay.

Ellipsoidal – elliptical in optical section.

EC – Emulsified concentrate.

Entomogenous fungi – fungi growing on insects.

EPA – Environmental Protection Agency (USA).

Epidemic rate – the amount of increase of disease per unit of time in a plant population.

Epidemiology – the study of the factors affecting the outbreak and spread of an infectious disease.

Epigeous – growing above ground or substratum.

Eradication – elimination of a pathogen or pest from the host or from the host environment or both.

Exudates – ooze from a part of plants, such as root exudates, leaf exudates or stem exudates etc.

e.g. – *exempli gratia* (for example).

et al – and others.

etc. – *et cetra* (and so on).

Effused reflexed – partly flat on the surface.

Fairy rings – a ring like structures formed of mushrooms on the ground representing the periphery of mycelium growth especially in basidiomycetous fungi.

Filiform – thread like , filamentous.

Food intoxication – diseases resulting from ingestion of poisonous food of any kind.

Freeze – *drying* – a technique used for the preservation of plant viruses, microorganisms or foodstuffs (mushrooms also) whereby water is removed under vacuum while the preserved material remains in frozen state.

Fructification – any fungal structure which contains or bears spores.

Fruiting body – a complex fungal structure containing fructification.

Fugacious – disappearing quickly.

Fumigants – volatile chemicals applied into confined space.

Fungicide – a substance that kills fungal spores or mycelium.

Fusoid – spindle shaped.

Farinaceous – an odor resembling that of freshly crushed wheat.

Fimbriate – fringed.

Floccose – covered with coarse woolly hairs.

Free – gills that do not tough the stem.

Fuliginous – sooty or dark brown.

Fumosous – smoky.

Furfuraceous – clothed with numerous minute scales.

Fulvous – tawny.

Genetic engineering – manipulation of the genetic composition of a cell by various procedures including transformation and protoplast fusion etc. in tissue culture.

Germ tube – the hyphae originating from germination of spore.

Germination – active growth by the embryo of a seed. The process of growing from a seed or spore.

Gill – the structure resembling plates bearing hymeruum in mushrooms.

Glabrous – naked, not covered with hair.

Gleba – the spore bearing tissue of puffballs and heir alleles.

Granular – lightly rough, covered with tiny grain like structures.

Gregarious – numerous individuals near each other but not tufts.

Habitat – the place where an organisrn grows or lives.

HETP – Hexa ethyl tetra phosphate. It is a substitute for nicotine and is effective against aphids, thrips, mealy bugs and red spider mites.

Hybrid – a plant resulting from the cross between parents of different species

Hygroscopic – with water, watery.

Hymenium (pl. hymenia) – a fertile layer consisting of asci or basidia.

Hymenophore – the fruit body.

Imbricate – overlapping, some thing like shingles on a roof.

Involute – rolled inward.

Immerged – embedded in fhe substratum.

In vitro – in the laboratory or in the experimental culture but not in living cells.

In vivo – in living cells but not in synthetic culture medium.

Incompatible – not capable of being mixed together. When two or more fungicides that are not compatible are mixed together, they become ineffective and may cause injury to plants.

Inhalation toxicity – poisonous effects of a fungicide/ chemical breathed into the lungs.

Insecticide – any substance intended for preventing, killing, repelling or controlling an insect pathogen.

Intervenose – with veins between, said of gills having on their sides, branched ridger that resemble veins.

Koch's postulafes – Three criteria were proposed by Robert Koch (1883) for proving the pathogenicity of any biotic pathogen. (1) The suspected causal organism must be constantly associated with the disease. (2) It must be isolated and grown in pure culture. (3) When inoculated into healthy plants it must reproduce the original disease and the (4) criterion was appended by E.F. Smith that the same organism must be re-isolated from the experimentally infected plants.

Lobed – having rounded divisions on the margins.

Lateral – stem attaehed at oneside of the cap.

Lamella – a plate like structure (gill) on which basidia are produced in some basidiomycetous fungi.

Larnellula – a short gill

Longitudinal – lengthwise.

Lunate – like a new moon, crescentric.

Luteous – egg-yellow.

Macroclimate – climate operating in larger heights and regions.

Malathion – a general purpose non systemic insecticide.

Mancozeb – a fungicide.

Maximam residue limit (MRL) – maximum concentration in mg/kg or ppm of a residue that is legally permitted in or on food at a specified post harvest processing stage.

Melleous – honey – yellow.

Miniatous – scarlet.

Murinous – mouse – coloured.

Mycorrhiza (pl. Mycorrhizae) – symbiotic, non pathogenic association of fungi and roots.

Mycotoxicosis – poisoning by fungi.

Micro flora – vegetation of microorganisms.

Microbial ecology – the field of study that examines the interactions among microorganisms with their biotic and biotic asurroundings.

Moulds – mycelial micro fungus or a visible growth of such fungus.

Necrophyte – an organism living on dead material.

Nematodes – vermiform animals.

Nematophagous – feeding on nematodes.

Obtuse – rounded, not tapering to a sharp edge.

Oblong – rounded.

Obovate – narrowest at base.

Obpyriform – the reverse of pear shaped.

Obtuse – blunt.

Ochraceous – ocher yellow.

Olivaceous – greenish brown.

Oval – widely elliptical.

Over composting – the condition of the compost where the decomposition has proceeded beyond the optimum point for mushroom growth and has resulted in excessive break down of the organic material.

Oxidation – a chemical reaction in which oxygen combines with another substance, or in which hydrogen atoms or electrons are removed from a substance.

Para sexuality – a process in which plasmogamy, karyogamy and haploidisation take place in sequence but not at specified points in the life cycle of an individual.

Pasteurization – reduction in the number of microorganisms by exposure to elevated temperatures but not necessarily the killing of all microorganisms in a sample.

Petridish – plates (Petri plates) as a simplest piece of equipment made of glass or plastic for culturing microorganisms.

pH – relative acidity of a solution.

Pellicle – the cuticle or thin skin forming the surface of a mushroom cap.

Pileus – the cap of a mushroom, the entire fruit body of any of stalk less fleshy fungus.

Pin head – a stage in the development of mushroom at or near the end of differentiation of the cap, but before any enlargement has taken place.

Poroid – resembling pores.

PPB – parts per billion (1,000 million).

Pre-emergence – before germination.

Post – emergence – after germination.

PPM – parts per million. One part per million is equal to I milligram in I kilogram.

pl. – plural.

Pure culture – a culture that contains cells of one kind.

Purification – the separation of organism in pure form.

Pubescent – covered with fine hairs.

Pulvervulent – covered with powder or dust.

Recurved – curved inwards and inwards.

Reniform – shaped like a kidney bean.

Reticulate – covered with a network of raised ridges.

Rhizomorphs – a cord like strand of fungal hyphae.

Rhizoid – root like structure.

Seceding – gills that at first are attached to the stem but separate from it later.

Separable – easily removed.

Serrate – with pointed teeth, like the edge of a saw.

Sessile – without a stem, shelf-like.

Sheath – a membrane of mycelium enclosing the stem of a mushroom.

Sinuate – gills notched at the stem.

Spatulate – shape of a blade of spatula.

Spore – a single to many celled reproductive body, in the fungi or lower plants which can develop into new plants.

Species – one short of plant abbreviated as *sp.* or *spp.*

Strain – an organism or group of organisms differing in origin and in physiology from other organisms of same species or variety.

Sterigma (pl. sterigmata) – projection for supporting a spore.

Striate – marked with tiny streaks, furrows or lines.

Striations – delicate lines or furrows.

syn. – synonym.

Testaceous – pale brick coloured.

Tomentose – clothed with dense, matted hairs.

i.e. – id *est* (that is).

Umbilicate – a small depression in the centre of the cap.

Undulate – wavy.

Ungulate – hoof shaped.

Volva – the cup shaped structure surrounding the base of the stem of some mushrooms.

Bibliography

(Author thankfully acknowledges having consulted the following books, in addition to many other research papers, training manuals and journals not included here).

Ainsworth, G.C.; Snssman, A.S. and Sparrow, F.K., Eds. **(1973).** *"The fungi"*, vol. 48, Academic Press, New York.

Arita, I. (1974). Genetic studies of white fruit bodies of *Pleurotus ostreatus* (Fr.) Kumar. *Rep. Tot. Myco. Inst.* **11**: 58–68 (In Japanese with English summary).

Atkinson, Ceo. F. **(1971).** *Mushrooms, Edible, Poisonous etc.* 3rd Edition, Henry Holt & Co., New York.

Ando, M. (1972). Fine structure of hyphae of *Lentinus edodes* Sing. *Trans. Mycol. Soc.*, Japan, **13**: 191–195.

Ando, M., Nukumizu, T. and Kubota, N. (1969). On the ecological and morphological characters of the strain of *Lentinus edodes*. *Experimentia*, **15**: 237–1238.

Barnet, H.I. (1937). Studies in the sexuality of the Heterobasidiae. *Mycologia*, **29** : 626–649.

Buller, A.H.R. (1932). *"Researchces in Fungi"* **Vol. IV** Longmans, Green, New York.

Bels, P.J. (1950). A comparison of mushroom cultivation in Switzerland, Belgium, England, Holland and Scandinavia. *Mushroom Sci.*, **1**: 9–19.

Bels-Koning, H.C. and Gerrits, J.P.G. (1962). Some fungi appearing towards the end of composting. *Mushroom Sci.*, **5**: 165–168.

Bano, Z. and Srivaṣtava, H.C. (1962). Studies on cultivation of *Pleurotus* species on paddy straw. *Food Sci.*, **12**: 363–365.

Bano, Z., Srinivasan, K.S. and Srivastava, H.C. (1963). Amino acid composition of the protein from a mushroom *(Pleurotus* species). *Applied Microbiol.*, **11**: 184–187.

Block, S.S. (1965). Carvage composting for mushroom production. *Applied Microbiol.*, **13**: 5–9.

348

Block, S.S., Tsso. And Han. I. (1958). Production of mushroom from sawdust. *J. Agric. Food Chem.* **6**: 923–927.

Block, S.S., Tsso. And Han. I. (1959). Experiments in ihe cultivation of Pleurotus ostreatus. *Mushroom Sci.* **4**: 309–325.

Chang, S.T. (1972). *"The Chinese mushroom"* The Chinese University of Hong Kong. Hong Kong.

Chang, S.T. and Lang, K.Y. (1970). Nuclear behavior in the Basidiomycetes – *Volvariella volvacea. Am. J. Bot.* **57**: 165–171.

Chang, S.T. and Yau, C.K. (1971). *Volvariella volvacea* and its life history. *Am. J. Bot.* **58**: 552–561.

Cochran, K.W., Nishikava, T. and Beneke, E.S. (1967). Botanical sources of infiuenza inhibitors. *Antimicrobial agents and chemotherapy.* pp. 515–520.

Calinga, R.H., Ballon, F.B. and Lumibao, I.R. (1976). Mushroom Culture. Bureau of plant industry, Philippines.

Chang, S.T. (1964). The influence of cultural methods of on the production and nutritive content of *Volvariella volvacea. Chung Chi,* J. **4**: 76–84.

Chang, S.T. (1965). Cultivation of the straw mushroom in S.E. China. *World crops,* **17**: 47–49.

Chang, S.T. (1966). Spore of *Volvariella volvacea. Nature* (London) **212**: 528529.

Chang, S.T. (1974). Production of the straw mushroom *(Volvariella volvacea)* from cotton waste. *Mushroom J.* **21**: 348–354.

Chang, S.T. and Yau, CK. (1970). A simple technique for indoor cultivation of straw mushroom. *Mushroom News.* **18**: 9–11.

Tripathi, D.P. and Shukla, H.P. (2002). Mushroom Cultivation (Hindi), Rama Publishing House, Meerut (U.P.)

Slements, F.C. (1910). Minnesota Mushroom-University of Minnesota, Minneapolis.

Elliott, T.J. (1972). Sex and single spore. *Mushroom Sci.* **8**: 11–18.

Esser, K. (1966). Incompatibility. "The Fungi" G.C. Ainsworth and A.S. Sussman .Vol. 2 pp. 661–676. Academic Press, New York.

Edwards, R.I, (1950). Synthetic Composts. *Mushroom Sci.* **1**: 62–63.

Edwards, R.I, (1961). Air conditions in commercial mushroom growing. *Mushroom Sci.* **6**: 379–387.

Edwards, R.I, (1973). Mushroom house ventilation in theory and practice. *Mushroom J.* 3 and 4: 117–131 and 166–176.

Food and Agricultural organization. (1967). Development of commercial mushroom production. No. T.A. 2331. FAO, Rome.

Gray, W.S. (1973). The use of fungi as food and in food processing. Part 11, pp. 182, CRC Press, Cleveland, Ohio, U.S.A.

Green, H.E. (1964). Mushroom growing in Japan. Boston Myco. Club, *Bull. No.*1

Gibson, W.H. (1895). Non Edible Toadstools and mushrooms. New Ed. 1903. Harper Bros. Co. New York. 8th edition.

Hawksworth, D.L.; P.M. Kirk; B.C. Sutton and D.P. Pegler (1995). Anisworth and Bisby's *Dictionary of fungi*

Hayes, W.A. and Naie, N.G. (1975). The cultivation of *Agaricus bisporus* and other edible mushrooms. *"The filamentous fungi"* (J.E. Smith and D.R. Betry ed.) Vol. 1, pp. 212–248, Wiley, New York.

Hayes, W.A. (1969). Microbiological changes in composting wheat straw/horse manure mixtures. *Mushroom Sci.* **7**: 173–186.

Hayes, W.A. (1972). Nutritional factors in relation to mushroom production. *Mushroom Sci.* **8**: 663–674.

Chang, S.T. (1968). Investigation of ultra low temperature on the viability of selected fungus strain. *Mycologia* **60**: 6133–621.

Huhnke, W. and Von Sengbusch, R. (1965). Active mycelium spawning affecting sporophore formation in *Agaricus bisporus.* *M.G.A. Bull.* **126**: 205–214.

Hussey, N.W., Read, O.H. and Hesting, J.T. (1969). "The pest of protected cultivation" Arnold. London.

Ho. M.S. (1972). Straw mushroom cultivation in plastic house. *Mushroom Sci.* **8**: 257–263.

Hard, M.F., (1908). Mushroom edible and other wise. Ohio Library Co., Columbus, Ohio.

Higuchi, T. (1953). Carbohydrate metabolism of wood destroying fungi. *J. Jap. For. Soc.,* **35**: 339–349.

Hussey, N.W. (1972). Pests in perspective. *Mushroom Sci.,* **8**: 171–181.

Klioshnikova, E.S. (1938). Sexual character in cultivated mushroom. *Bull. Soc. Nat.,* Moscow, **47**: 30–38.

Knee bone, L.P. (1968). Strain selection, development and maintenance. *Mushroom Sci.* **7**: 531–541.

350

Komatsu, M. and Kimura, K. (1964b). Studies on abnormal fruit bodies of the hypomycetous fungi. III Fruit bodies with brownish gills of *Lentinus edodes* (Berk.) Sing. *Rep. Tottori Mycol. Inst.,* 4: 21–28 (In Japanese with English summary).

Kaneda, T. and Takuda, S. (1966). Effect of different mushroom preparations on cholesterol levels in rats. *J. Nutri.* **90**: 371–376.

Kurtzman, R.H., Jr. (1975a). Straw, wood, paper and the cultivation of edible wild mushrooms. "Proceedings of seminars on mushroom research and production". pp. 23–42., *Agric. Research Counc.,* Karachi.

Kligman, A.M. (1950). Hand book of mushroom culture, Business Press Inc. Lancaster, Pennsylvania.

Lambert, E.B. (1932). Mushroom growing in the United States. U.S. Department of Agriculture., **251**: 1–34,

Lamberk, E.B. (1933). Effect of excess carbon dioxide on growing mushrooms. *J. Agric. Research,* **47**:350–608

Lambert, E.B. (1941a). Studies on the preparation of mushroom compost. *J. Agric. Research,* **62**: 415–422.

Lambert, E.B. (1950b). Comments on twenty years of research in mushroom culture. *Mushroom Sci.* **1**: 7–8.

Lambert, E.B. (1956). Mushroom growing in United States (Revised December 1955). U.S. Department of Agriculture. *Farmers Bull.* **1875**: 1–12.

Miller, R.E. (1971). Evidence of sexuality in cultivated mushroom, Agaricus bisporus, *Mycologia,* **63**: 630–634.

Miller, R.E. and Kananen, D.I., (1972). Bipolar sexuality in mushroom. *Mushroom Sci.* **8**: 713–718.

Marshall, W. and Jenison, W.M. (1959). Chemical and vitamin composition of the mycelium of wood rotting Basidiomycetes, *Mushroom Sci.* **4**: 183–185.

Mori, K. (1974). Studies on virus like particles in *Lentinus edodes.* Proceedings of the inter congress of IAMS. **3**: 396–401.

Naidu, N.R. (1971). Cultivation of paddy straw mushroom *Volvariella volvacea* (Fr>) Sing. Using oil palm bunch waste as a medium. *The Planter,* **47**: 190–193.

Park, Y.H., Chang, H.C., Jung, C.S. and Kim, D.S. (1974). Some experiments on the cultivation of straw mushroom *Volvariella volvacea* (Bull. ex. Fr.) Sing. IN Korea. *Korean J. Mycol.,* **2**: 21–24.

Patterson, Flora. W. and Vera K. Charles (1905). Mushroom and other common fungi. U.S. Agri. Bull. 175 – Washington, D.C.

Raper, C.A. and Kaye, G. (1978). Sexual and other relationships in the genus *Agaricus.* J. Gen. Microb. **105**: 135–151.

Rangaswami, G. Kanda Swami, T.K. and Ramaswami, K. (1975). *Pleurotus sajor caju* (Fr.) Sing. Protein rich nitrogen fixing mushroom fungus. Cur. Sci. **44**: 403–404.

Ramakrishna, K., Kumari, D.L., Shanmugam, N. and Krishnamurti, C.S. (1968). A simple technique for increasing yield of straw mushroom *Volvariella diplasia* (Berk. and Br.) Sacc. Madras Agri. J., **55**: 144–145.

Rettew, G.R., and Thompson, F.G. (1958). Manual of mushroom cultivation. Mushroom Supply Co. Tough Kenamon, Pa. U.S.A.

Robinson, W. (1970). Mushroom culture-Its extension and improvement Fredetick Warne & Co. Limited.

Rolef, R.T. and Rolete. F.W. (1925). The romance of the fungus world. Chapman & Hall Limited, London.

Seth, L.N. (1944). Cultivation of mushroom in Burma. *Indian Farming.* **5**: 520–522.

Singer, R. (1961). Shiitake and its cultivation in East Asia. *Mushroom and Truffles.* Leonard Hill, London. p. 132–146.

Sinden, J.W. and Schisler, I.C. (1962). Nutrient supplementation of mushroom compost at casing. *Mushroam Sci.,* **5**: 267–280.

Singer, R. (1961). *Mushroom and truffles.* pp 132–146. Leonald Hill Ltd. London.

Sinders, T.W. (1909). Mushroom and their cultivation. W.H. & L Colling ridge.

Summer School on emerging areas of mushroom Research and Production (2003). National Research Centre for Mushroom, chambaghat, Solan (H.P.).

White house, H.I.K. (1949). Heterothallism and sex in fungi. Biol. Rew. Cambridge, Phikos. Soc., **24**: 411–447.

Tokita, F., Shibukawa, N., Yasumoto, T. and Kaneda, T. (1972). Isolation and Chemical structure of the plasma-cholesterol reducing substance from shiitake mushroom. *Mushroom Sci.* **8**: 783–788.

Tripathi, D.P. and Shukla, H.P. (2003). Mushroom cultivation (in Hindi), Rama Publishing House, Meerut (U.P.)

352

Vogel, F.S., McGarry, S.J., Kemper, L.A.K, and Graham, D.G. (1974). Bacteriocidal properties of a class of quinoid compounds related to sporulation in the mushroom *Agaricus bisporus*. *Ame. J Pathl.* **76**: 165–174.

Yoshioka, P., Ikekawa, T., Noda, M. and Fukuoka, F. (1972). Studies on anti-tumer activity of some fractions from basidiomycetes. *Chemical Pharm. Bull.* **20**: 1175–1180.

Zadrazil, F., (1974c). The ecology and industrial production of *Pleurotus ostreatus, Pleurotus florida, Pleurotus cornucopiae* and *Pleurotus sryngi. Mushroom Sci.* **IX**: 621–652.

Zadrazil, F., (1975a). Influence of CO_2 concentration on the mycelial growth of three *Pleurotus* species. *Euro. J. Appl. Micro.*, **1**: 327–335.

Subject Index